NHS
UNDER
SIEGE

NHS UNDER SIEGE

The fight to save it in the age of Covid

JOHN LISTER
JACKY DAVIS
PLUS EXPERT CONTRIBUTORS
FOREWORD BY **MICHAEL ROSEN**

MERLIN PRESS

First published in 2022 by
The Merlin Press Ltd
50 Freshwater Road
Dagenham
RM8 1RX

www.merlinpress.co.uk

ISBN 978-085036-777-5

Royalites for this book will go to Keep Our NHS Public

A catalogue record of this book is available from the British Library

Printed in the UK by Imprint Digital, Exeter

Dedication

This book is intended to be used as a weapon to inform and strengthen the fight for the NHS. It is dedicated to the NHS workforce, past, present and future – in particular John's granddaughter Kaitlin who will begin her midwifery course in the autumn of 2022.

Contents

Acknowledgements

This book could not have been completed without the assistance of many people, most notably Michael Rosen and our thirteen expert contributors: Lobby Akinnola, Rehana Azam, Kevin Courtney, Sara Gorton, Colenzo Jarrett-Thorpe, Roger Kline, Roy Lilley, Michael Mansfield QC, Professor Sir Michael Marmot, Professor Martin McKee, Professor Neena Modi, Jan Shortt and Dr David Wrigley. We would also like to thank Peter Blackburn and Theo Chiles for additional material.

We also owe thanks to Tony and Adrian at Merlin Press who have encouraged and urged us on from the outset.

As joint authors and editors we have been able to draw on information and analysis from other campaigners, especially the resources brought together by Keep Our NHS Public and its People's Covid Inquiry in 2021. We have also made use of our own and colleagues' articles and publications over the years, including *Morning Star* columns; Health Emergency newspapers, research and reports; Health Campaigns Together newspapers (and online bulletins from 2020); and, since 2019, the fortnightly Lowdown. We have tried throughout to identify sources and offer urls to online publications: clearly any errors in the completed text are ours alone.

We have both also been lucky enough to enjoy the support and encouragement of friends and family, who have allowed us the time and space to work on and edit our own chapters, as well as the specialist chapters. Particular thanks for their patience and understanding are due to Rick Chiles and to Sue Lister.

Jacky Davis and John Lister, April 2022

Organisations and abbreviations

A&E Accident & Emergency.

AACE Association of Ambulance Chief Executives.

ACO Accountable Care Organisation – system devised to address problems of US health insurance system, in which providers are contracted at a fixed price to provide all services (and shoulder all risks) for a defined population. See https://lowdownnhs.info/explainers/4638/

ADASS Association of Directors of Adult Social Care.

BMA British Medical Association, http://bma.org.uk/

BMI BMI Healthcare was Britain's leading provider of independent healthcare with a nationwide network of 51 hospitals – subsequently taken over by Circle, before Circle was taken over by US-owned Centene.

BMJ British Medical Journal, http://www.bmj.com/

CAMHS Child and Adolescent Mental Health Services.

CCG Clinical Commissioning Groups, (Commissioners).

CHPI Centre for Health and the Public Interest, http://chpi.org.uk/

CQC Care Quality Commission, http://www.cqc.org.uk/

DHA District Health Authority – no longer exists in England.

DHSC Department of Health and Social Care.

ED Emergency Department.

FTTIS The introduction of an effective and comprehensive programme of case Finding, Testing, contact Tracing, Isolating and Support to contain infectious disease.

FYFV Five Year Forward View, http://www.england.nhs.uk/wp-content/uploads/2014/10/5yfv-web.pdf

GMC General Medical Council, http://www.gmc-uk.org/

Health Foundation Independent charity which funds and carries out research on health and health policy https://www.health.org.uk/about-the-health-foundation

Healthwatch http://www.healthwatch.co.uk/find-local-healthwatch

HCA Healthcare American for-profit operator of healthcare facilities that was founded in 1968. It is based in Nashville, Tennessee, and has established a network of private hospitals, outpatient centres and specialist clinics in England.

Health Campaigns Together Campaign, newspaper, online bulletin and website. See Chapter 6. https://healthcampaignstogether.com/

HSCIC Health and Social Care Information Centre, http://www.hscic.gov.uk/

Health Emergency A tabloid newspaper for campaigners defending the NHS. that was circulated from 1984 until 2015, and a website with archive resources. Subsequently merged Into Health Campaigns Together https://healthemergency.org.uk/

HSJ Health Service Journal, http://www.hsj.co.uk

HSSF Health System Support Framework, now expanded to list 200+ 'approved' companies and organisations to advise ICBs on the establishment of 'Integrated Care' without competitive tender. Most on the list are private companies, and over 20 are US-based. https://lowdownnhs.info/integrated-care/whos-cashing-in-on-icss/

ICB Integrated Care Board.

ICP Integrated Care Partnership.

ICS Integrated care System.

ISP Independent Service Provider.

IPPR Institute of Public Policy Research claims to be 'the UK's leading progressive think tank', (but often annoys progressives).

IRP Independent Reconfiguration Panel, https://www.gov.uk/government/organisations/independent-reconfiguration-panel.

i-SAGE Independent SAGE is a group of scientists established in 2020 to work together to provide independent scientific advice to the UK government and public (see also SAGE).

ISTC Independent Sector Treatment Centre.

ITU Intensive Therapy/Treatment Unit.

King's Fund An 'independent charitable organisation working to improve health and care in England'; but more often appearing to endorse government policy of the day than to question or oppose it.

Lowdown The Lowdown is a free access evidence-based online source of information, analysis and comment on the NHS and health policy primarily aimed at campaigners, union activists and academics, established in early 2019. https://lowdownnhs.info

NAO National Audit Office, http://www.nao.org.uk/

NHSCC NHS Clinical Commissioners, http://www.nhscc.org/

NHS Confederation Body representing NHS commissioners and providers including NHS, private sector and voluntary sector http://www.nhsconfed.org/

NHSE NHS England, http://www.england.nhs.uk

NHS Providers NHS Providers is the membership organisation for NHS hospital, mental health, community and ambulance trusts: it also offers associate membership to private sector providers. https://nhsproviders.org

NHS Support Federation (See chapter 6) http://www.nhscampaign.org/

NICE National Institute for Health and Clinical Excellence, http://www.nice.org.uk/

NPC National Pensioners Convention, https://www.npcuk.org/

Nuffield Trust The Nuffield Trust says it is an independent health think tank which aims ' to improve the quality of health care in the UK by providing evidence-based research and policy analysis'. http://www.nuffieldtrust.org.uk/

OBR Office of Budget Responsibility https://obr.uk/

OOH Out of Hours.

PCTs Primary Care Trusts, local level commissioning bodies established 2001, replaced in 2013 by Clinical Commissioning Groups – which will be replaced in July 2022 by 42 Integrated Care Boards.

PCI People's Covid Inquiry.

PFI Private Finance Initiative.

PHE Public Health England (abolished October 2021).

PHIN Private Healthcare Information Network, https://www.phin.org.uk/

PPE Personal Protective Equipment.

RCP Royal College of Physicians https://www.rcplondon.ac.uk/

RCPsych Royal College of Psychiatrists https://www.rcpsych.ac.uk/

RCEM Royal College of Emergency Medicine https://rcem.ac.uk/

RCN Royal College of Nurses, http://www.rcn.org.uk.

RCGP Royal College of General Practitioners, http://www.rcgp.org.uk.

SAGE British government's Scientific Advisory Group for Emergencies

SHA Strategic health authorities, abolished in 2013.

STP Sustainability and Transformation Plan/Partnership.

TSA Trust Special Administrator.

TTIP Transatlantic Trade and Investment Partnership.

TUPE Transfer of Undertakings (Protection of Employment).

Type 1 The most serious emergency patients, most likely to require swift admission to inpatient treatment.

UCC Urgent Care Centre.

UEC Urgent and Emergency Care.

UNISON Trade union with largest NHS membership, formed in 1992 from merger of NUPE, NALGO and COHSE. http://www.unison.org.uk

UNITE British and Irish trade union which was formed in 2007 by the merger of Amicus and the Transport and General Workers' Union http://www.unitetheunion.org/

WHO World Health Organisation.

WMAS West Midlands Ambulance Service.

Foreword

Michael Rosen

My parents' generation created a beautiful and wonderful thing. After centuries where access to treatment was a matter of how much money you had, a majority of British people put a government in power which said that everyone should be able to get treatment and care from the cradle to the grave on the basis of need. Easy to say, incredibly difficult to put in place but it happened. It wasn't magic. It came about as the result of people's thoughts, wishes and struggles in many different ways across the country. We can find the roots in places as diverse as self-help and mutual aid organisations, miners' 'welfares', socialist health practitioners' associations, womens' health associations, the co-operative society and of course the Labour Party, the party which created the NHS.

I am just too old to have been born in the NHS (1946) but throughout my life the NHS has been there for me, whether it was our family doctor coming to see me when I knocked myself out falling off my bike, spells in hospital with a broken nose (cricket match!), a broken pelvis (car accident), hypothyroidism (auto-immune disease), bringing my children into the world, seeing my parents out of it, and then, in 2020 when the NHS saved my life by putting me into an induced coma for more than 40 days (Covid-19). If I hadn't realised before, I certainly realised it as I woke up out of intensive care, that in order to save my life and the lives of thousands of us during that phase of the Covid pandemic, the work, training, knowledge and experience of hundreds of thousands of people had to be engaged. I thought at that moment, this was and is an example of the greatness of what we humans can do: we can muster all we've got to look after each other. If only, I thought, we could use that principle and apply it to every part of our life, work and leisure!

Instead, I see governments that have spent years using every trick in the book to import into the NHS the systems and methods used by humans to compete against each other, do each other down, squeeze resources and wealth out of others. The shorthand word for that is 'privatisation', though of course we are often subjected to bits of jargon like 'contestability' or 'the efficiency of the market' and the like. This is paraded in front of us as a great virtue as if this 'market' has a proven track record of being good at providing all humans with what we need! Didn't this market bring the world economy to the brink of collapse in 2008 – an event that inflicted and continues to inflict hardship and poverty on millions? If the market is so 'efficient' why can't it make sure that everyone in this rich country can 'eat and heat'? Why do people talk of 'inflation' as if it is a monster from outer space rather than something that the market itself creates? I could go on.

This book is a superb reply to what is happening with our beloved NHS. We need it to help us in our struggles to push back against those who are snatching it away from us. All struggles need resolve, solidarity and hope, but they also need information. Information helps us see what is really going on and it helps us see over the hill to what is possible, just as my parents' generation saw when they won the NHS in the first place.

This is the book for the job.

Introduction

Crisis point ... again

To say that the NHS is in or is facing a crisis has sadly become something of a cliché: it is no longer enough to excite news editors, even though it is true. Unfortunately, despite best efforts by campaigners and unions the NHS is still facing an existential crisis. We have previously co-authored two books* on the fate of the NHS under successive Conservative governments, but the situation has significantly changed since *NHS for Sale* was published early in 2015.

So now, with some reluctance, we have had to look at a different way of expressing the threat to the NHS posed by the combination of two years of a global pandemic with the relentless policies pursued by Tory-led governments since 2010.

The title proclaims '**NHS Under Siege**'. The siege has taken the form of a full decade of austerity imposing real terms cuts on the NHS in England. This has effectively wiped out the decade of growth from 2000-2010, and left a weakened NHS that is now so lacking in capacity and investment that all of its longer-term plans routinely involve one-sided 'partnerships' with the private sector.

The siege has remained in place while the NHS has also been hit by the still-unresolved pandemic, which accelerated the changes already under way. The pandemic

- deepened the crisis of morale amongst NHS staff who had already been ground down by constant pressure and dwindling real terms pay, and who now have no visible prospect of relief.

---

* *NHS SOS* (2013) One World, London, and *NHS For Sale* (2015) co-edited with David Wrigley, Merlin Press

1

It currently has 110,000 posts vacant, an unknown number of staff suffering from long Covid, and growing numbers leaving to escape the stress and frustration of not being able to deliver quality care.

- greatly increased the crisis of capacity, with the abrupt closure of thousands of beds to enable social distancing in March 2020 (followed by the need to accommodate – and isolate – thousands of Covid inpatients). This drastic loss of regular capacity followed the cash-driven closure of almost 9,000 frontline beds since 2010, which had already left England with fewer beds per head than comparable countries.
- resulted in a record 26% increase in spending on private hospitals and private providers in a single year (2020), which we know will be followed by similar inflated levels of spending on private providers until at least 2025.

The besieging forces – right wing politicians, private hospital corporations, contractors, management consultants and others – don't want to eradicate the NHS, but to subordinate it.

They don't want to replace the tax-funded system, but to exploit it more fully, to ensure the maximum flow of profitable activity to private providers, while also maximising the numbers who will opt to pay privately for elective treatment rather than face long delays. So they still need a core NHS, to treat the emergencies, the pregnancies, the complex and chronic cases that offer no profit, to train nurses, doctors and other professionals, and to foot the bill for poor, sick and elderly patients who will never be allowed to threaten the profit margins of private insurers.

Rhetoric

While the siege continues, ministers' rhetoric could not be more surreal. The reality of a massive and growing £9 billion-plus bill for backlog maintenance, and the danger of a number of 1970s-built hospitals falling down is concealed behind an inane repetition of Boris Johnson's empty promises to build first 40, and now 48 'new hospitals'. In truth, all the grandiose schemes are at a standstill and facing cutbacks, while dozens of trusts are still struggling to make payments on PFI hospitals** built in the 2000s.

Ministers continue to gaslight about spending 'more than ever before' on health, while the truth is quite the reverse. Each year since 2010 the health budget has grown by less than previous average increase in spending, bringing real terms cuts as resources lag behind rising costs.

Any specific gap in service or failure to fulfil a promise – on mental health, primary care, children's services, maternity – is met by some meaningless and distorted government statistic on spending, which always somehow seems enough to satisfy poorly-briefed and deferential TV and radio interviewers.

But the statistics and the state of play on the ground are shocking, and far from routine.

- Over 6 million patients and rising are on the biggest-ever waiting lists in England.
- There are chronic failures in performance in A&E, and growing numbers of 12-hour trolley waits.
- Performance on cancer care is disastrous and still deteriorating.
- Mental health is desperately under-resourced, with 1.5 million people needing mental health care, but not getting it.
- And there are huge delays in assessment of patients' need for social care, and huge gaps in provision of care.

In these circumstances Rishi Sunak's decision in last autumn's spending review to reimpose tight spending limits is steering the NHS to an even worse place, one in which staff, patients and the general public can begin to lose confidence that it will ever be restored to the performance levels achieved in 2010.

Reality

This book therefore looks at the policies, decisions and circumstances that have brought us to this situation, the actual and real terms cuts in spending, the fragmentation, the privatisation, the so-called reforms,

** Funded through the Private Finance Initiative, in which a consortium of finance houses, service providers and construction firms design, finance, build and operate support services in the hospital, which is then effectively leased to the NHS for an index-linked fee, commonly for 30 or more years.

reorganisation and plans that have weakened the NHS and made it more dependent on the private sector.

A major section, drawing extensively on the evidence and findings of the Peoples Covid Inquiry led by Keep Our NHS Public in 2021, looks in detail at the way these issues played out in the course of the pandemic and its aftermath. Areas examined include the government's lack of preparedness, its sluggish response, its failure to protect frontline workers and the vulnerable, its preference for the private sector over public services, cronyism and corruption and finally its lack of accountability for the tens of thousands of avoidable Covid deaths in the UK.

And we are not out of the pandemic yet, despite the governments cavalier abandoning of all public health measures. At the time of writing, Covid case numbers and hospital admissions are rising again.

The impact of Covid on hospital capacity means cancer treatment faces worsening delays, and NHS waiting lists are set to rise until 2024 as a hidden backlog of as many as 13 million people begin to seek care they put off during the peak of the pandemic. Over 300,000 patients have already waited over a year for treatment and the government's own elective recovery plan admits that people will be waiting over 18 months for treatment until 2023 at the earliest.

Reforms

Sajid Javid now claims the government is at a crossroads: 'a point where we must choose between endlessly putting in more money, or reforming how we do healthcare.' He opts for more 'reforms', even before the Health and Care Bill is on the statute book.

But none of the reforms he proposes are new, and none addresses any of the big problems facing the NHS. He talks about three Ps: prevention, personalised care and performance.

But prevention has been undermined by a decade of austerity that has deepened the health divide between rich and poor, ended improvements in life expectancy, slashed public health budgets and replaced Public Health England with the rhetoric of an 'Office for Health Promotion'.

Personalised care can't be done without enough staff to attend to patients' needs. Under this heading Javid also revives the idea of personal health budgets, which proved unpopular and impractical when proposed by NHS England in 2014, and the 'right to choose' which hospital to go to for elective care, which is already in the NHS Constitution, but does nothing to address the shortage of capacity in the NHS.

Javid's call to improve performance without any plan to solve the shortage of staff centres on expansion of digital systems that require more cash (and private sector expertise) to put in place, and which threaten to further isolate the millions of people who have significant health needs but remain 'digitally excluded'.

Response

Rejecting this nonsense, this book offers a concerned reader an up-to-date guide to the ruins, spelling out the scale of the crisis that has been created since the NHS was at its peak performance in 2010, explaining the main policies and plans, analysing the extent and impact of privatisation, and pointing to the campaigns and initiatives that offer ways to do something about it.

However, we have not attempted the bigger task, which is impossible in a book of this length, of seeking to integrate an analysis of the process of privatisation and decline that has led to the current chronic crisis in social care. Since Sainsbury boss Roy Griffiths first identified long-term care of older people as a suitable target for means-tested charges and privatisation in 1988, the previous public provision of NHS geriatric beds and council-run home help services has been replaced by a nightmarish chaos of profit-seeking care homes and brutally exploitative home care companies paying minimum numbers of staff minimum wage, often on zero hours contracts. Since 2010 the massive year by year cuts in funding to local government have compounded the problem – and opened yawning gaps where a service should be in place.

We recognise that the crisis in the NHS can't be completely solved without a radical reform of social care, but there is no consensus on what this should look like, and no substantial campaign that unite the various interest groups into a common fight to rescue and transform a care sector that spans a variety of specific areas from children's homes and child protection, through support for people with disabilities, to care of the frail elderly and elderly mentally ill. We have not felt able to do justice to these issues, and don't wish to appear to be telling campaigners what they should be doing, so this has to remain a missing element in our analysis.

One aspect of social care is, however, taken up in the Chapter by Jan Shortt of the National Pensioners Convention, which is one of over a dozen shorter chapters that we have included to allow well-known experts and leaders – from the trade unions, public health, child health, pensioners, management experts, and Covid-19 Bereaved Families for Justice – to explore specific issues and aspects of the crisis. We are delighted that so many people have accepted our invitation to submit a chapter, and their contributions are important in lending extra dimensions and depth to the analysis.

Resistance

It's very important to stress that the siege has been resisted. Almost every measure at national or local level that has attacked, eroded or undermined the NHS has been met by a level of resistance unmatched in any other public service.

This book is intended to arm and fuel that resistance rather than concede defeat. So we conclude with a brief chapter on what can be done to strengthen the defences, and reach out as widely as possible to build the kind of broad, inclusive movement that is needed to drive back the encroaching forces.

In January and February 2022 a new, broad alliance, SOSNHS was established at the initiative of Health Campaigns Together and Keep Our NHS Public. It links campaigners with trade unions and has won the endorsement of over 50 organisations. It has staged a major online rally, a Day of Action spanning 85 events across the country on 26 February 2022 and launched a 175,000-strong petition handed in to Downing Street on the eve of the Spring Budget. The alliance centres on three key demands:

- the need for a massive £20 billion injection of emergency funding to kick-start the recovery of the NHS and its performance;
- the need to invest in a significant above inflation pay in-crease for NHS staff to ensure the workforce can grow to meet the needs of the NHS;
- the need to ensure that all of the investment is channelled into reopening, rebuilding and expanding the NHS and its capacity, and is not squandered on private providers.

The initial success of this campaign points the way forward to building a popular movement big and powerful enough to get Tory backbenchers to break ranks and put pressure on the government to change course.

It's important that the campaign runs under the positive slogan SOSNHS. The NHS is deep in crisis, it's under siege, it has been eroded and undermined; the private sector has made significant inroads – but there is still a lot of NHS left to rescue and defend. At stake is the availability of emergency treatment, comprehensive treatment, services that can be planned according to local needs, and treatment based on patients' needs rather than the prospect of profit. This book is our contribution to that defence.

Our hope is that it will help lift the siege and keep our NHS public!

Jacky Davis and John Lister, 21 March 2022

Chapter 1

The first decade of austerity: 2010-2019

John Lister

This chapter charts the decade of decline in the NHS that followed New Labour's decade of investment and privatisation. It begins with the change of political and financial regime in 2010 as the Cameron coalition took over, and its brutal austerity regime slammed the brakes on NHS spending, using the McKinsey report commissioned by Labour after the banking crash.

It looks briefly at the Health and Social Care Act) that broke the Tory promise of 'no more top-down reorganisation', but was passed in 2012 with backing from the LibDems. It shows the scale of "efficiency savings" that began to force closures of NHS hospitals, and cuts and centralisation of services, and reviews the Act's impact on privatisation, especially of mental health and community health services.

It discusses the subsequent efforts of NHS England to work around the Act, beginning with the Five Year Forward View in 2014 – which lacked any workforce strategy. In 2016 England's NHS was carved into 42 Sustainability and Transformation Plans (STPs), which attempted to force through more cuts by claiming local 'affordability gaps' totalling £23bn. When STPs were toxified as a concept by campaigners warning they meant 'Slash, Trash and Privatise' they were replaced by so-called 'integrated care'. In each case new structures were being created that stood outside the law and lacked any local legitimacy or accountability.

As waiting lists and waiting times increased, in 2018 Theresa May followed an apology for the state of the NHS with a 70th birthday funding settlement for the NHS that promised an extra £34bn over five years, worth just £20bn in real terms, nowhere near enough to compensate for eight years of frozen funding. A year later Boris Johnson took over as PM and ran a Brexit-focused election promising an 'extra' 40 hospitals, but with nowhere near enough money to pay for them, or to implement the NHS Long Term Plan published in January 2019.

The first decade of austerity ended (and the pandemic began) with almost 9,000 'general and acute' beds having closed along with 22% of mental health beds, and England's waiting list increased by 2 million to 4.5m.

* * *

The change of regime

The transition from feast to famine in NHS funding was swift, as one decade ended and the new one began. Even prior to the change of government in May 2010 it was already obvious from New Labour's plans, warnings and more guarded promises that the decade of record growth in NHS spending from 2000 was coming to an end.

The impact of the 2008 banking crisis had brought an economic slump, coupled with a huge increase in government borrowing, with up to £137bn of public money – around 7.5% of GDP[1] – used as loans and capital to stabilise the banks. And while Labour ministers committed to honour their promise of above inflation funding in 2009-10 it was already clear that the years of record increases in real terms spending on the NHS were over.

The change of government, as Gordon Brown lost the election in 2010 and David Cameron's 'ConDem' coalition with the Liberal Democrats took over, opened a prolonged period of 'austerity', imposing severe limits on spending on public services and welfare benefits,[2] and what proved to be a decade of decline in resources and performance.

The high-priest of austerity, George Osborne, one of the coterie of 23 millionaires in Cameron's 29-strong cabinet, was keen to pass off the borrowing (much of which has subsequently been repaid) as deficits left behind by Labour, and use the scale of this 'deficit' as the excuse for squeezing down spending on public services, while cutting taxes for big business. In six years as chancellor he never admitted that the economy was already recovering when he took over and slammed on the brakes in 2010.

The Cameron government's claim was that NHS spending was being 'ring-fenced' and protected from cuts; by comparison with other departments, which faced deeper cutbacks to spare the NHS, this was obviously true. However, this still left the NHS facing five years of record low increases in spending, and real terms cuts as cost pressures and population increased.

While total spending on government departments was to be slashed on average by around 10% between 2010 and 2015, with some departments losing 20% or more, NHS spending was to grow, but only by 6%. This was well below the average levels of spending increase in the previous 62 years.[3]

Misleading manifesto

The new austerity had not been advertised in the Conservative 2010 election manifesto, which had claimed that they would 'outspend' New Labour (who had outlined no commitment going forward and largely downplayed the NHS as an issue). The Tories also promised (falsely, as we discovered within weeks of the election) that there would be 'no more top-down reorganisation' of the NHS.

But the tightening spending squeeze from 2010 was grimly predictable from previous periods of Tory government. Former Nat West banker Derek Wanless, in reports for Gordon Brown in 2001 and 2002,[4] had shown that successive governments in the 25 years to 1998 had underinvested in the NHS by up to £267bn; in all but six of those years the Tories were in office. Indeed in 62 years of the NHS only one ruling party had shown the courage to pump significant and sustained increased resources into health care, to improve performance dramatically – and it wasn't the Tories.

From 1979 to 1997 the NHS had endured outright spending cuts, the privatisation of hospital support services (with disastrous results), and Margaret Thatcher's wasteful and ideologically motivated 'internal market' reforms. Long term care for older people, now referred to as 'social care', was transferred from the NHS, where it was free at point of use, to local government social services, where it has been almost completely privatised and remains subject to means tested charges, more cuts and soaring waiting lists.

New Labour's record – more spending, more privatisation

By contrast, 13 years of New Labour, and most significantly the ten years from 2000, had brought a real, positive transformation. Huge new resources had been pumped into the NHS, with spending rising at the fastest rate in 60 years. Health spending almost trebled in cash terms between 1997 and 2010, with generous above inflation year-on-year increases from 2001, pushing the share of national wealth spent on health up towards the European average.[5]

Waiting times were dramatically reduced, with the 18-week

maximum wait putting the NHS among the best health systems in Europe; staff numbers were increased.

There were also over 100 new hospitals, built, or begun, although almost all of these were funded through the controversial Private Finance Initiative (PFI), the most expensive and ridiculous possible way to raise the money. The costs of this are still being shouldered by trusts into the 2020s and 2030s.[6]

PFI was just one of many flaws in New Labour's record. Another was that instead of sticking to their promise to sweep away Margaret Thatcher's costly and wasteful 'internal' market system, Blair and Brown hung on to it, made it more complex and bureaucratic, and brought in far more private sector involvement than the Tories ever dreamed of.

So it was New Labour, not the Tories, who first began contracting out NHS clinical care to private hospitals and providers and who first established an 'NHS Commercial Directorate' in 2003 to promote greater involvement of the private sector. This was headed initially by Texan Ken Anderson, who staffed the 200-strong directorate almost exclusively with management consultants and contractors. From 2007 he was succeeded by another American, former United Health director R. Channing Wheeler, who told the *HSJ* in 2008 of his ambition that:

> Independent sector providers will weave and integrate with the NHS and I hope we will start to just think of NHS-registered providers of care, so it doesn't matter whether they are acute trusts, foundation trusts, independent sector or voluntary providers.

Overhead costs of this increasingly complex and bureaucratic market system mushroomed (eventually estimated at £4.5 billion per year in 2014[7]), while the talk of 'efficiency' had never been louder as NHS commissioners and providers sought to cut spending by centralising and reorganising services.

With the market system came an indecipherable jargon on 'World Class Commissioning',[8] and a swarming of private sector management consultants, who were among the corporations welcomed by Tony

Blair into an ever-widening 'NHS Family'. In 2008, 14 giant private sector corporations, including four big American health insurers and care managers – Aetna, Humana, UnitedHealth and Health Dialog Services – along with KPMG and McKinsey and UK-based private companies including BUPA and Axa PPP were added to a list of firms pre-approved to bid for contracts to help local Primary Care Trusts spend their £75bn NHS commissioning budgets as part of the 'Framework for Procuring External Support for Commissioners' (FESC).[9]

There had also been a relentless drive to draw in private providers to deliver clinical services and even community and mental health services through the 'Transforming Community Services' policy, and the expensive irrelevance of 'Independent Sector Treatment Centres'.[10]

But while Labour could obviously have spent much of the extra money more wisely, it was clear from their previous 18 years in office that the Tories wouldn't have spent that extra money at all. Left to them, the waiting list would have remained at least at the sky-high level it was under John Major in 1997, with hundreds of thousands of people waiting 18 months or more for treatment.

And while Labour stupidly rolled out the red carpet for private providers, the Tories were no opponents of privatisation; they had been the first to begin contracting out NHS services, and have since proved their determination to drive it further.

Nonetheless, New Labour's flawed record had severely weakened the party's standing by 2010. Many angry Labour and trade union activists, frustrated at the government's adherence to Thatcher's anti-union laws and continuation of her privatisation offensive, even argued that there was 'no choice' between the main parties.

McKinsey and the £20bn challenge

The cynicism was compounded by the fact that New Labour ministers, despite public denials and a refusal to publish the report, were known to have commissioned management consultants McKinsey in 2009 to investigate how £20 billion of 'savings' could be squeezed from the NHS by 2014.[11]

The £20bn savings target was embraced from the outset by NHS

Chief Executive Sir David Nicholson, who warned, on the basis of the economic crisis, that NHS trusts and commissioners should be prepared 'for a range of scenarios, including the possibility that investment will be frozen for a time'.

In what became known as the 'Nicholson challenge' he told NHS leaders to 'plan on the assumption that we will need to realise unprecedented levels of efficiency savings between 2011 and 2014 – between £15 billion and £20 billion across the service over three years'.[12]

It was therefore no coincidence that George Osborne's first Spending Review in 2010 also set a £20bn target for the NHS, requiring year-on-year efficiency gains of 4 per cent for the next four years – a level of savings never achieved previously (or since).

In reality the 'Nicholson Challenge' should have been called the Banker's Bonus or the Tax Dodgers' Legacy. The cuts had been triggered by the banking crisis and continued despite the fact that uncollected tax alone added up to £120bn a year, six times the £20 billion target for cuts by 2014.[13]

A National Audit Office report to the Commons Health Committee in 2011 explained that the challenge was more complicated because the NHS was certain to face significant additional demand for services arising from the age and lifestyle of the population as well as the need to fund new technologies and drugs, but it would have to cope without any real terms increase in funding from 2011 to 2015. The NAO warned that the government had asked the NHS to make efficiency savings of up to £20 billion by 2014-15 whilst simultaneously driving up the quality of services and the outcomes it achieved.[14]

The cutbacks fell unevenly on England's ten Strategic Health Authorities (SHAs).[15] Two were required to make savings of 17.3%, others all faced higher targets, with four SHAs facing cuts of more than 20% in their planned regional budgets.[16]

These underlying targets and plans to rein in spending after a decade of growth meant hospital trusts across the country had already drawn up plans to axe large numbers of jobs before the May election in 2010. By April 2010 cuts of over £300m, axing beds and jobs, had been announced, including hospitals in Leicestershire, Southampton, Salford, Oxfordshire, Gloucestershire, Nottingham, Gateshead, Wirral and Cambridge.[17]

So by the time George Osborne began drawing up his first budget the NHS had already got the message: the good times were long gone, and the financial squeeze was on for the indefinite future.

To underline the fact that the first plans for austerity had been laid by New Labour, Health Secretary Andrew Lansley triumphantly published the McKinsey report in July 2010,[18] making rather less noise about the fact that many of the plans it contained were to be rolled out under the coalition.

McKinsey formula for cuts and closures

Centralisation of emergency and other hospital services was one of the core suggestions advocated by McKinsey. This inevitably resulted in cuts, downgrades and closures. By the end of July 2010 Lansley ended the brief 'moratorium' on hospital closures he had opportunistically announced a few months earlier, when hospital cutbacks and closures had become an issue in the run-up to the election.

Just two months after the election NHS Chief Executive David Nicholson told Strategic Health Authorities they should decide on contested closures and warned against 'potentially vexatious objections' from stakeholders who remained opposed.[19]

The NHS Confederation, the body representing both com- missioners and providers, happily accepted the new approach, telling NHS bosses that they had to 'think big' and seek large-scale changes if they were to meet tough targets to squeeze down costs and spending. This could mean that 'beds and wards need to be closed, but also entire buildings and possibly whole sites'.

An even more blunt message came from the King's Fund's chief economist John Appleby, who defended the 'ring-fence' protection of the NHS from the wider public spending cuts by spelling out the scale of threat to the NHS posed by the coming cash squeeze. If the NHS were not protected, he argued, it would have to find actual cuts amounting to around 14% of its budget (£18 billion), and suggested five ways it could do this:

- 30% real pay cut for all staff;
- Abolish the NHS in London;
- No drugs;
- Sack all consultants and general practitioners;
- Abolish the NHS in Scotland and Wales.

A different approach would be 'for whole services to close down':

- no NHS dentistry (£2bn);
- no community services (£9bn);
- no ophthalmic services (£0.5bn);
and still another £6.5bn to find.[20]

None of these were palatable options for NHS bosses or the politicians. But some of the plans drawn up by managers 'thinking big' were also daunting. By Autumn 2010 London's five Strategic Health Authorities had each published blood-curdling projections of their spending gaps. They added up to £3.3 billion, which the SHAs argued had to be addressed with major cutbacks and savings.

- North-East London wanted to close 827 acute beds (about one in five), decommission services, make £237m cuts in non-acute services and 'efficiency savings' from the McKinsey list in order to save up to £540m by 2017.
- North-West London estimated its gap at £796m and looked to a similar combination of cuts in beds and hospital closures and 'efficiency savings'.
- North Central London, projecting a smaller gap of £560m by 2017, was planning to axe 250-500 acute beds, cut mental health beds, and find 'efficiency savings'.
- South-West London was looking to save £300m by 2017.
- South-East London was projecting a £467m shortfall by 2014 and a monster £810m-£1,090m gap by 2017, and using these as reasons to contemplate cutting the tariff prices paid for each treatment to NHS trusts, to save £224m on acute services and £62m on mental health.[21]

Mental health was also facing cutbacks with a quarter of beds set to close in Sussex, major cuts in Oxfordshire and psychology services being put out to tender to save money in Camden.

Around 11,000 job losses had been announced by 106 acute Trusts, with a specialist children's unit at Frenchay in Bristol to be closed, and hospital cuts also looming in Plymouth, Reading, York, Aintree, and the North-East.

So by the autumn of 2010, just six months after the election, the government had fully imposed austerity.

Limits on cutbacks

However, three factors impeded the implementation of such large cutbacks. The first two were political and linked: the strong likelihood, if not certainty, of local resistance to closures of hospitals and services; and the coalition government's concern not to stir up political pressure as they pushed through legislation for a massive top-down reorganisation of the NHS that did not reach the statute book until spring 2012.[22] The third factor is a more practical one: local NHS bosses have in most cases pulled back from agreeing to cuts in acute services that are likely to result in embarrassing failures of emergency services – even if this means running up financial deficits.

The third factor was the continued pressure on NHS services and the impracticability of cutting back capacity without an immediate and obvious impact on emergency care, waiting lists and waiting times. It was not until the summer of 2012, once the Health and Social Care Act was on the statute book, that the extended standstill on cuts in pursuit of the £20 billion 'efficiency' target came to an end.

Then the list of cuts grew longer week by week. Hospitals in Stafford, Rugby, Kidderminster, Redditch, Trafford General in Greater Manchester, Newark, Northallerton and Hartlepool were under threat, with cutbacks in East Sussex.[23]

In north-west London four A&E units – Ealing, Central Middlesex, Charing Cross and Hammersmith – faced the axe; St Helier hospital in the south-west was also to be run down, along with King George's hospital in Ilford, north-east London, and Chase Farm in north central.[24][25]

The biggest crisis was in south-east London. Queen Mary's hospital in Sidcup, which had already been largely dismembered in futile attempts to balance the books of the South London Healthcare Trust (SLHT), was facing the axe. The trust was wrestling with ruinous PFI payments for two hospitals (Queen Elizabeth in Greenwich and Princess Royal in Orpington) which had together cost about £210m to build, but had been on the brink of bankruptcy for years. In 2012, with over £500m already paid off, there was still another £2 billion to pay. These inflated PFI costs were dragging down health services for a million people in south-east London. In the autumn of 2012, a 'trust special administrator' was brought in, who called for not only the dismemberment of the failing SLHT, but also proposed major cutbacks in the neighbouring, quite separate, Lewisham Hospital Trust, triggering a massive, and ultimately successful campaign to defend it.[26]

2013 began with more drastic cuts, including

- Hertfordshire – £276m (17%) to be cut over four years.
- Rotherham Foundation Trust – 20% of the workforce to be cut to save £50m from its £220m budget.
- and Norfolk & Suffolk Foundation Trust cutting mental health services, axing 21% of jobs (33 consultants, 60% of staff grade doctors, 200 Band 6 and 34 Band 5 nurses and therapists) and 86 beds over four years.[27]

Meanest ever

In March 2013 new figures from the NHS Confederation confirmed that the four years 2011-2015 were set to be the meanest-ever years for funding since the NHS was established in 1948. Real terms spending was to rise by just 0.1% per year over the 4-year period, far short of the increase in demand for health care from the aging population, inflation in the costs of goods and services required by the NHS, and the cost pressures of new technology and new drugs.

The curse of PFI was also driving cuts in Dewsbury in Yorkshire, which had been unlucky enough to be merged into the Mid-Yorkshire Hospitals Trust, whose newly completed £320m PFI deal fell immediately and deeply into crisis. Dewsbury faced the loss of its A&E, while Pontefract's brand new urgent care centre, run by the same trust, had already been scaled back, and the main PFI hospital in Wakefield, short of beds, was struggling to cope.[28]

Hospital trusts also faced a year-by-year demand for 4% 'efficiency' savings. Acute trusts were being penalised with a 30% reduction in payments for every additional emergency patient treated above the contracted level.[29] However, promises of alternative services, including improvements in community health and primary care, remained simply promises.

The claim had always been that 'savings' were to be recycled back into the NHS: but in 2010-12 £3 billion of NHS unspent 'surpluses' were clawed back into Treasury coffers, while thousands of nurses had lost their jobs, beds had closed, and over a million NHS staff had suffered a hefty real terms cut in pay.[30]

The situation was made worse by the inexorably rising costs and consequences of Private Finance Initiative contracts, which each year were milking even larger payments and profits from the shrinking NHS pot. Twelve of the 30 trusts most challenged on emergency performance were saddled with large and growing commitments to service PFI bills: these dozen PFI hospitals had cost £2.7 billion to build, but would cost upwards of £16.7 billion in PFI charges.[31]

By autumn 2013 it was clear that the 'challenge' of saving £20 billion by 2015 (most savings for which had come from effectively cutting the pay of over 1 million NHS staff) was to be followed by an even steeper 'challenge' of saving another £30m by 2020. Crisis management had become a permanent way of life for the decade.

The medical director of the obscure new 'London Area Team' of NHS England, Dr Andy Mitchell, emerged from the shadows to claim that London's hospital services were 'unsustainable', and that swift action was needed to close half its A&E units and many of its maternity and children's services. On closer examination it was clear Dr Mitchell was concerned first and foremost with finances, since his warning was that action had to be taken to prevent London's NHS running up a £4 billion deficit by 2020, and he went on to argue that the capital's trusts could 'not afford' to staff wards safely.[32]

Desperation was clear in cash saving plans when Worcestershire, where hospital beds averaged 99% occupancy (compared with the safe occupancy level of 85%) decided to close beds. Services were to close in Redditch and Bromsgrove and relocate to Worcester,[33] with no serious consideration of the problems, especially for elderly and low-income patients who would be forced to make ever-longer cross-county journeys to access care, while those with the most trivial need would still be catered for locally in 'urgent care centres'.

In January 2014 the Nuffield Trust published figures which showed the scale of the gap that was looming between NHS resources and demands, warning of a further £30 billion gap by 2022 if the current spending plans were left unchanged.[34]

Early in 2014 Bart's Health, the biggest health trust in England was found to be deep in debt, sinking deeper, with projected deficits for 2014-15 rocketing upwards from £43m in December 2013 to £93m by its February board meeting – or even as much as £100m, according to the *Health Service Journal*.[35]

The financial problem had been a ticking time bomb ever since the Trust was given the go-ahead in 2006 to sign up for the £1.1bn PFI scheme to redevelop both Bart's and the Royal London hospitals. The trust had taken over Newham and Whipps Cross hospitals,[36] and their combined turnover, to increase Barts Health's total revenue by over 50%. This appeared to reduce the PFI payments as a proportion of trust turnover, from 16% to a less scary – but still unaffordable 11%. However East London Clinical Commissioning Groups had drawn up a joint strategy 'Transforming Services, Changing Lives'[37] requiring local NHS trusts to find 'savings' totalling £434m, of which £324m had to come from Barts Health. There seemed to be no way out, short of massive cuts in the two non-PFI hospitals, Newham and Whipps Cross.

By April 2014 the impact of austerity on mental health services was again highlighted, as actual spending levels fell. 1,700 beds had closed since 2010, leaving dire shortages in various parts of the country, not least for child and adolescent mental health, where young people were often transported hundreds of miles to find a spare bed, or even placed on adult wards. In Norfolk and Suffolk the mental health trust was simultaneously cutting back on both beds *and* community mental health provision, while dispatching dozens of patients to beds many miles from their homes and families.[38,39]

The gaps in social care were perhaps even greater, with massive cuts across the board hitting mental health the hardest: by 2014 the numbers of people with mental health problems receiving social care had been cut by 48% since 2005; one in three councils had cut mental health services by 50% or more.[40]

Widening gap

Even George Osborne's own Office of Budget Responsibility (OBR) was warning of the widening gap between required spending and available resources. OBR figures showed that the share of national wealth (GDP) spent on the NHS, which had grown in the 2000s, was set to decline from 6.5% in 2012 (already low in comparison to similar countries in Europe) to 6.2% in 2015. John Appleby of the King's Fund warned it could fall to 6% or less by 2021, wiping out all the extra investment under Labour.[41]

A large majority of hospital trusts had ended 2012-13 with deficits, and 19 financially troubled trusts had been referred by the Audit Commission to Jeremy Hunt.[42] University Hospitals Leicester, £41m in the red, was borrowing money to open extra beds; Lincolnshire health bosses, seeking to 'save' £105m by 2018, were looking to cut 300 beds and 'centralise' A&E, maternity and paediatric services to save money. Nottinghamshire's Sherwood Forest Hospitals FT revealed it was forking out almost £1 in every £6 it received (£3.56m each month) to service the PFI contract on the new £320m King's Mill Hospital. The total repayments, including some support services, would be a staggering £2.5bn – eight times the initial cost.[43]

The NHS cutbacks brought a private sector bonanza: in July 2014 the Nuffield Trust published damning figures showing the rapid increase in the share of NHS spending on private sector community and mental health services that had been scooped up by the private sector. Non-NHS provision in mental health services had increased by 15% in real terms between 2011/12 and 2012/13 alone, and:

One pound in every five spent by commissioners on community health services in 2012/13 was spent on care provided by independent sector providers, an increase of 34 per cent in one year alone. Along with the money spent on voluntary and other providers of community services, this means that nearly one third of the £9.75 billion the NHS spends on community health services is now with non-NHS providers.[44]

Also in 2014 new NHS England chief executive Simon Stevens launched a 'Five Year Forward View' – calling for an extra £8bn funding to 2020, and promising to deliver an improbable £22bn more in 'efficiency savings'. We now know NHS England was not permitted by the Treasury to talk about future capital investment, social care or workforce training, without which the plan was a largely empty statement of aspirations.[45]

In 2014 a new Immigration Act involved the NHS in a nasty extension of the 'hostile environment' which Home Secretary Theresa May had unleashed in 2012, notionally to make life miserable for 'illegal' immigrants, but in fact cranking up racist hostility to all who might appear to be immigrants. The new legislation, which took effect from 2015, expanded the pre-existing – and previously widely ignored – regulations requiring 'overseas visitors' to be charged for using the NHS.[46]

It broadened the group of people who were subject to charges, introduced a new £200 'immigration health surcharge' for anyone seeking visas to enter the UK, and allowed NHS Trusts to charge up to 150% of the cost of treatment in secondary care. NHS Trusts were now in theory required to question everyone's eligibility for care upfront; but of course it was people of colour who were always the most likely to be checked, potentially blocking or delaying their access to care. The new law, subsequently further toughened, struck a major blow at the notion of the NHS as a universal service, covering all who need care, and funded not from user fees but from general taxation. As the Patients Not Passports campaign explained, this undermined the patient-healthcare provider relationship, not least because it soon became clear that NHS Digital was systematically sharing patient data with the Home Office for immigration enforcement purposes.[47]

Winter crisis 2014

By December 2014 the headlines were unrelenting: hospital after hospital declared 'Black alerts' as they ran out of beds and diverted blue light ambulances to hospitals miles away. Beds filled up as older patients stayed on after treatment for lack of social care to support them if discharged. Delays in A&E were the worst since weekly records began. Waiting times for operations began to increase as numbers on waiting lists hit 3 million.

In January 2015 NHS Providers, representing the majority of NHS hospital Trusts, refused – for the first time ever – to sign off the proposed 'tariff' of fees the NHS paid for each patient treated, arguing that a fifth successive year of cuts would mean trusts could no longer guarantee the safe care of patients.[48]

Five years of cuts amounting to almost 40% in spending on social care had also prompted council leaders and the NHS Confederation to jointly sign a letter to *The Observer* with health professional bodies, warning of the dangers to patients if more cuts continued. GP leaders had been warning for some time of the growing shortage of GPs and the falling real terms budget for primary care.[49]

Every story revealing the growing crisis was met by a routine knee-jerk denial by the Department of Health, or NHS England, which had jacked up its spending on PR and communications staff to 'spin' the bad news by 37% in the previous 12 months, to £6.1m.[50]

Meanwhile, despite the looming general election there was little if any political opposition to the pressures on the NHS. Labour lacked even the boldness of the Blair years, mounting no real challenge in its election campaign to the continued brutal austerity, and therefore failing to make electoral capital from the Tory cuts. The party still echoed Blair's claims that the NHS needed the support of the private sector, although they did promise to scrap the competition rules in Lansley's 2012 Act, re-establish the NHS as 'preferred provider' and reimpose the limits on the amount of private patient income Foundation Trusts could raise.[51]

Another Tory victory – new threats to NHS values

The Tory victory in the 2015 election, albeit with a majority of just 12, predictably cranked up more pressure on the NHS. Newly-appointed Tory Minister for NHS Productivity, Lord Prior, wanted to force through a massive round of hospital closures, and axe 50,000 acute beds; he even set up an inquiry into the possibility of funding the NHS through user fees for service.[52],[53]

The Chartered Institute for Public Finance and Accountancy – which dismissed any likelihood of the NHS making the required £22 billion of savings over the next five years – also produced a report arguing that the government had to either come up with more money for the NHS, or reduce services, or ... charge users more: 'To choose none of those is not a realistic option.'[54]

Monitor, the NHS regulator, also argued there was simply not enough money to maintain NHS services as before – again proving that Cameron's bland pre-election promises of an extra £8 billion for the NHS by 2020 were no guarantee that services would not be slashed to ribbons and the most potentially profitable services privatised. Monitor wrote to trusts, which were facing deficits totalling £2bn, telling them all financial penalties for missing targets were being suspended, enabling them to disregard targets for waiting times, and tear up guidance on safe staffing levels, in a desperate effort to balance the books, regardless of the consequences.[55]

In London, the claimed NHS 'affordability gap' had risen still further – to £4.8bn by 2020, of which £3bn was down to London trusts (25% of their turnover, with two thirds of them projecting deficits), and £1.74bn from commissioners whose savings would almost certainly mean cutting contracts with trusts.[56]

By November 2015 a survey of members of the Healthcare Finance Management Association found 88% of NHS finance chiefs were unconvinced that their organisations could deliver the target of 2-3% efficiency savings. More than 84% believed the Five Year Forward View was unachievable because trusts lacked the resources required. However, George Osborne's Spending Review statement soon afterwards offered the NHS an even bleaker prospect, with extremely lean years from 2017 onwards.[57]

A new reorganisation

Just before Christmas 2015 NHS England sent out new instructions to NHS leaders – telling them to begin a wholesale reorganisation of the NHS. This involved dividing England into far fewer 'footprints', within which providers and commissioners were required to work together at speed to draw up 'Sustainability and Transformation Plans' (STPs), with a focus on how to bridge the huge financial gap between needs and resources.[58]

In March 2016 NHS England published a map identifying 44 STP areas. The STPs were from the outset a formula for enforcing cuts. Before the STPs areas were announced Trusts had already been told to consider all measures, including staffing cuts, to tackle their deficits, which were at all-time record levels, averaging £15m per acute trust. Twenty financially challenged trusts had been forced into a 'turnaround' process, costing each trust an average £500,000 on management consultants, with little result. In mid-March the Commons Public Accounts Committee (PAC) criticised the government for being too slow to address growing hospital deficits.[59]

The American professor Don Berwick, world expert on developing effective healthcare systems and improving quality of care, who had been brought in to give advice to David Cameron's coalition government, warned that government funding policy for the NHS was an 'experiment'. He told the *Health Service Journal* that to try to run 'a universal health system, free at the point of care, government funded, [with] ever increasing excellence' for about 7% of GDP was 'risky', and 'way out on the edge compared with any other Western, developed democracy I know'.[60]

Chris Hopson, chief executive of NHS Providers, which represents foundation trusts and NHS trusts, warned: 'The events, reforms and policies of recent years have created a climate where it is nearly impossible to maintain a balanced budget while maintaining quality of care and meeting rising demand.'[61]

Renewed squeeze on spending

Worse, from 2018, George Osborne's miserly budget would mean two more years with increases of less than 1 per cent. This was not altered by the result of the 23 June Brexit referendum, despite the ludicrous claim on the side of the Brexit bus that the UK was paying £350m a week to Brussels, and that some or all of this could be spent on the NHS if Britain left the EU. Barely had the votes been counted before UKIP's Nigel Farage admitted on GMTV that he had never agreed with the idea – and leading Tories began to distance themselves from it.[62]

Of course, the tight-fisted policies did not originate in Brussels but in the UK Treasury. There was no reason why the Tory government could not have simply decided to spend more money on the NHS, rather than impose George Osborne's brutal austerity regime. And the policy was not changed despite Brexit, and the subsequent change of prime minister and chancellor as Theresa May and Phillip Hammond took over.

The squeeze meant that more CCGs were drawing up lists of which services they would cease to fund for elective treatment. These ranged from relatively 'soft' targets, such as IVF treatment (incurring high costs for few people), to more mainstream services like joint replacements, hernia repair and cataract operations – the type of treatments which private hospitals find profitable to take on for paying patients.[63]

Social care was also still under the axe. A survey of all councils in England by social services directors (ADASS) warned of further reductions of £371m in services for people needing care and for their carers. This followed five years of funding reductions totalling £4.6bn. Worse, almost half the savings would be made through outright cuts.[64]

All 44 STP Footprints had been required to draw up five-year plans at rapid pace. NHS England insisted any consultation on the plans would only come at the end of the year – after the plans had been finalised and vetted by NHS England bureaucrats. So obsessive was the level of secrecy that in North-West London council leaders were pressurised to sign a 2-page document which was (falsely) claimed to be a 'summary' of the local STP – without seeing the full document! The full text, still confidential and unfinished, was draft 39, indicating the number of versions already discussed behind closed doors. It had 51 densely packed pages, containing repeated commitments to close Ealing and Charing Cross Hospitals.

Reset – more centralisation

NHS England published a 'Reset' plan which argued that hospitals and services which depended on locums and agency staff should be closed, and services centralised in 'nearby' larger units:

> By the end of July STPs should have reviewed services which are unsustainable for financial, quality or other reasons [...]. They should have developed plans to re-provide these services in collaboration with other providers to secure clinically and financially sustainable services, both for 2016/17 and for future years.[65]

As the first STP drafts began to emerge, it was clear many were seeking savings through 'reconfiguration', despite the lack of any capital for investment in alternative services for the hospitals that were to be closed or downgraded.[66] This weakness undermined their credibility.[67] Shropshire's STP, for example, wanted to axe an A&E (to 'save' £22m per year), but the scheme would cost £300m.

In October 2016 Sally Gainsbury and Mark Dayan of the Nuffield Trust demolished government claims that the NHS was getting an extra £8bn, revealing that it could be as little as £800m over five years.[68] Sarah Wollaston, Tory Chair of the Commons Health Committee joined those openly criticising the government's deception.[69] And a senior NHS England director, Julia Simon, resigned, denouncing the 'mad' STP process as shameful, and the plans as full of lies.[70]

An NHS Providers survey showed just one in six NHS finance directors believed they could deliver on STP plans, because there was just not enough money in the pot.[71]

When all of their plans were finally published at the end of 2016, the 44 STPs between them were forecasting a combined deficit of over £23bn by 2020. 82% of this was for the NHS, the remainder for social care. The plans called for capital investment totalling over £14 billion[72]. Twenty-three STPs were proposing to close acute and community beds. 18 STPs had plans to close A&E services. But by the autumn of 2017 many STPs had begun to retreat from these proposals as trusts warned of the likely consequences in the coming winter.

Doctors' petition

In February 2017 a petition to ministers signed by over 2,000 senior doctors was prematurely publicised before even more could sign up.[73] They were demanding the government back down on its relentless squeeze on NHS funding, after a winter of near-misses and system failures. In some areas Tory MPs, wary of more cuts looming and the threat to close or downgrade hospitals, had also begun pressing Theresa May's government to reconsider its refusal to relax the vicious austerity policy.

Instead ministers admitted funding was set to fall further behind in 2017 and actually drop by 0.6% per person in 2018. Health minister Philip Dunne argued NHS England's per capita real terms budget had increased by 3.2% in 2016-17. However, much of this had already been swallowed by deficits. Moreover, growth would fall sharply in 2017-18, to just a 0.9% increase in 2017 – and then go negative by 2018-19 with a 0.6% fall in real spending per head.[74]

NHS Providers produced a hard-hitting report, *Mission Impossible*, insisting that ministers who decide to impose austerity cuts on NHS spending must be forced to face the actual consequences, and take responsibility for the chaos that results. Its CEO Chris Hopson said:

> NHS Providers has analysed what NHS trusts have to deliver from 1 April 2017 and compared it to the available funding. The result is an unbridgeable gap, with worrying implications for patients and staff.[75]

The Health Foundation also published a report which warned that private providers were growing at the expense of NHS trusts: 'NHS providers received just £650m of the £2bn of extra funding for commissioners in 2015/16. This was less than the £900m of additional funding that went to pay for care provided by non-NHS bodies.'[76]

With an increased proportion of its own beds taken up with emergency cases, and more of the profitable elective services going to private hospitals, the NHS was being forced into becoming an emergency only service.

2017 election

As a snap election was called by Theresa May to exploit what seemed to be a runaway lead in the polls, NHS Providers, representing NHS trusts and foundation trusts, issued its own manifesto. It called on all parties to end the austerity funding of the health service, and inject an extra £5 billion a year until 2020, as well as £10bn in capital to pay for backlog maintenance and upgrading.[77]

Labour's manifesto, largely carried over from the one that had made so little impact in 2015, was nowhere near as radical, with just over a page of vaguely worded waffle and few clear commitments.[78] It made no commitment to repeal the 2012 Health and Social Care Act, and failed to exploit the scale of the Tory failures on the NHS, not least the woeful failure to invest in diagnostics and capacity. This left Britain as 30th out of 32 wealthier countries on provision of CT scanners, 29th out of 31 on MRI scanners – and 33rd out of 35 on provision of hospital beds.

On the eve of the election, the *Health Service Journal* leaked the news that NHS England and the regulator NHS Improvement had for months been secretly discussing draconian measures to force down spending to comply with the tightening cash freeze. NHS managers in debt-ridden trusts and commissioning groups in 14 areas had been told to 'think the unthinkable', including 'changes which are normally avoided as they are too unpleasant, unpopular or controversial'.[79]

One chief executive told the *HSJ* some of the proposals 'challenged the value base' of NHS leaders. But the NHS bosses lacked the courage to release or even leak these details to the public and to the politicians in time to allow voters to react to this new threat of major cuts.

Soon after the election more details emerged of the plans that were still being developed as part of NHS England's new 'Capped Expenditure Process' (CEP) to restrict spending to the 'control totals' set for each area for 2017/18. Key suggestions identified by the *HSJ* included:

- systematically drawing out waiting times for planned care, including explicit consideration of breaching NHS constitution standards;
- stopping NHS funding for some treatments, including extending limits on IVF, adding to lists of 'low value' treatments that would no longer be provided, and seeking to delay or avoid funding some treatments newly approved by NICE;
- closing wards and theatres and reducing staffing, while seeking to maintain enough emergency care capacity to deal with winter pressures;
- closing or downgrading services;
- and selling estate and other 'property related transactions'.

The *Guardian* obtained a leaked 21-page document from Cheshire detailing proposals including an arbitrary 25% reduction in endoscopy examinations, which could put the lives of patients with early stage cancers at risk. In North Central London another series of damaging cuts were proposed to make savings by denying patients treatment, extending waiting times for operations and even closing A&E and maternity units.[80 81]

These proposals struggled to survive as soon as they became public knowledge. A huge public backlash forced rapid retreats in both Cheshire and London, and within a couple of weeks NHS Improvement (NHSI) was forced to step in and dilute the process. They announced a series of additional regulations effectively restricting what cuts could be made, while describing the CEP demands as merely 'proposals'.[82]

By October 2017 the scale of the real squeeze on mental health was revealed by Freedom of Information requests from Labour shadow minister Luciana Berger. They showed that far from the promised increase in funding for mental health, half of the 129 Clinical Commissioning Groups had published plans that intended to cut spending, ignoring official guidelines from NHS England and fine words from politicians. This was just three months after Health Secretary Jeremy Hunt's July 2017 announcement of a £1.3bn plan for better mental health services, including the recruitment of 21,000 extra staff by 2021, to treat an extra million people and deliver 24/7 services.[83]

Also in October, as a consequence of the Brexit vote, and while the first revelations were exposing the shameful, unlawful treatment of the Windrush generation under the 'hostile environment', racist regulations requiring overseas visitors and migrant workers to be charged for treatment, or pay up front for access to the NHS were further toughened. The new laws introduced charges for some community services, NHS Trusts were given a legal duty to check the eligibility of all patients before providing treatment in secondary care, and, for certain non-urgent treatments, patients were to be asked to pay upfront or risk being turned away.

Ministers cynically claimed that the charging regulations were not intended to be part of the government's 'hostile environment' for migrants, but in order to recover much-needed costs for the NHS. However, the government's own figures revealed that deliberate 'health tourism' accounted for only 0.3% of the NHS budget.[84] As Patients Not Passports summed up, the erosion of the principles of the NHS and putting thousands of patients' lives at risk was a high price to pay to combat such a minimal problem.[85]

May's apology

On 4 January 2018, its 70th anniversary year, Theresa May joined Health Secretary Jeremy Hunt in issuing a hollow apology for the state of the NHS.[86] Even as May spoke news was emerging of an 81-year-old Essex woman who died waiting for an ambulance which took 4 hours to arrive, and of two deaths of older patients waiting to be seen in an overcrowded A&E in the West Midlands.

But there was no change of policy even after almost eight brutal years in which the population had grown by 4 million, but 8,000 front line beds and 20% of mental health beds had closed. Below inflation pay settlements had been a factor contributing to 100,000 vacant NHS posts, increasing the pressure on the dedicated staff who remained.

A February 2018 blog ('With strings attached') by Nuffield Trust analyst Sally Gainsbury explained why in practice much of the 'extra' £1.6 billion that was announced by Chancellor Phillip Hammond could only be used to bail out deficits – and virtually none of it could be used as extra spending to expand services.[87] One of the more shocking facts to emerge was the reduction in the real terms value of the 'tariff' that fixes the prices paid to hospitals for patient care. As a result, Gainsbury explained:

> … this year, NHS trusts will make an average 5% loss on each patient they treat, reflecting the gap between how much they are paid to treat each patient and the actual costs of providing that care.

The following month Nottingham University Hospitals chief executive Tracy Taylor was one of the first to call for a review of plans drawn up by the local STP, dismissing them as just 'an aspiration'. Nottinghamshire's plan to close 200 hospital beds had been exposed as unrealistic after the area's health services were overwhelmed by 'extraordinary' winter pressures.[88]

Figures compiled by the House of Commons Library showed that winter 2017/18 had been the worst ever for the NHS. With 1,100 fewer front-line beds open than the previous year, emergency admissions soared by 6%, reducing capacity for elective care, and lengthening delays in A&E. Numbers of patients kept waiting over 4 hours in A&E rose to a new peak – 846,000 (22.9%) – almost four times the level they were at in 2010/11 when the spending freeze began.[89]

June 2018 figures showed 4.1 million people were waiting for operations – the highest for 10 years. 3,464 patients had waited over a year for treatment, more than nine times the number in 2013. And 130,553 people in England had waited over two weeks for their first appointment with a cancer specialist. The Royal College of Surgeons found 84,000 fewer consultant-led NHS operations had been delivered in England in the first seven months of 2018 compared with 2017.[90]

More cuts were planned, and on July 4, the day before the NHS's 70th Birthday, NHS England discussed a new far-reaching plan to further limit access to a growing number of so called 'clinically ineffective' treatments. A 'relatively narrow' initial list of 17 treatments to which access would be restricted for all but private patients was published as the basis for a 3-month public 'consultation'.

Birthday present

Under intense pressure Theresa May announced that her government would mark its 70th birthday by giving the NHS in England a 'long-term settlement'. The 'extra' money was a paltry £20 billion real terms increase by 2023/24, later misleadingly rebranded as a '£34bn' cash increase. Every expert immediately agreed this was better than nothing but nowhere near enough. Theresa May's settlement fixed the core funding for the NHS through to the beginning of the pandemic in 2020.

At the end of 2018 a new cunning plan from NHS Improvement was revealed. They wanted trusts to consign thousands more NHS elective patients to the questionable care of private hospitals, even though they lack the intensive care, emergency response and multi-disciplinary teams of NHS hospitals. NHS Improvement had even drawn up a list of 54 trusts which it thought would need to contract out operations to hold down waiting lists and cope with pressures on beds. A third of them were in London, with other major hospitals listed in Leeds, Kent, North Lincolnshire, Oxford, Derby, Leicester, Staffordshire, Plymouth, Southampton, crisis-ridden Worcestershire and many more.[91]

The list, which was leaked to the *HSJ* in early December 2018, had not been intended to go to the trusts, few of whom were aware of its existence. Instead, it was to be sent to private hospital chains such as Spire Healthcare, BMI and Nuffield Health, effectively giving them the nod to pressure the target trusts for lucrative business to fill their otherwise empty beds. They were predictably delighted. But it was a disastrous deal for NHS trusts, which would still be left with inadequate capacity to get through an average British winter. And it would hand a bonanza of extra income to the private hospitals, even though many would need to poach even more NHS staff to cope with any significant increase in caseload.

Meanwhile a powerful TUC report on the decline in mental health services revealed a serious reduction in staffing levels of doctors and nurses since 2013, and in the number of beds available in mental health trusts since 2009. Funding for mental health trusts had risen in cash terms since 2016–17, but in real terms mental health trusts were receiving £105m *less* than in 2011–12. And there had been an exodus of demoralised staff, with 23,686 mental health staff leaving the NHS (one in eight of the total workforce in mental health) between June 2017 and May 2018.[92]

In December 2018, as another negative spin off from the Brexit vote, the blatantly unfair and unjustified £200 Immigration Health Surcharge, introduced in 2015, was doubled to £400, creating yet another barrier to recruitment of vital staff to the NHS. It was cynically sold by the government as a means to give the NHS 'extra funding',[93] but the limited extra cash came in a brutally unfair way, and at a considerable long-term cost. Few could fail to notice that the measure was designed to appease racists and also other Brexit voters who wanted to keep any immigrants out, since the exemption for EU citizens would end once Britain finally left the EU. The staffing problems in the NHS were already worsening[94] as more overseas staff began to feel unwelcome. Recruitment of qualified staff from the EU rapidly declined in the run-up to Brexit.

Long Term Plan

2019 began with the publication of NHS England's 'Long Term Plan'[95] which, like previous and subsequent plans, lacked either a workforce strategy or sufficient funding to enable it to deliver its relatively limited ambitions. It also involved a contradictory approach to the private sector.

On the one hand the plan proposed new legislation that would reverse the clauses and regulations in the 2012 Health and Social Care Act which compelled local commissioners to put increasing services out to competitive tender and enforced competition between NHS providers. On the other it also proposed to set up large-scale networks with private sector 'partners' to provide pathology and imaging services.

NHS England was already driving through highly contentious contracting-out and privatisation of services, notably the first of a series of eleven major contracts for PET-CT scanner services in England, which in Oxfordshire had been secretly awarded to a private company. Immediate and furious opposition from local consultants, campaigners, and MPs of all parties led to a few meaningless concessions, but also the threat that NHS England would take legal action against anyone raising concerns about clinical standards and care.[96]

A similar contract in South-East London had also been awarded to a private-led consortium, and in Bristol, North Somerset and South Gloucester the CCG had decided, with no intervention from NHS England, to put all the adult community health services out to tender, as a single 10-year, legally binding contract.[97]

The final 'sitrep' report for the 2018-19 winter showed only 20 out of 131 acute trusts had managed to contain bed occupancy below 90% on 3 March. 36 trusts were running on or above 97% – well above the already increased NHS England target level. Five were running completely full, at 100%. A key factor was the inadequate provision of frontline beds.

Mental health in crisis

The dire state of mental health services was again underlined by shocking new findings from an NHS Providers survey of mental health trust leaders, which revealed that fewer than 10% of trusts reported that they currently had the right staff in the right place to deliver services. 95% of trust leaders responding to the survey did not believe overall investment would meet current and future demand.[98] The most recent increases had only raised the share of NHS funding spent on mental health by 0.5%; and too little of the new money was reaching the front line of service delivery. NHS Providers warned: 'This raises questions about how much of the NHS Long Term Plan can be delivered and how fast.'

Over two thirds of mental health leaders said they were worried about maintaining the quality of services over the next two years, with 81% of trust leaders saying they were not able to meet current demand for community Child and Adult (CAMHS) services and more than half (58%) saying the same on adult community mental health. 85% of trust leaders either disagreed or strongly disagreed with the statement that there were adequate mental health community services to meet local needs.

In several areas there were strong campaigns against plans for hospital closures and downgrades. Telford council voted to seek a judicial review of the controversial 'Future Fit' plan in Shropshire;[99] while in north-west London the stubborn resistance of Hammersmith & Fulham and Ealing campaigners and councils to the 'Shaping a Healthier Future' plan to axe Charing Cross and Ealing hospitals won the day as Health Secretary Matt Hancock finally threw out the plan.[100]

Paying for NHS treatment

The summer of 2019 brought a new scandal. Warrington and Halton Hospitals Foundation Trust decided to cash in on frustration at the growing list of treatments that had been excluded from the NHS by cost-cutting local CCGs. It decided to launch its own private NHS patient service, under the supremely inappropriate label of 'My Choice'. The scheme offered patients whose painful and debilitating health problems had been included by local CCGs on a list of 71 treatments branded as 'Low Clinical Priority', despite their proven value, the chance to purchase some of these operations from the NHS – for cash up front.[101]

The trust initially congratulated itself on its 'affordable self-pay service', charging customers 'the local NHS price, previously paid for by commissioners'. But, of course, it meant that, just as before the NHS was founded, patients who could afford it were urged to stump up the cost of treatment themselves, while for the many who couldn't afford to pay there was not even a sympathetic shrug. The trust's website boasted that whereas 'My Choice' had originally been created in 2013, 'the service has been significantly extended to include the large number of procedures no longer available on the NHS'. It offered an extensive price list, including hip replacements at £7,050; knees at £7,179; and cataracts at £1,624 each.

Chief executive Mel Pickup, promoting the scheme, said: 'Procedures of low clinical priority do not mean low value to our patients, and we are pleased to be able to make a large number available at a really affordable price, at their local hospitals'. But patients were warned not to expect any special treatment; they would simply be paying out of pocket for NHS treatment that had once been free: 'There are no private rooms .... The major benefit is access to outstanding NHS treatments at a fraction of the cost of those undertaken by private providers.'

Trust bosses retreated from the scheme almost immediately after it was splashed across the front page of the *Mirror* and suspended the scheme while they 'reviewed its impact' on waiting lists.[102] However there were fears that this was the new, increasingly commercial face of the NHS, with policies shaped by almost a decade of austerity, and six years of legislation that urged Foundation Trusts like Warrington to make up to 50% of their income from private medicine.

Johnson's 'new hospitals' promise

Boris Johnson's arrival as Tory leader in summer 2019 brought an apparent change of rhetoric, especially on the NHS, with eye-catching promises to build 40 new hospitals, even though from the outset they lacked any real conviction.[103] Only six of the projects were in theory to start at once, and even these would mostly be rebuilds and extensions rather than new hospitals; it was promised £2.7bn would be allocated to them by 2025.

Campaigners warned that the other promised schemes might well never happen at all; 21 of the schemes (one of which was for up to 12 small community hospitals, hence the inflated numbers) would not be funded or begin construction until at least 2025. The misleading promise of a 'capital injection' had to be set against the rising £6bn backlog maintenance bill, £3bn of which was for urgent work to make crumbling hospitals safe.[104]

But the squeeze was not only on capital. After nine years of effectively frozen funding, NHS trusts up and down the country had racked up massive cumulative deficits, in the form of loans from the Department of Health and Social Care, which they were in no position ever to repay. Many trusts had no plan to return even to a break-even position and were relying on continued rounds of 'cash funding loan finance' to stave off bankruptcy. On many annual reports, auditors warned 'a material uncertainty that may cast significant doubt on the Trust's ability to continue as a going concern'.

The *HSJ* estimated that, because so many loans had been issued, 'trusts' combined debts to the department reached £14bn by the end of 2018-19'.[105] This was to be acknowledged as the pandemic took hold in April 2020, when Matt Hancock announced a 'write-off' of £13.4bn of historic debt across the NHS.[106]

107 trusts had debts that averaged £100m, often incurred as a result of shortfalls in revenue, with the two largest debtors between them owing a total of £1bn. The debts were clearly never going to be repaid, so it was converted into an extended loan known as 'public dividend capital', subject to an annual charge, typically 3.5% – above the current bank rate. It was all done as a book-keeping exercise, loading hospitals' debts on to the Department of Health's balance sheet without drawing on Treasury cash – so offered no fresh freedom or resources to cash-strapped trusts, and was greeted with no visible celebrations.[107]

The decade ends with promises – but no new cash

Tight financial pressures since 2010 had driven the closure of almost 9,000 'general and acute' beds and a 22% reduction in mental health beds, while the waiting list in England had risen by 2 million to 4.5m. One in five cancer patients had waited up to 2 months for hospital treatment, and 70% of hospital trusts were missing the target to treat cancer patients within 2 months of referral.

Johnson fought the General Election in December 2019 under the banner of 'getting Brexit done' with its tacit promise of more steps to reduce immigration, but he but also offered false promises of new funds and support for the NHS. By then virtually all the gains in NHS performance that had been made during the 2000s had been wiped out.

The £33.9bn 'extra' that Boris Johnson boasted would be spent on the NHS over the next three years was the same money Phillip Hammond had come up with for Theresa May's 'birthday present' for the NHS almost 18 months earlier. Treasury figures revealed that in real terms the increase was not £33.9bn, but £20.1bn, according to the Treasury. This was an increase, but nowhere near enough to meet the growing cost pressures on the NHS. It was not the end but the continuation of austerity, with at least three more years to come of increases below the level needed even to stand still.

A grim decade of austerity, privatisation and ideologically driven 'reforms' had severely weakened the NHS on all fronts. It left it fragmented, lacking coordination and planning, lacking investment, staff and beds, saddled with debts, chronically dependent on private hospitals and contractors, and falling ever further behind on elective treatment, emergency care, mental health and long-term care for frail older people.

This was the enfeebled NHS that would have to do battle within months with the Covid pandemic that was already emerging in China. And, as the next chapter will show, that did not end well.

NOTES

1   https://fullfact.org/economy/1-trillion-not-spent-bailing-out-banks/
2   https://www.nytimes.com/2019/02/24/world/europe/britain-austerity-may-budget.html
3   https://researchbriefings.files.parliament.uk/documents/SN00724/SN00724.pdf
4   https://www.kingsfund.org.uk/publications/our-future-health-secured
5   https://www.kingsfund.org.uk/projects/general-election-2010/money-spent-nhs
6   Unhealthy Profits: Amazon.co.uk: Lister, John: 9780244734428: Books
7   https://chpi.org.uk/wp-content/uploads/2014/02/At-what-cost-paying-the-price-for-the-market-in-the-English-NHS-by-Calum-Paton.pdf
8   https://healthemergency.org.uk/workingwu/Healthworkersguide.pdf
9   https://www.whatdotheyknow.com/request/22335/response/57949/attach/3/456084%20FESC%20practical%20guide.pdf?cookie_passthrough=1
10 https://healthemergency.org.uk/articles/Newdimensionsinprivatisation.pdf
11 https://healthemergency.org.uk/pdf/McKinsey%20report%20on%20efficiency%20in%20NHS.pdf
12 https://www.hsj.co.uk/finance-and-efficiency/health-select-committee-calls-for-evidence-on-meeting-the-nicholson-challenge/5029746.article
13 https://www.taxjustice.net/wp-content/uploads/2013/04/hmrc_tax_report_pdf.pdf
14 https://www.nao.org.uk/wp-content/uploads/2011/12/NAO_briefing_Delivering_efficiency_savings_NHS.pdf
15 Between 2002 and 2013 SHAs were the regional bodies steering local level trusts and commissioners (Primary Care Trusts)
16 https://www.nao.org.uk/wp-content/uploads/2011/12/NAO_briefing_Delivering_efficiency_savings_NHS.pdf
17 https://healthemergency.org.uk/he-issues/Springbulletin2010.pdf
18 https://healthemergency.org.uk/pdf/McKinsey%20report%20on%20efficiency%20in%20NHS.pdf
19 https://assets.publishing.service.gov.uk/government/uploads/system/uploads/attachment_data/file/216051/dh_118085.pdf

20 https://www.bmj.com/bmj/section-pdf/186071?path=/bmj/341/7769/Head_to_Head.full.pdf

21 Information collated from published plans by Health Emergency at HE 69 https://healthemergency.org.uk/he-issues/he69.pdf

22 https://healthemergency.org.uk/pdf/UnpickingthespinBriefing.pdf

23 https://healthemergency.org.uk/diary.php?rn=95

24 https://healthemergency.org.uk/he-issues/he71.pdf

25 https://healthemergency.org.uk/he-issues/he72.pdf

26 https://healthemergency.org.uk/pdf/LondonHealthEmergencyResponsetoTSA-Dec2012.pdf

27 https://healthemergency.org.uk/he-issues/he72.pdf

28 https://healthemergency.org.uk/pdf/DeadWeight.pdf

29 https://www.kingsfund.org.uk/sites/default/files/field/field_publication_file/payment-by-results-the-kings-fund-nov-2012.pdf

30 https://www.hsj.co.uk/finance-and-efficiency/exclusive-nearly-3bn-returned-to-treasury/5051242.article

31 https://www.gov.uk/government/uploads/system/uploads/attachment_data/file/503954/current_projects_as_at_31_March_2015.xlsx , accessed February 16 2018

32 https://www.dailymail.co.uk/news/article-2458378/Boss-NHS-London-says-wards-parts-UK-unsafe.html

33 https://redditchstandard.co.uk/2013/11/12/news-Cutting-hospital-services-will-hurt-poor-report-warns-89394.html

34 https://www.nuffieldtrust.org.uk/files/2017-01/2014-payment-reform-policy-response-web-final.pdf

35 https://www.hsj.co.uk/barts-health-nhs-trust/barts-deficit-doubles-to-93m/5081842.article

36 https://webarchive.nationalarchives.gov.uk/ukgwa/20130513202839/http://ccpanel.org.uk/cases/Merger_of_Barts_and_The_London_NHS_Trust_Newham_University_Hospital_NHS_Trust_and_Whipps_Cross_University_Hospital_NHS_Trust.html

37 https://www.redbridgeccg.nhs.uk/Downloads/About-us/Governing-body-meetings/2014/Redbridge%20Governing%20Body%20Papers%20B%20November%202014.pdf

38 https://www.bbc.co.uk/news/health-26957435

39 https://www.bbc.co.uk/news/uk-england-29936392

40 https://www.communitycare.co.uk/2014/03/12/thousands-people-mental-health-needs-denied-social-care-due-cuts/

41 https://www.kingsfund.org.uk/sites/default/files/field/field_publication_file/the-nhs-productivity-challenge-kingsfund-may14.pdf

42 https://www.publicfinance.co.uk/2014/08/health-alert

43 https://www.bbc.co.uk/news/uk-england-nottinghamshire-29636743

44 https://www.nuffieldtrust.org.uk/news-item/sharp-increase-in-non-nhs-provision-of-community-and-mental-health-services-whilst-private-provision-in-hospital-care-slows

45 https://hansard.parliament.uk/lords/2022-01-24/debates/AB5351C6-2935-

446D-847E-CB3C193CDE45/HealthAndCareBill#contribution-DF9AA920-86D6-4DC8-B6C0-CF6EEDB953F1

46 https://www.legislation.gov.uk/uksi/2015/238/pdfs/uksi_20150238_en.pdf

47 https://www.patientsnotpassports.co.uk/learn/what-are-the-rules-on-immigration-checks-and-upfront-charging.html

48 https://nhsproviders.org/news-blogs/news/nhs-providers-opposes-tariff-objection-mechanism-changes

49 https://www.theguardian.com/healthcare-network/2015/jun/02/nhs-no-more-cuts-to-social-care

50 https://morningstaronline.co.uk/a-aa12-nhs-sos-1

51 https://manifesto.deryn.co.uk/wp-content/uploads/2021/04/BritainCanBeBetter-TheLabourPartyManifesto2015.pdf

52 https://www.independent.co.uk/news/uk/politics/the-principle-of-a-free-taxpayerfunded-nhs-must-be-questioned-says-tory-health-minister-10395991.html

53 https://www.nationalhealthexecutive.com/News/half-of-nhs-beds-could-face-the-axe--lord-prior

54 https://www.theguardian.com/society/2015/aug/05/nhs-patients-may-face-widescale-charges-warns-financial-thinktank

55 https://www.hsj.co.uk/home/providers-ordered-to-take-tough-new-measures-to-cut-deficits/5089390.article

56 https://healthemergency.org.uk/peoplesinquiry/pdf/SecondReport.pdf

57 https://www.independent.co.uk/life-style/health-and-families/health-news/simon-stevens-nhs-england-chief-executive-says-george-osborne-s-funding-plans-for-health-service-are-unworkable-a6727611.html

58 https://healthcampaignstogether.com/pdf/NHS%20England%20planning-guid-16-17-20-21.pdf

59 https://committees.parliament.uk/committee/127/public-accounts-committee/news/98298/deepening-concerns-over-financial-future-of-national-health-service/

60 https://www.hsj.co.uk/finance-and-efficiency/exclusive-don-berwick-warns-current-level-of-nhs-funding-is-risky/7002876.article

61 https://nhsproviders.org/news-blogs/blogs/how-do-we-clear-the-provider-side-deficit

62 https://www.independent.co.uk/news/uk/politics/eu-referendum-result-nigel-farage-nhs-pledge-disowns-350-million-pounds-a7099906.html

63 https://www.birminghamandsolihullccg.nhs.uk/about-us/publications/get-involved/consultations-and-engagement/procedures-of-limited-clinical-value/139-procedures-of-lower-clinical-value-engagement-report/file

64 https://www.adass.org.uk/media/5379/adass-budget-survey-report-2016.pdf

65 https://www.theguardian.com/society/2016/jul/21/nhs-england-bosses-launch-reset-plan-tackle-deficit-financial-special-measures

66 https://www.nuffieldtrust.org.uk/news-item/so-much-to-do-so-little-time-turning-stps-into-action

67 https://www.hsj.co.uk/finance-and-efficiency/exclusive-officials-warn-over-extremely-constrained-capital-for-stps/7010136.article

68   https://www.nuffieldtrust.org.uk/resource/behind-the-numbers-nhs-finances

69   https://www.theguardian.com/society/2016/oct/31/how-much-extra-money-tory-government-really-giving-nhs

70   https://www.gponline.com/shameful-pace-stp-rollout-risks-financial-meltdown-warns-former-nhs-commissioning-chief/article/1410546

71   https://www.nationalhealthexecutive.com/Health-Care-News/just-16-of-finance-directors-think-sustainable-stps-achievable-by-2021

72   https://healthcampaignstogether.com/pdf/sustainability-and-transformation-plans-critical-review.pdf

73   https://healthcampaignstogether.com/pdf/HCTNo5.pdf

74   https://www.bmj.com/content/356/bmj.j586

75   https://nhsproviders.org/mission-impossible

76   https://www.health.org.uk/publications/a-year-of-plenty

77   https://nhsproviders.org/media/3019/nhs-providers-briefing-2017-general-election-party-manifestos.pdf

78   https://www.bbc.co.uk/news/election-2017-39933116

79   https://www.hsj.co.uk/daily-insight/daily-insight-nhs-managers-told-to-think-the-unthinkable/7018489.article

80   https://www.kingsfund.org.uk/blog/2017/06/will-capped-expenditure-process-help-keep-lid-nhs-finances

81   https://www.theguardian.com/society/2017/jun/21/cheshire-cancer-patients-could-die-sooner-if-nhs-cuts-are-forced-through

82   https://keepournhspublic.com/wp-content/uploads/2017/08/NHS-Into-the-Red-Zone-web.pdf

83   https://healthcampaignstogether.com/pdf/HCTNo8.pdf page 3

84   https://fullfact.org/health/health-tourism-whats-cost/

85   https://www.patientsnotpassports.co.uk/learn/what-are-the-rules-on-immigration-checks-and-upfront-charging.html

86   https://www.independent.co.uk/news/uk/politics/theresa-may-nhs-crisis-winter-apology-patients-cancelled-operations-latest-updates-a8141591.html

87   https://www.nuffieldtrust.org.uk/news-item/with-strings-attached-taking-a-closer-look-at-the-new-nhs-money

88   https://www.hsj.co.uk/nottingham-university-hospitals-nhs-trust/trust-chief-stp-must-be-reviewed-after-extraordinary-winter/7021883.article?

89   https://commonslibrary.parliament.uk/research-briefings/cbp-8210/

90   https://www.theguardian.com/society/2018/sep/13/nhs-treatments-in-england-fall-by-675-a-day-despite-waiting-list

91   https://www.hsj.co.uk/quality-and-performance/exclusive-regulators-give-private-firms-list-of-trusts-which-may-outsource-ops/7023960.article

92   https://www.tuc.org.uk/research-analysis/reports/breaking-point-crisis-mental-health-funding

93   https://www.gov.uk/government/news/increase-to-immigration-health-surcharge-gives-nhs-extra-funding

94   https://ukandeu.ac.uk/the-impact-of-brexit-on-nhs-staff/

95 https://www.longtermplan.nhs.uk/wp-content/uploads/2019/08/nhs-long-term-plan-version-1.2.pdf
96 https://healthcampaignstogether.com/pdf/HCTNo14.pdf page 8
97 https://www.bristolpost.co.uk/news/bristol-news/1billion-adult-health-contract-go-2411487
98 https://nhsproviders.org/mental-health-services-addressing-the-care-deficit
99 https://newsroom.telford.gov.uk/News/Details/14598
100 https://www.nationalhealthexecutive.com/News-Archive/monstrous-500m-scheme-to-close-london-aes-scrapped-by-hancock-after-seven-year-campaign-
101 https://lowdownnhs.info/comment/warrington-warning-nhs-says-no-then-offers-private-care/
102 https://www.mirror.co.uk/news/uk-news/nhs-hospital-demands-18k-hip-16544619
103 https://www.itv.com/news/2019-09-28/boris-johnson-promises-40-new-hospitals-as-he-boosts-spending-on-the-nhs
104 https://lowdownnhs.info/analysis/6619/
105 https://www.hsj.co.uk/finance-and-efficiency/nhs-trusts-owe-government-14bn/7025771.article
106 https://www.thetimes.co.uk/article/matt-hancock-wipes-13-billion-of-nhs-debt-to-bolster-hospitals-6knpxx2rc
107 https://www.hsj.co.uk/finance-and-efficiency/government-writes-off-13bn-debts-and-pledges-to-review-annual-charges/7027305.article

Chapter 2

The perfect storm – an NHS in crisis meets the Covid pandemic

Jacky Davis

By the end of 2019 the NHS and other public services, weakened by a decade of austerity, were in no fit state to cope with the challenges of the Covid pandemic. This fact, combined with the careless and fatalistic attitude of the Johnson government, meant that far too many people have died avoidable deaths from Covid – over 180,000 to date.

More shocking still is the fact that the government failed to protect the vulnerable in society – the poor, the disabled, the elderly, the minority ethnic – who died at many times the rate of the rest of the community.

This chapter examines why the UK performed so badly – the effects of the preceding decade of austerity on public health, the lack of preparation for a pandemic, the willingness to accept deaths in order to protect the economy, and the deliberate choice to use the expensive and largely inept private sector rather than the trusted NHS. It looks at the corruption involved in the awarding of contracts worth billions to political cronies and donors. It examines the mixed messaging coming from lawmakers who have proved to be egregious law breakers. It asks how we can hold to account those who are to blame. Because, with a world class NHS and public health system, we should have done much better.

We would like to acknowledge the outstanding work done by the People's Covid Inquiry (www.peoplescovidinquiry.com) in uncovering much of the information presented in this chapter. By talking to over 40 witnesses, from front line workers to international experts, they captured an invaluable snapshot of the pandemic in real time. And by doing so they proved that the government could have held an inquiry during the pandemic which would have resulted in lessons learned and saved lives.

There is still little sign of a formal government inquiry, and Johnson will surely be planning to avoid accountability with any eventual findings being published after the next election. But it is the responsibility of those who remain to keep asking the questions on behalf of those who died.

* * *

We have at every stage tried to minimise the loss of life, to save lives, to protect the NHS and we have followed the best scientific advice that we can.
Boris Johnson to Parliament 26.5.21

One of 'the most important public health failures the United Kingdom has ever experienced.
Coronavirus: Lessons Learned to Date, report from the Health and Social Care/Science and Technology parliamentary committees

The UK has fared badly during the pandemic. At the beginning of 2022 the UK's Covid-19 death toll passed 180,000 (which is almost certainly an underestimate).[1] That figure amounts to an average of 250 deaths a day during the pandemic, the equivalent of a commercial airline crash every day for the last two years. In the first wave England had the highest excess all-cause mortality rate among 23 European countries and at that time 44% of all excess deaths had occurred in care homes.[2] People died not only from Covid but also because they didn't receive healthcare for other life-threatening illnesses during this time.

As early as May 2020 Professor Martin McKee and others called for a 'rapid and transparent review'[3] as did Covid-19 Justice for Bereaved Families. The government didn't want to know. Faced with appalling death rates they continued to make the same mistakes – prioritising the economy over the health of the population, showing an antipathy to lockdowns which they then lifted too early, and failing to protect frontline workers and the vulnerable.

Most informed commentators outside government – from the *BMJ* to the Prime Minister's ex chief advisor Dominic Cummings – have acknowledged that 'thousands of people have died needlessly as a result of the government's mistakes'.[4] We will never know how many avoidable deaths should be laid at the government's door.

How a decade of austerity pushed the NHS into crisis

'We had lost a decade with regard to health equity.'
Professor Sir Michael Marmot to the People's Covid Inquiry

How is it that the UK, the sixth richest nation in the world with an established national health service and a renowned public health service, has done so badly? To understand why it is first necessary to look at the preceding decade, during which, as outlined in Chapter 1, the government ran down public services. In 2010 the new Conservative-led coalition's ambition was to 'roll back the state'[5] and between 2010 and 2019 public spending fell from 42% to 35% of GDP. This was achieved by their fiscal policy of austerity. As a result the NHS was already in crisis when the pandemic struck at the beginning of 2020. Targets were routinely missed and waiting lists had risen.*

Learning disability and mental health services, including child and adolescent mental health services (CAMHS) were also in a dire state, with a lack of beds and staff. Mental health services were chronically dependent on private sector beds and too many patients were being sent hundreds of miles from home in search of an in-patient bed. Often there were no beds available at all for children at significant risk.

The government's deficit reduction policies also resulted in a slowing down, and in some cases a reversal, of social progress made in the previous decade. As a result, health gains slowed, stopped or even reversed and this affected lower income groups in particular.[6] The increase in health inequalities meant that when the pandemic struck, the vulnerable in society suffered to a disproportionate degree.

The NHS was not the only public service that was suffering. Social care had not been seriously overhauled since Margaret Thatcher's privatising reforms took effect in 1993, despite promises from successive governments. By the end of 2019 there were 120,000 staff vacancies in the care sector. Care homes were particularly badly affected, due to underfunding and staff shortages. The National Pensioners' Convention had repeatedly asked the government to

* See the damning report by the Institute for Public Policy Research, which found that austerity had 'ripped the resilience out of the health and care service'. It noted that the NHS was 'extremely fragile' before the onset of the pandemic, with unsafe bed occupancy levels, too few ITU beds and severe understaffing (https://www.ippr.org/news-and-media/press-releases/austerity-ripped-resilience-out-of-health-and-care-service-before-covid-19-crisis-hit-says-ippr)

reform and fund social care, but to no avail.

Schools too had seen their funding cut dramatically, and the schools with the poorest children suffered the largest cuts.[7] Class sizes increased with no compensatory increase in space which meant that once the pandemic took hold it was more difficult to achieve social distancing when children finally went back to school.

Despite warnings the government failed to prepare for a pandemic

The danger of a pandemic has long been recognised, and in 2006 the Government Office for Science predicted a global pandemic within the next 30 years due to a virus mutating from a wild animal to humans. In 2016 the government conducted Exercise Cygnus to look at preparedness for a possible influenza pandemic.[8] They did not make the report public, nor did they act to deal with the many weaknesses it uncovered, including predicting a crisis in care homes if a pandemic hit the UK.[9]

The government claimed that Cygnus was the only pandemic planning they had carried out and that it was not relevant for a coronavirus pandemic, but this was not true. In the same year they also conducted Exercise Alice, which looked at a possible outbreak involving a MERS-CoV virus.[10] It uncovered many potential problems which accurately predicted the failures that plagued the response to Covid-19. These included concerns about border controls, inadequate plans for test, trace, quarantine and self-isolation, insufficient bed capacity and inadequate supplies of personal protective equipment (PPE). The government, obsessed with holding down public spending, ignored its recommendations and withheld the report. Jeremy Hunt, health secretary at the time, claimed afterwards to know nothing about it, and the government's shameless cover-up was only exposed due to the persistence of transparency campaigner Dr Moosa Qureshi.[11]

Thus it turned out that the government had done plenty of planning, which had resulted in good advice, but ministers had failed to implement any of the crucial recommendations. Public Health England (PHE) subsequently argued that national security would have been damaged by the release of these reports, but their release would at least have put pressure on politicians to respond to them.

Too little, too late – the government's response to the pandemic

> 'The government wasn't on top of this in January/February. The Prime Minister wasn't talking about it.'
> Stephen Cowan, leader of Hammersmith and Fulham Council, to the People's Covid Inquiry

> 'We thought – this is major, and waited for something to happen in the UK. We saw only absolute inaction.'
> Dr Michelle Dawson, consultant anaesthetist, to the People's Covid Inquiry

By mid-January 2020 Wuhan, Hubei and other Chinese cities were in lockdown. The *Lancet* carried articles confirming the presence of a dangerous new coronavirus in China which included details of its alarming infectivity and death rate. On 30 January the World Health Organisation (WHO) declared a public health emergency of international concern and on 31 January the first UK case was identified. At that stage the government and Public Health England should have been preparing for the arrival of the pandemic.

There are international guidelines for responding to a global pandemic. In the absence of any treatment or vaccine the response depends on standard public health strategies aimed at eliminating the virus. The advice is straightforward – find the virus, isolate those who have it, trace and test their contacts and act quickly. Lockdown may be needed until a find, test, trace, isolate and support system (FTTIS) is in place and may require closing international borders.

The Westminster government did not act quickly – on the contrary they were complacent and criminally slow off the mark. The Prime Minister Boris Johnson was described as 'missing in action' from the start and did not bother to attend the first five meetings of COBRA (the emergency committee convened in crises).[12] One senior adviser was quoted as saying that Johnson 'didn't work weekends' and 'didn't do urgent crisis planning'.[13] Rumour had it that during that crucial early period he was closeted in Chequers in order to meet an urgent publishing deadline on a promised book about Shakespeare.[14] And of course he was preoccupied with Brexit.

From the outset Johnson had a cavalier attitude to Covid, boasting publicly about shaking hands with Covid patients[15] before catching it himself, and requiring hospitalisation for a reportedly near fatal episode. His chief adviser at the time, Dominic Cummings, stated that Johnson initially dismissed Covid as 'a scare story' and had no plan beyond 'taking it on the chin' and herd immunity.[16] While claiming that he would 'follow the science' Johnson repeatedly ignored it. By February 2020 it was known that the virus had a likely 80% infection rate and a 1% mortality rate, and by the start of March Covid cases were doubling every 3-4 days. Pandemic modelling suggested the possibility of 200,000 deaths but despite this Johnson refused to impose a lockdown until the end of March. In the meantime the government allowed national and international sporting events to go ahead, including the Cheltenham racing festival, attended by a quarter of a million people.

Before lockdown was finally introduced the government had failed to follow WHO advice (seen as only for 'developing countries') and rejected public health measures that other countries were taking as 'only appropriate for low and middle-income countries'.[17] As a result, hospitals were soon overwhelmed by Covid patients. In order to free up beds hospital patients were discharged back to care homes without being tested, leading to very high death rates among the elderly (see below). Johnson appeared fatalistic, and acted from the outset as though large-scale deaths were inevitable, warning that 'many families were going to lose loved ones before their time'.[18] His words proved grimly prophetic for the UK. This was because Johnson consistently prioritised the economy over the nation's health, resulting in the late lockdown in March 2020. He ignored his scientific advisers again in September 2020 after they urged him to impose a 'circuit breaker' lockdown because Covid cases were surging.* As we now know, countries that acted quickly and refused to tolerate the virus circulating in the community had much lower

---

* The Resolution Foundation estimated that delaying the winter 2020 lock down caused up to 27,000 extra deaths, a 'huge mistake'.

mortality rates than the UK and suffered less economic damage in the long run.* Johnson's laissez-faire attitude in the face of a pandemic cost many lives.

Not only did the government ignore the advice of its own pandemic planning exercises, it lied about them and then reacted too slowly when it was clear that we faced a genuine pandemic. These mistakes would prove fatal for tens of thousands of people.

The £37 billion failure that was 'test and trace'

*'We at iSAGE** were simply amazed. In the middle of the biggest pandemic in over 100 years we set up private companies with no healthcare experience to run (the FTTIS) from scratch.'*
Professor Sir David King to the People's Covid Inquiry

A reliable find, test, trace, isolate and support system (FTTIS) is a vital part of the public health response to a pandemic, but – according to Professor Sir David King of iSAGE - 'from the beginning we have never had a proper FTTIS'.[19] The government's attempts to set one up started badly and went downhill from there. The government had abandoned widespread testing by 12 March 2020 because of 'a lack of capacity'. Thereafter they failed on four occasions to launch a system, so that for several weeks during a critical period of the pandemic there was no functioning FTTIS at all. This lack of early testing meant frontline NHS and social care staff had to isolate unnecessarily, leading to acute staffing shortages, and many elderly patients were discharged into care homes without being tested, with devastating results.[20]

Faced with the urgent need to set up a test and trace system the government could have reinforced local public health networks, already in place but much weakened by the preceding decade of spending cuts. Instead, they chose to ignore them. They passed over local structures (including 44 public health laboratories) and GPs, whose community connections should have made them an

* 'The trade-off between the economy and public health is a false one. The smaller the mortality from covid the smaller the hit to the economy.' Professor Sir Michael Marmot to the People's Covid Inquiry.

** Independent Scientific Advisory Group for Emergencies

obvious choice for running the FTTIS, and turned to the private sector. They outsourced the system to private companies with no relevant healthcare experience, who had to set up from scratch a parallel system, with no local links or networks. Thus 'NHS Test and Trace' had little to do with the NHS, and was largely delivered by outsourcing giants like Serco, Sitel and Deloitte, commissioned directly by the Department of Health and Social Care.[21] The resulting centralised model, described as 'bizarre and ineffective',[22] was not efficient. One study showed that local public health teams typically had contact rates of over 90% compared to 60% for services run by Serco,[23] despite receiving only a fraction of the billions handed to the private sector.

Under the outsourced model patients often had to travel miles for tests, and those who didn't have a car were advised to request home testing kits from Randox, dispatched by Amazon. Much to health secretary Matt Hancock's embarrassment, 750,000 of these kits were found to be unsafe and had to be withdrawn.[24] A Channel 4 Dispatches investigation of the Randox superlab in Northern Ireland uncovered lost and leaking samples, cross contamination and dangerous disposal of waste.[25] An NHS consultant microbiologist commented: 'we would be shut down if we performed that way'.[26] Meanwhile Randox was paying former Tory minister Owen Paterson MP £100,000 a year to advise (and lobby for) them.[27]

Elsewhere local hospitals asked if they could take over testing after 'severe failings' were reported at a flagship centre run by Deloitte at Chessington World of Adventures.[28] Tests on NHS staff were being lost or sent to the wrong person and some test results were still not available three weeks later. Epsom & St Helier hospital trust decided it would be more efficient and convenient for their staff if they took the testing in-house and they quickly acquired the necessary equipment. A paramedic was asked about the involvement of Deloitte, which specialises in management consultancy, tax and accounting. They replied 'I'm not sure what an accountancy company can bring to this', a sentiment echoed by many caught in the nightmare of delayed, lost and misdirected tests.

Inexplicably the contract with Deloitte (the lead consultancy) did not oblige them to share test results with Public Health England (PHE) nor with local authorities, so GPs didn't know which of their patients had Covid.[29] Hospitals, GPs and local public health teams were understandably frustrated at being excluded from test and trace.[30] It was clear to all but the government that an effective FTTIS needed people with expertise, local knowledge and good community relationships – Germany for instance employed 400 local authorities and public health teams.[31] But English politicians were obsessed with involving the private sector.

The 44 NHS labs were not working at full capacity and major centres such as the Francis Crick Institute and Oxford University were offering expertise and resources. The government however proposed developing a new network of three Lighthouse Laboratories with private sector involvement, all to be co-ordinated by Deloitte.[32] NHS staff were worried that this parallel system would lead to competition for supplies and reduce the capacity of established laboratories. There were concerns about a lack of transparency in the commissioning of the Lighthouse labs, lack of regulation of the services they provided, including yet again lost samples and leaking test tubes, delayed results and the diversion of resources from NHS labs.[33] In the event some of these labs were scaled back and others were decommissioned, leading to more criticism of public money being wasted. The same pattern would be seen time and again during the pandemic.

Crucially, the government failed to address an important component of FTTIS – the need to isolate and support people who had Covid or who were contacts of those who did. The statutory sick pay available to those who had to stay at home (£97/week) was totally inadequate (one of the lowest in the developed world)[34] and many had no choice but to continue working in order to pay the bills. The government talked airily of patients and contacts using 'separate bathrooms' with seemingly no idea of the circumstances of multi-occupancy households. No alternative accommodation was offered for those who couldn't self-isolate at home. Once again, ministers chose not to call upon local solutions and community engagement that could have solved these problems.

Few were surprised when FTTIS proved to be a very expensive failure. The Public Accounts Committee couldn't have been more damning when it concluded that there was no clear evidence that it had made 'a measurable difference to the progress of the pandemic' despite the 'unimaginable' cost of up to £37 billion (more than a fifth of the core annual NHS budget).[35] The committee criticised the vast sums spent on private consultants – 2,500 Deloitte management consultants at an average daily rate of £1,000. Some were being paid £6,000/day,[36] meaning that in five days they earned the average annual salary of a nurse. This money should have gone to increasing local public health capacity and supporting people to self-isolate. Local teams would have done an infinitely better job than the private sector if they had been given the huge sums of money handed over to the likes of Deloitte and Serco.

The dismal failure of FTTIS, outsourced to massive private companies and overseen by those with little or no relevant experience, stands in stark contrast to the vaccine roll out, implemented and administered efficiently by the NHS. We will never know how many avoidable deaths were caused by the FTTIS fiasco.

PPE – the criminal failure to protect frontline workers

'We were talking to local businesses, veterinary practices, anyone we could think of, because we couldn't get (PPE) from the government. It was a complete dereliction of duty.'
Dr Rachel Clarke, palliative care consultant, to the People's Covid Inquiry

'The issue with PPE was so appalling. They (ITU) were receiving second-hand PPE, some of which had blood on it.'
Michael Rosen, author, to the People's Covid Inquiry

The government had been warned four years previously that it needed to stockpile personal protective equipment (PPE). Its own Exercise Alice noted the vital role of PPE during a possible coronavirus pandemic, stating that it would be 'of crucial importance for frontline staff', and it recommended ensuring sufficient quantities were available. The government didn't act.

Worse, the government had outsourced much of the PPE procurement and storage systems to a complex web of private companies such as DHL and Unipart, and some of these activities had been further subcontracted out. In essence the government had allowed the private sector to take over the vital business of ensuring sufficient up-dated stocks of PPE along with timely access to them.[37] The resulting fragmentation and increased bureaucracy spelled chaos when the pandemic struck. An inventory of the emergency stockpile published in May 2020 showed that it did not contain any gowns, and that 20 million out of 26 million respirators and nearly half the stock of surgical masks had passed their use-by dates, with some showing signs of deterioration.[38] Despite knowing that stocks were inadequate the government did not take advantage of the short grace period to obtain more before the pandemic arrived in the UK. On the contrary, the UK shipped quantities of PPE to China in Feb 2020.[39]

The subsequent scramble for equipment led to overpayment, contracts being awarded to political contacts without transparency and huge wastage. The acute shortage of PPE resulted in failure to protect frontline staff, including those in care homes. Staff were forced to see Covid patients without adequate protection and were photographed wearing bin bags and other makeshift items.[40] Porters had to move infected bodies with no body bags, masks or gowns. This inevitably led to a high rate of hospital acquired infection amongst both staff and patients, with many deaths among frontline NHS staff.* Scottish data reported that patient-facing clinical staff and their families were significantly more likely to be admitted to hospital with Covid than other workforce groups.[41] No fewer than 880 health and social care staff died from Covid between March and December 2020[42] while other countries had largely managed to avoid deaths among healthcare workers by employing rigorous infection control measures. Hospital in-patients also caught Covid. Members of Bereaved Families for Justice estimated that 40% of their loved ones had contracted the infection in hospital.[43]

* Data on the numbers of NHS and social care staff who have died is hard to come by but an FoI request in July 2021 received the response that it was 1,500
https://www.mirror.co.uk/news/politics/more-1500-nhs-care-workers-24536105

The advice about PPE changed frequently – 40 times in 6 months – suggesting that it was tailored to suit the stocks that were available rather than the scientific evidence. Healthcare workers were understandably terrified of catching Covid at work, and in hospitals, hospices and the social care sector desperate staff improvised PPE and accepted donations from local businesses, schools and veterinary practices. Many, including 1500 doctors, logged reports of inadequate PPE.[44] Hundreds subsequently described being unsupported, threatened, or even disciplined for highlighting the shortages, although NHS trusts subsequently denied this.[45] * Given the dangers facing staff every day it must have been particularly galling to hear the Secretary of State for Health Matt Hancock claim that there had never been a national shortage of PPE.[46] Health professionals knew to their cost that this was a brazen lie.

Institutions which were forced to look for their PPE outside the normal NHS supply chain were later told by the government that they would not be reimbursed for these costs. It was reported that hospitals concerned were out of pocket to the tune of tens of millions of pounds.[47]

Further scandals continue to dog PPE, including corruption and cronyism around contracts, millions of pieces of equipment that have had to be discarded as not fit for purpose and huge sums lost to fraud (see page 16). But the biggest scandal remains the fact that our government failed to protect frontline workers and as a result there were many avoidable deaths. No one in government has yet thought to apologise or suggested recompense for their families.

A bonanza for the private sector

'There have been too many failures and too much taxpayer money has been squandered by this government to avoid accountability in the way they have at the moment.'
Matt Western, Labour MP, to the People's Covid Inquiry

* 130 trusts were asked under Freedom of Information requests whether they had limited the availability of PPE for their staff. 66 replied. 60 denied issuing instructions to limit PPE, 5 refused to provide information, and 1 said the information was not available https://www.bmj.com/content/372/bmj.n438

The UK NHS is deservedly famous for its primary care network and system of public health, but we have seen how the government chose to turn its back on these established public services when it made the disastrous decision to outsource FTTIS to the private sector. This is only one instance of the government favouring the private sector over the NHS during the pandemic.

As a result of the funding cuts and closures described in other chapters the NHS faced the pandemic with 100,000 staff vacancies, a crumbling infrastructure and too few hospital beds. To make matters worse a further 5,000 hospital beds were closed in March 2020 and have remained unused ever since.[48] Hospitals soon faced being overwhelmed, and in March 2020 the government announced they had contracted with 26 private hospital companies to block book up to 8,000 beds in private hospitals. The contract also undertook to cover 100% of the operating costs of the private hospitals regardless of activity.[49]

Health campaigners, led by the Centre for Health and the Public Interest (CHPI), subsequently called for the Public Accounts Committee to look into these deals, noting that there was a complete lack of transparency about how much the government had paid and plenty of evidence that the private sector had underperformed in terms of activity. CHPI estimated that the contract was costing the taxpayer between £170m and £400m a month, while there was on average only one Covid patient a day in the private beds, which accounted for only 0.08% of the 3.6 million bed days for Covid patients.[50]

The Department of Health defended their decision, saying that the intention was to allow the NHS to use the private beds to deliver non-Covid care but even this didn't stand up to scrutiny. In the year before the pandemic the private sector delivered 3.5 million NHS funded procedures, but this dropped to 2 million in the first year of the pandemic. At a time when the NHS needed the private sector to step up, and indeed had paid it handsomely to do so, it underperformed to a shocking degree.

Why were huge and undisclosed amounts of taxpayers' money spent on contracts which allowed the private sector to fall so far short of expectations? While representing very poor value for money to the NHS and the taxpayer, the contracts in effect provided a subsidy to the private sector which otherwise might not have survived the pandemic. As it is, they are well set to profit from the back log of non-Covid work, either through NHS contracts or increased numbers of self-funding patients.[51]

For the next four years the government will continue to pay to use private sector beds for NHS patients at a cost of up to £2.5bn a year, double the amount spent in 2018 and 2019.[52] In January 2022 Sajid Javid instructed Amanda Pritchard, CEO of NHS England, to pay £270m to private hospitals to reserve beds for three months in case of a surge in Covid cases, despite her warnings that the NHS would be financially exposed and likely to pay for 'activity that is not performed'.[53] All this money would be better spent increasing the capacity of the NHS.

Alongside these contracts the government built seven Nightingale hospitals, supposedly to deal with Covid patients. The buildings went up commendably quickly, at an estimated cost of between £420m and £500m (proving that there was a magic money tree in a crisis). It has proved impossible to establish how much of this money went to the private sector.[54] The Nightingale in London's ExCel centre, designed for those requiring intensive care, had 4,000 beds, equal to the entire pre-pandemic intensive care bed base in England. There were 15,000 beds in other Nightingale sites, set up for post-acute patients.[55] In the end Nightingale hospitals admitted fewer than 1,000 patients, which works out at £50,000 a patient. The reason? Hospital beds are no use without staff and there simply weren't enough doctors, nurses and allied health professionals to provide the medical cover needed. If the government had thought to consult with NHS frontline staff they would not have wasted £500 million on beds they couldn't staff.* Much better if they had ensured adequate staff and bed numbers in the NHS in the first place.

* The Birmingham Nightingale, the most expensive one to set up at £66.4m, did not treat any patients throughout the pandemic.

Pandemic contracts – chumocracy, cronyism and corruption

'Never again should any government treat a public health crisis as an opportunity to enrich its associates and donors at public expense.'
Jo Maugham, director of the Good Law Project

When Covid struck the government panicked. They had no plan for a pandemic apart from herd immunity or the 'let it rip' attitude favoured by Johnson, and knew that they were not prepared for the coming demand on hospital beds and equipment such as ventilators and PPE. In May 2021 Dominic Cummings, the Prime Minister's chief adviser at the beginning of the outbreak, confirmed to the Health Select Committee that there had been no pandemic plan, no plan for emergency procurement, not even a plan for disposing of bodies. There had been 'no sense of any urgency' until the last week of February.[56]

Having run down the NHS and the UK public health system in the decade prior to the pandemic the government turned to the private sector. By March 2020 the government had struck deals for the use of thousands of private hospital beds, as described above. Spire Healthcare's contract was reportedly worth £466 million and that of Circle Health £463 million.[57] At the same time the government signed off large uncontested contracts for undisclosed amounts of money with an array of private companies. Some of these companies immediately turned around and subcontracted out the work, presumably after taking their cut.

Strict rules are supposed to govern the spending of public money. Government procurement must be transparent and provide value for money, and the details of all contracts must be published within 30 days of being awarded. Yet under cover of the pandemic the government ignored the basic rules. Many contracts were not put out to tender and campaigners and public interest lawyers have struggled to find out how much was spent on what and how much activity it bought. For example, the government set up a fast track 'VIP lane' for PPE providers. Contracts worth billions were awarded, many without competitive tendering, to companies who too often had little or no relevant experience of procuring or making PPE or medical grade equipment. 47 companies were awarded contracts totalling £4.7bn after being fast tracked by ministers, MPs, peers and officials. Suppliers directed into the VIP lane were ten times more likely to be awarded a contract than those using the normal channels.[58] Almost all had connections with the Conservative Party.

David Meller, a Tory party donor and backer of Michael Gove, won PPE contracts worth £164m.[59] Tory peer Baroness Michelle Mone, best known for her lingerie business, referred a company called PPE Medpro to the VIP lane and it was awarded two contracts worth £203m. At the time of her referral the business had not yet been incorporated as a company. Baroness Mone and her husband were later accused of being secretly involved with PPE Medpro, although they both consistently denied any 'role or function' in the company.[60]

£840,000 went via Michael Gove's office to a company called Public First, one of whose owners had worked for Gove. The contract wasn't advertised and it was only three months later that any written record of it appeared.[61]

Matt Hancock was asked to 'set the record straight' after his former pub landlord won a contract for over £40m for Covid related work despite having no previous experience of producing medical supplies.[62] Hancock had to set it straight again after he was found to have broken the ministerial code by failing to declare a stake in a family company that won an NHS contract.[63]

In April 2021 a report from Transparency International noted that one in five Covid contracts raised red flags for possible corruption and that there had been 'systemic bias' in favour of firms with political connections.[64]

There was no pretence that a referral to the VIP lane had anything to do with track record or quality. A £250m contract for PPE went to a Miami jewellery designer[65] who had paid £21m to a 'consultant' to broker the deal.[66] A Turkish T-shirt manufacturer failed to deliver most of the 400,000 gowns that had been ordered and paid for, and when they did finally arrive they were not fit for purpose.[67] Also unusable were 50 million face masks, part of a contract for which a company specialising in currency trading was paid £252m.[68] PestFix, a pest control company, was awarded a £32m contract for surgical gowns despite having listed assets of only £18,000. PestFix is not a manufacturer and was obliged to order the gowns from China. Because they had no assets to speak of the government had to give them a deposit worth 75% of the contract (thus breaking its own rules).[69] Months later the gowns had still not been made available.

Meanwhile companies and individuals with established track records of procuring and manufacturing PPE (but without connections to Tory politicians) were unable to get through to the government. Dr Michelle Dawson, a consultant anaesthetist who set up a charity to make and deliver PPE wherever it was needed, described how the government failed to take up a contract for millions of items of PPE that she had managed to negotiate. There was no mark up and no middle man involved. The result was that – at a time of acute shortage – the items were sold to other countries.[70] The BMA reported being contacted by over 70 companies who said they could supply high quality PPE but had received no response from the government. The BMA forwarded these offers to the Department of Health who never replied.[71] In PPE procurement, as in Test and Trace, it wasn't what you knew but who you knew.

The National Audit Office investigated the procurement process and concluded that 'standards of transparency and documentation were not consistently met during the first phases of the pandemic'.[72] It took a legal action brought by the Good Law Project and EveryDoctor to reveal the sordid details of at least some of what went on. Together they crowdfunded enough money to make a case against contracts awarded to PestFix, Clandeboye (a confectionary wholesaler), and Ayanda, a private equity firm owned through an offshore holding company in Mauritius. The court noted that the majority of the products supplied by Ayanda and PestFix could not be used by the NHS and those from PestFix were all defective in some way. The judge also ruled that the fast-track lane used by ministers, MPs and officials was unlawful.[73]

Julia Grace Patterson, CEO of EveryDoctor said, 'We brought the government to court because NHS staff and other frontline workers were woefully unsupported and unprotected by this government.

Many were provided with no PPE and many died.'

Perhaps the most egregious case of chumocracy involved the overlapping interests of politicians, the horse racing industry and certain related private companies. As MP for Newmarket, Matt Hancock has received tens of thousands of pounds in political donations from the racing fraternity.* Newmarket racecourse is owned by the Jockey Club, and eyebrows were thus raised when Hancock appointed Baroness Dido Harding, on the board of the Jockey Club, to head the critical Test and Trace programme. Baroness Harding had no training in public health but she was a Tory peer and an old chum of David Cameron. Subsequently Randox Healthcare was awarded an uncontested £133 million contract to produce and process Covid testing kits.[74] Randox was paying Tory MP Owen Patterson £100,000 to lobby on their behalf, while his wife was chair of Aintree racecourse, home of the Grand National, sponsored by Randox.

If you thought there was something rather fishy about all of this you could always take your case to the UK Anti-Corruption champion, MP John Penrose, who also happens to be Baroness Harding's husband. Her appointment as head of Test and Trace was eventually ruled 'unlawful' by the High Court,[75] and she failed in her subsequent bid to become CEO of NHS England.

In February 2022 the government quietly reported (on page 199 of its Annual Report) that it had written off £8.7bn of taxpayers' money spent on PPE, either because it was faulty or it was not used by its expiry date.[76] The government was also heavily criticised for overpaying for equipment. A government spokesperson said, 'We are seeking to recover costs from suppliers wherever possible'. They didn't say whether that included the Conservative politicians and donors who had profited handsomely from the corrupt awarding of contracts.

* £68,000 between May 2019 and June 2020 according to the House of Commons register of members' interests.

Frontline workers betrayed

'I feel hugely let down by the government, cannon fodder absolutely nails it.'
Nurse quoted by a witness to the People's Covid Inquiry

'Every single day there was an NHS worker in tears in the changing room because we were seeing colleagues dying. We saw them dying and we were terrified we would be next.'
Dr Michelle Dawson, consultant anaesthetist, to the People's Covid Inquiry_

While Johnson and his ministers dithered and delayed about everything apart from lining the pockets of their chums and donors, frontline workers had no choice but to get on with the job. The fact that the NHS didn't collapse in the face of the pandemic was largely down to the efforts of NHS staff who worked long hours in gruelling and dangerous conditions, often to the detriment of their own mental and physical health. It was soon apparent who were the real 'essential workers' in a crisis. Along with NHS staff they include transport workers, supermarket shelf stackers, care home staff, teachers and postal staff. Many of these frontline workers are poorly paid, often on zero hours contracts or minimum pay and conditions, and they cannot work from home. Many fell into other risk categories apart from poverty, including co-morbidity, ethnic minority backgrounds[77][*] and living in crowded accommodation. Most could not survive on £97/week if they got Covid or came into contact with it, and so couldn't afford to self-isolate.[**]

NHS staff quickly found themselves dealing with illness and death on a previously unknown scale. Not only were their patients dying

---

[*]   21% of NHS staff are from ethnic minority backgrounds but non-white ethnicities accounted for 75.8% of deaths https://www.bmj.com/content/372/bmj.n602

[**]   Professor Jonathan Portes, giving evidence to the People's Covid Inquiry, felt the government's worst policy error had been their failure to raise sick pay so that people could afford to stay at home if they needed to. He saw it as a false economy which had led to poor compliance with more people getting sick and prolonging the pandemic.

from Covid at a shocking rate, but so also were their colleagues. Because of the lack of PPE, NHS workers had a seven-fold increase in their risk of getting – and thus dying from – Covid. Most NHS staff were working longer hours to cover absent colleagues (exacerbated in the early stages by the lack of testing) and some were redeployed into unfamiliar roles. Annual leave was cancelled. It is no wonder that many were soon suffering from burnout, moral distress and moral injury.

Burnout involves physical and emotional exhaustion as a result of working long hours in stressful circumstances. Moral distress is the psychological harm that occurs when people are forced to act in ways that contradict their core professional and moral values. Both have been widespread during the pandemic, often due to resource constraints – too few staff, too few ITU beds, inadequate PPE, having to turn away patients with urgent but non-Covid health needs. The professional responsibility felt by highly trained frontline staff, combined with their powerlessness to change the situation, gave rise to corrosive feelings of guilt, shame and anger.[78] If sustained, such moral distress can lead to moral injury, a deeper and more lasting harm.[79]

Years of underfunding meant that even before the pandemic many staff were struggling with jobs in which they had responsibility without autonomy. There was already evidence of early retirements and a crisis in recruiting and retaining staff.[80] Covid only served to exacerbate existing pressures. 80% of doctors who responded to a BMA survey said that the term 'moral distress' resonated with their experience of working during the pandemic.[81] The 2020 NHS Staff Survey found that 44% of NHS staff had reported feeling unwell because of work related stress, a third had considered quitting their job and a fifth said they might leave the NHS completely.[82] The BMA's mental health and support services experienced a 40% increase in their use in the first three months of the pandemic.[83]

It was no surprise that a report by the Health and Social Care Committee in June 2021 concluded that 'burnout is a widespread reality in today's NHS' and had been a problem even before the pandemic. They recommended tackling the root causes with robust workforce planning and dealing with chronic excessive workloads.[84] There is no sign yet of that happening.

Employers have a duty of care and a responsibility (Health and Safety at Work Act 1974) to protect the health and safety of their workforce 'as far as reasonably practical', which begs the question as to why the government didn't protect workers better. Risk assessment for example can reduce hazards and risks but there was little or no attempt to risk assess, even for those who were quickly seen to be at greater risk, such as the minority ethnic community.[85] There was also little in the way of moral or psychological support offered to frontline NHS staff. Dr Elaine Kinsella and Dr Rachel Sumner, both psychologists, looked at the support that frontline workers had received during the pandemic and found that there had been very little in the UK. Dr Kinsella told the People's Covid Inquiry: 'When we asked our participants how they were doing, many of them said "God, that's the first time somebody's asked me" and broke down, were really really emotional.'

Not only did staff have to work under inhuman pressures while at the same time risking their lives, some were also subjected to harassment and vitriol from the public, in particular from campaigners against vaccinations. Some of those speaking to the media had to contend with threats of physical violence and even death threats.[86][87] A GP practice in London which sent out text reminders about vaccines got a number of abusive responses including 'Contact me again and I will take u to court personally for crimes against humanity' and 'Go fuck yourself with ur poisonous cocktail which is killing people'.[88]

As the pandemic continued unchecked and deaths mounted Johnson and Hancock, along with most of the nation, banged pots on their doorsteps in support of NHS staff. But for the politicians it was an empty gesture. Quite how empty was revealed when the government made their insulting offer of a 1% pay rise. Staff felt overworked and undervalued and for many this was the last straw.

NHS staff do not want the public to bang pots on doorsteps, to be praised as heroes and congratulated for their resilience. They would prefer to work in a properly funded system without facing daily burnout and moral distress due to chronic staff shortages and lack of resources.[89] One witness to the People's Covid Inquiry felt that staff would give up even the paltry 1% pay rise if they could only get the resources to do their jobs properly. But there is little sign of any improvement on the horizon. On the contrary, NHS staff now face the biggest backlog and waiting lists since records began,[90] with Sajid Javid, Hancock's replacement as Health Secretary, threatening the NHS with 'tough new targets'.

Other frontline workers did not fare any better. The People's Covid Inquiry took evidence from representatives of teachers and transport workers and from union leaders and it was clear that many employers shirked their responsibility for making workplaces safe. Instead, it fell to trade unions to establish safe environments and to conduct risk assessments, especially for at-risk groups such as ethnic minority workers. London bus drivers, whose services had been largely privatised, had to take their own safety measures such as erecting plastic screens and reducing access by closing the front doors on buses. One employer sent out a notice saying that these measures had not been agreed and threatening disciplinary action if they continued. London Underground staff had to fight for basic measures like masks and hand gel, and had to use threats of suspending the service in order to get them.[91] 21 transport workers died within a month of lockdown and 88 had died by May 2021.[92]

Primary Care

> 'I have a horrible feeling that if some patients had been passed on to their GPs we might have saved some lives. People died at home because they didn't get the medical attention they needed quickly enough.'
> GP Dr Helen Salisbury to the People's Covid Inquiry

Primary care is the foundation of the NHS, handling 80% of patient contacts while receiving only 9% of the budget. Like the rest of the service, it had endured well over a decade of under-investment and was already creaking at the seams before the pandemic struck. Promised increases in GP numbers had never materialised despite

15% year-on-year increases in appointments.[93]

From the very start the government decided to bypass NHS GPs, who run one of the best primary care systems in the world. Instead, they redirected all patients with possible Covid symptoms to NHS 111, the phone and online service for urgent healthcare advice. Patients with Covid symptoms were told to ring NHS 111 call centres and not to trouble their GPs. If a patient did contact their GP because they were worried about Covid symptoms, the GP was not able to arrange for them to be tested, nor did they get the results for patients who had been tested through Test and Trace.

NHS 111 had to take on new staff to deal with the rise in callers, and there was limited training, with a steep learning curve. There was a list of inflexible scripted questions which didn't take account of the varied symptoms of Covid. In particular there was little understanding that patients could be dangerously short of oxygen and yet not be breathless. People were asked whether their lips were blue (as an indication of hypoxia) which was not an appropriate question for Black people. Many who were dangerously ill with Covid were told to stay indoors and 'take a paracetamol' when they should have been directed to hospital, with the result that some people died at home without ever having seen a doctor.

Thus GPs were effectively barred from managing their own patients with Covid, and excluded from the local public health response to the pandemic (see Test and Trace above). But they still had their hands full. With the arrival of the pandemic they had to adapt quickly and almost overnight. In March 2020, under direction from NHS England, they rapidly introduced remote consultations via phone and online consulting for the great majority of patients. This had the effect of removing some of the barriers previously faced by patients when trying to get an appointment with a GP and resulted in a sharp rise in requests for consultations. One GP reported patients 'submitting many e-consultations in a 24-hour period, often for problems they might never have consulted their GP about previously'.[94]

Some GPs also had to source their own PPE, often from local charities or knitting clubs,[95] continue to offer safe face-to-face appointments to patients who needed them and arrange to care for the patients who couldn't been seen in secondary care. Many of these were waiting with painful or life-threatening conditions after hospitals suspended specialist services. They also had to take on the challenge of patients with exacerbation of their mental health problems and patients with long Covid while enduring micromanagement by NHS England.[96] They took responsibility for the lion's share of the vaccination programme, which was one of the few success stories of the pandemic. And, of course, they also had to keep all of this going while contending with high rates of staff absences.

It was thus extraordinary that, with the pandemic still in full swing, Sajid Javid should have chosen to side with a far right and *Daily Mail* campaign demanding that all patients should be able to have a face-to-face appointment with their GPs.[97]* Javid even threatened to 'name and shame' (in local and national league tables) GPs who failed to co-operate, and to send in 'hit squads'.[98] It would be hard to imagine a more damaging populist stance against the profession, with the less well-informed asking when GPs 'were going to start work again'. GPs and their staff had to face daily verbal abuse and even physical violence, and many accused the government of shifting blame on to the same workforce that had worked so hard throughout the pandemic.[99]

Javid had to back-pedal on his belligerent stance when it became clear that GPs were going to lead the massive roll-out of booster jabs that began in October 2021. The overall success of the vaccine campaign, run by the NHS via GPs, pharmacists and dedicated centres, has been in stark contrast to the abysmal failure of the privately run Test and Trace system. There is a lesson there which should not be lost on politicians.

---

* GPs were quick to point out the irony when Sajid Javid cancelled his own face-to-face appointment with 1,500 of their representatives at their annual conference. https://www.mirror.co.uk/news/politics/sajid-javid-mocked-failing-defend-25213580

Secondary care

'We weren't prepared. We didn't have the PPE, we didn't have the protocols, we didn't have the rapid response systems we didn't have the infrastructure. I think the NHS has been starved of funds for the last 12 years.'
Dr Chidi Ejimofo, NHS consultant in Emergency Medicine, to the People's Covid Inquiry

Hospitals also had to act quickly. Changes that would normally take months happened in the space of days as wards and operating theatres were repurposed and emergency departments reorganised into high and low risk areas. Hospitals also had to cancel elective procedures and operations, move outpatient work online and severely restrict visits, all without any help from higher up the NHS chain of command. As Dr Chidi Ejimofo, Emergency Medicine consultant, told the PCI, 'We were having to create our own guidance, we weren't getting anything nationally'. That also included PPE, which his staff had to scramble to find for themselves.

The pre-pandemic chickens came home to roost. Too many hospital buildings are old and not fit for purpose, with poor ventilation and crowded common areas. There were too few hospital beds, in particular a shortage of single rooms, and the government wasted millions on Nightingale hospitals because they overlooked the fact that there was nobody to staff them. There was a criminal lack of PPE. Not enough testing was available in the early days for staff or for patients being discharged. All these factors meant that – despite the best efforts of health professionals – hospital in-patients still caught Covid. In June 2021 a survey of NHS trusts reported that 32,307 patients admitted to hospital with other conditions had contracted Covid, and of these 8,747 (27%) had died within 28 days. 45 trusts refused to release their figures despite being legally obliged to do so.[100]

Jeremy Hunt, chairing the Health and Social Care select committee, commented, 'these figures are devastating and pose challenging questions on whether the right hospital infection controls were in place'.[101] This was particularly ironic as Hunt had been in charge when the pandemic preparedness exercises were shelved, and had presided over the reduction in hospital bed numbers.

We have already seen how staff had to work in dangerous conditions with inadequate or non-existent PPE, and some faced extra stress by having to work in unfamiliar areas. Burnout and moral distress were rife and remain so. One particular war zone involved Accident and Emergency (A&E) departments. Initially attendances fell by up to 57%,[102] possibly because patients were afraid to visit crowded departments, but that soon reversed.

By September 2021 the Royal College of Emergency Medicine (RCEM) reported that A&E targets had long since fallen by the wayside. Dr Katherine Henderson, President of the RCEM, said that the NHS was short of 15,000 beds needed to cope with emergencies, and there was 'literally no room at the inn' for ambulances arriving with critically ill patients.[103] Half of all departments left sick patients outside in ambulances or even turned them away. Half of casualty wards were treating patients in corridors every day and 48 hour waits for an in -patient bed were not uncommon.[104] Trusts declared critical incidents as they were forced to cancel planned surgery.

Part of the problem, aside from the chronic lack of beds, was the difficulty of applying infection control measures in crowded spaces and part was due to the growing demand for urgent and emergency care as non-Covid patients returned. These included not only those with typical acute problems such as heart attacks and strokes, but also those who had become seriously ill during the 18 months of the pandemic, and patients who had been on waiting lists for months and who were 'stressed and fed up with waiting'. There was also a significant increase in mental health admissions, especially among young people, whose dedicated services simply could not cope with the demand.

At the time of writing (February 2022) there are still not enough hospital beds, not enough staff, ambulances are queuing outside A&E and there is a backlog of 6 million people waiting for procedures and elective surgery. Despite this Boris Johnson has thrown caution to the winds and announced that public health measures will no longer be mandatory from the end of this month. Sajid Javid, secure in his

Whitehall fastness, continues to tell exhausted staff and patients waiting (and dying) in the back of ambulances[105] that the NHS is still not under 'unsustainable pressure'.

What happened to vulnerable people

'We all face the same storm but we are not all in the same boat.'
Dr Sonia Adesara (after Damian Barr) to the People's Covid Inquiry

'It makes me angry. Boris Johnson has forgotten this whole group of people who have died at six times the rate of their peers in the general population.'
Clare Phillips, manager supported living services for adults with learning difficulties, to the People's Covid Inquiry

We have seen what happened to NHS staff and other frontline workers, unable to work from home and exposed to the virus without adequate protection, but other vulnerable groups also fared very badly. The poor, the elderly, the disabled, those with mental health problems and learning difficulties, migrants and the minority ethnic community all faced particular challenges and died in disproportionate numbers.

In March and April 2020 thousands of older people were discharged from hospitals back into their care homes without being tested.[106] Care homes are 'institutional amplifiers' and, once introduced, the virus spread rapidly amongst the frail and elderly. This seeding of Covid from hospitals into care homes was made worse by the fact that there wasn't enough PPE or testing available. Some staff who worked on multiple sites were catching Covid and taking it to other communities. During the first wave elderly people living in care homes were twenty times more likely to die of Covid than those living in the community.[107] It is difficult to ascertain the overall percentage of Covid deaths in care homes, but it is likely to be somewhere between 25% and 30%. Early in the pandemic Matt Hancock claimed to have put a 'protective ring' around care homes.[108] These figures show that he did nothing of the sort, and it was no surprise when he later denied saying it, despite having made the claim on live TV and to parliament.

Another group of vulnerable people who died in disproportionate numbers were the disabled, and those with learning difficulties. People with learning difficulties were five times more likely to be admitted to hospital and eight times more likely to die.[109] There was a suggestion that the clinical frailty score was used overzealously in order to avoid images in the media of hospitals being overwhelmed, as had been the case in Italy. Old prejudices emerged and those in this vulnerable group, along with those with mental health problems, were afraid that their lives would count for less in the pandemic.

The People's Covid Inquiry heard that people with a range of disabilities were driven to creating 'hospital passports' to persuade medical professionals that they deserved admission to hospital and life-saving treatment. These passports contained the patient's diagnosis, medications and the needs of individuals who might not be able to advocate for themselves if separated from their usual support workers.[110]

Between 800,000 and 1.2 million people in the UK are classed as 'undocumented' and their immigration status is checked whenever they need to access public services. They are fearful of using the NHS because it shares patient data with the Home Office, and also imposes charges – up to 150% of the cost of care, with some non-urgent care requiring payment up front. The People's Covid Inquiry heard of instances of undocumented migrants dying at home with Covid as they were afraid to seek help. They were in fact entitled to free care for Covid but they didn't know this as the government hadn't publicised the fact.[111] Covid also ripped through centres holding asylum seekers, where there was no ready access to GP services and no possibility of social distancing.[112]*

The minority ethnic community was also at greater risk – by April 2020 30% of those admitted to ITU were of non-white ethnicity, although they constitute only 14% of the population. The increased risk was due to a number of factors including a high rate of co-

* Professor Martin McKee told the People's Covid Inquiry: 'In our modern economy prisons, care homes and immigrant detention centres are a means of monetising the storage of human beings. They have a different set of objectives and the idea that they're there to look after people is missing the point. They are essentially financial vehicles which happen to have people in them.'

morbidities such as diabetes and cardiovascular disease, crowded living conditions and multigenerational households, and working in frontline jobs, meaning increased exposure. BMA surveys had already shown that minority ethnic doctors were more at risk from discrimination and bullying and they were therefore less likely to raise concerns such as inadequate PPE.[113]

Children and young adults also suffered during the pandemic and continue to do so.[114] Their education was interrupted (the determination of exam grades has been criticised as 'farcical'), and many from poor households had little space and few resources at home. There have been particular problems around the mental health of children and adolescents. The pandemic exacerbated pre-existing problems such as eating disorders, self-harm and depression, which thrive on isolation. In February 2021 it was estimated that a sixth of children had a probable mental health problem and only a quarter of those estimated to need help were receiving treatment. Anne Longfield, the children's commissioner for England, warned that the damage caused to children's mental health could last for years.[115]

The pandemic has also exacerbated many chronic gender inequalities. While men were more likely to die from Covid, women have suffered a greater social and economic impact. They are more likely to be poor, to work in sectors such as hospitality which were affected by the pandemic, and they are responsible for 60% more unpaid work than men. As a result they were more likely to be made redundant, more likely to be furloughed, have suffered a big increase in their unpaid work and are more likely to be in serious debt.[116] There has also been a significant increase in domestic violence towards girls and women.[117]

Finally there are the clinically vulnerable, who at the beginning of the pandemic were advised to self-isolate. A report by MPs found that due to 'poor data and lack of joined up systems' the government failed to reach 800,000 of them and argued that support was subject to a postcode lottery.[118] At the time of writing, when Boris Johnson has just announced the end of mandatory public health measures to control the pandemic, there is no sign of a plan to deal with the estimated 3.7 million extremely clinically vulnerable people in the UK.

Covid has shone a spotlight on the social inequalities which had already worsened over the previous decade. People woke up to the effects of long-term underinvestment in areas such as public health, social care services, schools, public housing, alcohol and drug services. The big challenge will be to start to address social inequalities and their causes once the pandemic is over.

As Dr Mary Ann Stephenson told the People's Covid Inquiry: 'Covid has highlighted problems that existed long before the pandemic ... we don't want to go back to the way things were, we have an opportunity to do things differently and this is the moment to do that.'

Lack of coherent guidance and poor messaging

The People's Covid Inquiry heard criticism from many witnesses about the lack of guidance and clear messaging from the government.[119] This meant that in the early stages of the pandemic those in the firing line, for instance in the NHS, in local government and those responsible for public transport, were forced to take matters into their own hands.[120]

When government guidance was issued it was often incoherent and not fit for purpose. For instance, 96% of people said they understood the instruction to 'stay at home' but only 30% thought they understood 'stay alert'. What did that mean in practice? Others were confused by 'stay at home, protect the NHS'. Many obeyed, either because they were afraid of catching the virus in crowded A&E departments, or because they didn't want to burden the NHS.[121] As a result people didn't present with serious and life-threatening conditions such as heart attacks and cancer. The government were warned this was a danger but they didn't change the messaging. Minority ethnic groups were particularly at risk, but messaging was not tailored to their particular needs and was felt to have been poor to non-existent.

The government's erratic behaviour and policy U-turns led to mistrust. Schools were deemed safe one day but had to be closed the next. The infamous change of policy when Johnson tried to 'save

Christmas' 2020 only to have to cancel it at the last minute was followed by the UK's worst daily death toll, which peaked at 1,359 on 19 January 2021.[122] People were especially confused by advice to exercise caution and common sense while at the same time the government was relaxing restrictions. For instance, the policy of 'eat out to help out' (renamed 'eat out to spread the virus') made no sense to frontline workers,[123] and is thought to have been responsible for a sixth of new Covid cases in the summer of 2020.[124]

Unclear and inconsistent messaging also led to some members of the public refusing to observe basic safety measures such as wearing masks in public spaces. The BMA heard from a number of GP practices who had been threatened with legal action under the Equalities Act for asking patients to wear a face covering,[125] and in Northern Ireland doctors reported increasing numbers of patients refusing to wear face coverings or to have a Covid test before assessment or admission to hospital.[126]

Failure to listen, failure to take advice, failure to trust the public

'(the government's) paternalistic psychology, that people are weak and frail and can't do things for themselves, their positioning of their best asset as a problem, is one of the fundamental failures of the whole pandemic.'
Professor Steven Reicher to the People's Covid Inquiry

Before and then during the pandemic the government have shown themselves unwilling to listen to professionals and experts. The People's Covid Inquiry heard from a range of individuals and professional organisations who said the government had never consulted them nor heeded their advice.

Well before the pandemic the National Pensioners' Convention had written repeatedly to the government asking them to reform social care but had never received the courtesy of a response.[127] Kevin Courtney, Joint General Secretary of the National Education Union, said the teachers' unions were 'completely blanked by the Prime Minister' when they tried to give advice and felt there would have been less disruption of education and fewer deaths if the government had listened to them.[128] Even those responsible for the vulnerable in the community, who as we have seen were dying in high numbers, could not get the government's ear.

This failure to listen to experts, unless they were saying what the government wanted to hear, was rooted in their general distrust of professionals and in their misplaced belief in the private sector. As we have already seen, this manifested itself in their failure to trust GPs, the NHS and public health bodies to run the FTTIS system. Instead they outsourced a vital service to private companies who had little or no relevant experience, with disastrous consequences for patients.

Tragically the government didn't trust the public either, viewing them instead as a problem with a poor grasp on reality. Because of this they never tried to engage the public, to mobilise communities nor the 750,000 volunteers who had come forward to offer their help at the start of the pandemic. But then, as a letter to the *BMJ* pointed out, volunteers, with their unpaid good will, can't be outsourced to the private sector.[129]

The government did accept advice early on, from non-behavioural scientists who argued that the British public would not cope with a lockdown, and they delayed imposing one. There was little or no evidence for this assumption, which resulted in many avoidable deaths. Research shows that it is important to trust the public in times of crisis. They are more likely to react with solidarity than panic and will come together and support each other if given the chance. The public were never involved in decision making and were told what to do rather than being mobilised to help.[130]

Research also shows that the public's willingness to co-operate and adhere to restrictions depends on trust in their government. The stream of confused messaging and contradictory policies did not engender public trust but the real problem arose when those in power were seen to disobey their own rules. From Dominic Cummings testing his eyesight with a drive to Barnard Castle,[131] through Matt Hancock's career-ending clinch under a CCTV camera[132] to the scandal of #partygate,[133] those who were making the rules were increasingly seen to be breaking them. The government talked about pandemic fatigue and claimed that the public were tired of restrictions, but they were wrong. The vast majority have been heroic, prepared to abide by tough measures for extended periods as long as they thought we were all in it together. Their attitudes changed dramatically when they saw egregious rule breaking going unpunished.

Failure to tell the truth

'I have lost confidence in the secretary of state's honesty.'
Cabinet secretary to Dominic Cummings

When Dominic Cummings gave evidence to the joint select committee hearings in May 2021, he accused the then health secretary Matt Hancock of 'lying to everybody on multiple occasions'. He said Hancock had lied over the availability of PPE, over putting a shield around care homes, over testing patients before discharging them to care homes and when he claimed that everybody who needed treatment was getting it.[134] When Hancock appeared before the same committees a few weeks later he defended himself and blamed 'clinical advice' for several major government failings. His memory let him down over a number of important matters involving testing and PPE.[135]

The truth matters in a national crisis. People are prepared to adhere to tough restrictions and sacrifice much if they think they can trust the government. Unfortunately, senior advisers, ministers and the prime minister himself have shown themselves to be untrustworthy during the pandemic. The public have generally behaved better than the people who set the rules, but lost faith when they understood politicians were lying to them.

Public health

'One of the most important public health failures the United Kingdom has ever experienced.'
Corona Virus: Lessons Learned to Date[136]

'Public health in general became a lesser interest of the government. If the system had been operating well and run by public health people … we would have coped much better. We have governments that have no real interest in the health of the population.'
Professor Gabriel Scally to the People's Covid Inquiry

Andrew Lansley's deeply flawed Health and Social Care Act resulted in, among other things, a massive re-disorganisation of public health. Responsibility for public health went to a new national body, Public Health England (PHE) with services devolved to local authorities. The following decade saw big cuts in the funding of both. Since 2015 £850m has been cut from government public health grants to local authorities. PHE's operational budget has been cut by 40% in real terms since 2013.[137]

The result was an under-resourced and fragmented public health service which was already struggling to cope before the pandemic. Some areas such as sexual and mental health services and dependency services suffered extreme cuts. Staff who were used to making progress in vital areas such as teenage pregnancy and substance misuse, found that some public health indicators were stationary or actually going backwards. Life expectancy stalled and even started to decline in some areas.[138] As Sir Michael Marmot noted: 'We were in a very bad state, and then came the pandemic.'[139]

Public Health England (PHE), which had become an integral part of the Department of Health as part of Lansley's Act, proved a handy scapegoat when the government's pandemic response proved woefully inadequate. Politicians blamed it for problems outside its remit, such as a lack of adequate PPE and the failure to roll out mass testing.[140] Then came the bombshell; in the middle of the most serious public health crisis in decades the government made the decision to scrap Public Health England.

Typical of the government, PHE's demise was first announced not in the House of Commons but via the *Daily Telegraph*.[141] A government source told the paper that PHE should have been on the alert for pandemics instead of trying to prevent ill health. The former Conservative leader Iain Duncan Smith claimed that PHE was guilty of 'arrogance laced with incompetence', and Boris Johnson pointedly said that 'some parts of government' had responded to the pandemic 'sluggishly'.[142] *The Sun* newspaper joined in the chorus of criticism, claiming that PHE had spent too much time 'banging on about the dangers of fizzy drinks'.[143] Duncan Selbie, the ousted chief executive, pointed out that there had never been an intention for PHE to provide mass testing and it was the Department of Health and Social Care's responsibility to deliver a national testing programme,[144] but the government had found a scapegoat.

The new agency that took over – the National Institute for Health Protection – would be responsible for protecting the country from future pandemics. People noted with concern that the words 'public health' had disappeared from its title, and that the government had replaced the term 'health inequalities' with 'health disparities', a concept which sounded more bland and less in need of government intervention.[145] The new agency would not apparently be responsible for promoting health and reducing health inequalities, possibly because the government had long felt that many public health measures constituted intrusions by a nanny state. When he was Secretary of State for Health Matt Hancock promised to embed health inequality reduction across government, but he is long since banished and little has been heard of this goal since.

Why did the UK, with a reputation for an excellent public health system, end up with one of 'the most important public health failures the United Kingdom has ever experienced'? The fact was that a decade of deep cuts and the dismantling of infrastructure had decimated the public health system. Structures responsible for pandemic planning had been weakened or abolished and the system simply didn't have the resources to mount a successful pandemic response. This could have been remedied quickly – many countries gave their public health organisations more powers and resources during the pandemic – but true to form the UK government did just the opposite. They scrapped Public Health England, turned to the private sector to run vital public health functions such as Test and Trace and failed to resource and use local public health teams and local authorities. The blame for the public health disaster that followed lies squarely at the door of government.

The Audacious Data Grab

'Data protection laws require your explicit consent to what happens to your data. The obligation is on the Secretary of State and NHS Digital to seek your consent and to notify you about this proposal. Currently their notification is simply a webpage and a link to how you can opt out.'
Rosa Curling, CEO of Foxglove, to the People's Covid Inquiry

The NHS is a highly centralised system. Its unique mass of patient data has been estimated to be worth £10bn a year to the private sector, which is well aware of its value and its potential to generate profits. In March 2020 the government set up the Covid-19 data store, to collate in a single place all the data needed to support the Covid response. This was done quietly, announced only via an NHS blog which listed Deloittes, McKinsey and Palantir among the private companies involved.[146]

There was no transparency around these contracts but campaigners (Open Democracy and Foxglove) understood that all GP records would go into the store unless patients opted out. This was unlikely to happen as there had been no public consultation and most patients knew nothing about it.

Part of the process involved a two-year £23m contract with Palantir, a controversial firm described as 'the scariest of America's tech giants'. The deal was presented as an emergency and short-term Covid response, but campaigners got wind of mission creep extending beyond the pandemic and took the government to court. Government lawyers insisted that the public have no right to a say in NHS contracts with big tech, but were forced to postpone the transfer of data indefinitely and to agree not to extend Palantir's contract beyond the end of the pandemic without consulting the public.[147]

Patients have a legal right to know what is happening to their data – where it is being stored and by whom, whether it is secure, who has access to it and what it is being used for. NHS data has been very important during the pandemic, for instance for research on treatments for Covid and vaccine effectiveness, for identifying and contacting the clinically vulnerable for shielding purposes and for prioritising early vaccinations. Patients are by and large willing to share their data for planning and research but do not want it used for marketing or insurance purposes. They are also entitled to know that it is being stored securely.

Transparency and trust are necessary if the public are to agree to the collection and storage of their clinical data. They must be consulted and allowed to opt out. Rushing changes through, awarding contracts to the likes of Palantir with no details available, and failing to inform and consult the public are retrograde and dangerous steps, and must not become the new post pandemic norm.

The cost to the country

'The death of one man is a tragedy. The death of millions is a statistic.'
Attributed to Joseph Stalin

At the time of writing the number of Covid deaths in the UK stands at just over 180,000. It is easy to become inured to statistics; indeed, with such shocking figures the government counts upon it. But, to finish where we began, that is equivalent to a commercial planeload of people crashing every day over the last two years. It is shocking and demands investigation. Even more shocking is the fact that the poor and the vulnerable died in such disproportionate numbers.

At the same time, the economic cost to the country is estimated to be between £315bn and £410bn.[148] The government has squandered billions of taxpayers' money, most noticeably on the failed test and trace system. It has written off up to £10bn spent on PPE, overpaying for some things while having to discard millions of items which were out of date or not fit for purpose. More recently news has emerged of over £200m lost when Sajid Javid cancelled a non-refundable contract with French vaccine manufacturer Valneva.[149]

At no stage has it been too late to change course and many voices called for an early and thorough investigation. Johnson declined, saying 'We must not inadvertently divert or distract people on whom we depend ... in our struggle against this disease'.[150] Oddly enough this didn't seem to be a problem for him when the government scrapped Public Health England and introduced sweeping new NHS reforms in the middle of the pandemic.[151]

Johnson did promise a public inquiry starting in spring 2022 but at the time of writing (February 2022) there is little sign of this happening.* In the absence of any initiative from the government others took matters into their own hands. The campaigning group Keep Our NHS Public (KONP) conducted its own comprehensive investigation, the People's Covid Inquiry, which ran from January to June 2021.[152] Michael Mansfield QC presided and the inquiry heard from over 40 witnesses including international and UK experts, frontline workers, bereaved families, trade union leaders and representatives of disabled people's and pensioners' organisations. It invited the government to participate but received no reply.

The conclusions of its final report, aptly entitled Misconduct in Public Office, are as follows:

- The government was not prepared for a global pandemic despite warnings that one was likely.
- When it arrived they ignored clear warnings and then did too little too late.
- During the decade before the pandemic successive Conservative governments had run down public services including the NHS, public health, and care services with the result that these were already in crisis when the pandemic struck.
- The pandemic has highlighted and exacerbated long-term problems in society around inequalities and discrimination.
- As a result of these the poorest and most vulnerable were hit the hardest and died in disproportionate numbers.
- The government failed to fulfil its basic duty of protecting frontline workers, at-risk groups and the public.
- The government made disastrous decisions about FTTIS and NHS 111.
- The government consistently favoured the private sector over the NHS. There was a lack of transparency around these dealings and huge sums of taxpayer's money have been wasted.

* Although Johnson has paid Deloittes £900,000 to prepare evidence for an inquiry, which will look - among other things - at Deloittes handling of the failed Test and Trace service.

- The government failed to consult or heed the advice of professionals, experts, civil society including unions and the public, and what's more actively distrusted them.
- The government have shown themselves unwilling to acknowledge and learn from their mistakes, or to change course where appropriate.
- They ignored calls from many quarters for an urgent inquiry and thus missed the opportunity to avoid further unnecessary deaths.

The findings of the People's Covid Inquiry were soon echoed by parliament. In October 2021 the Commons Health and Social Care and the Science and Technology committees produced a joint report, 'Coronavirus: Lessons Learned to Date'.[153] It was highly critical of the government's response to the pandemic, labelling it one of 'the most important public health failures the United Kingdom has ever experienced'. The report accused the government of complacency, fatalism and exceptionalism. It concluded amongst other things that management prior to the vaccination programme had been derailed by 'group think', care homes had effectively been abandoned, the hugely expensive test and trace had had only a 'marginal impact on transmission' and the government's initial response had failed so miserably because they had viewed the impending crisis through 'a veil of ignorance'. Unfortunately, the many pandemic procurement scandals fell outside its remit.

The report acknowledged the success of the vaccine programme but felt that should not be used to brush aside the many failures it had identified. On the day the report was published Stephen Barclay was the only minister available to do the media rounds defending the indefensible (the prime minister being conveniently on holiday in Spain). Barclay repeatedly refused to apologise for the avoidable deaths.[154]

At the time of writing Boris Johnson has announced he will abolish all mandatory Covid regulations a month earlier than anticipated, including self-isolation for those with a positive Covid test and mask wearing. Free testing will no longer be available.[155]

The announcement has come at a time when there are still over 60,000 new cases and more than 200 deaths a day.

Johnson has been under increasing political pressure over 'partygate' (the breaking of lockdown rules in Downing Street), as well as from the libertarian faction of his party who want a return to pre-pandemic 'business as usual'. The announcement abolishing mandatory Covid regulations was widely seen as politically expedient, red meat for his back benchers to keep them onside during the scandals besetting the prime minister. No government scientist supported the decision, which has been widely criticised by union leaders, representatives of the vulnerable and leading scientists including the World Health Organisation.[156]

The government seemingly have no plan to support the 3.7 million clinically vulnerable people who now face an uncertain future. The NHS is still overwhelmed, with ambulances queuing outside A&E departments, more than 11,000 hospital beds still occupied by Covid patients and a record-breaking backlog of 6.1 million people waiting for treatment. It seems that Boris Johnson still refuses to learn any lessons.

Accountability and responsibility

'The first responsibility of any Government is to protect its citizens and threats to public health are amongst the most important of all.'
Matt Hancock, Secretary of State for Health, on social media 18.8.2020[157]

By any standards, including those of Matt Hancock himself, the UK government failed to protect its citizens and tens of thousands died avoidable deaths. By February 2021 half the world's Covid death toll had occurred in 5 nations and the UK was one of them. Four of them had populist leaders, including Trump, Bolsonaro, Modi and our prime minister Boris Johnson. The handling of the pandemic is inextricably linked to politics.

We could and should have done much better and at this stage we urgently need to know why we didn't. We need answers to the following questions

- what happened?
- why did it happen?
- who is to blame?
- what can be done to prevent it happening again?

This can only be done through a credible, independent and wide-ranging public inquiry. It will need to address not only the specific failures identified above but also the broader issues such as the pre-existing health and social inequalities which were responsible for disproportionate death rates in some groups. It will need to look at scandals such as procurement and FTTIS along with the possible misuse of public funds. It will need to address the running down of vital public services in the decade leading up to the pandemic.[158]

In the meantime the question arises of who was responsible and how we hold them to account. In February 2021 Dr Kamran Abbasi, then executive editor of the *British Medical Journal* (*BMJ*) started asking the hard questions in a powerful and much quoted editorial entitled 'Covid-19: Social murder they wrote – elected, unaccountable and unrepentant'.[159]

He argued that the UK government had shown 'a premeditated and reckless indifference' to human life when it accepted tens of thousands of premature deaths in the pursuit of herd immunity or for the sake of saving the economy.

He asked whether it was lawful for politicians to wilfully neglect historical experience, scientific advice and their own statistics and modelling because to act on them would go against their political ideology. He proposed that public health malpractice during a pandemic could become a crime against humanity.

He also suggested that what has happened to vulnerable groups during the pandemic should be classified as 'social murder'. The term was first coined by Friedrich Engels, who argued that the conditions created by the privileged classes inevitably lead to premature and 'unnatural' death amongst the poorest classes. Today 'social murder' aptly describes 'the lack of political attention to social determinants and inequities'. This, exacerbated by the pandemic, has resulted in disproportionate deaths in vulnerable groups.

Abbasi asked where citizens can turn for accountability and redress when their government fails them. He concluded that the answers lie in pushing for a public inquiry, in broadening the mechanisms of global governance such as the International Criminal Court to include state failings in pandemics, and in voting out governments that are unrepentant. This latter means that voters need to understand the enormity of the government's failings, rather than being deceived by bluster and gaslighting from our political leaders.

The government has tried to deflect criticism for their gross mishandling of the pandemic by claiming that they got 'the big calls right', but they didn't.[160] [161] They made error after egregious error, beginning with their failure to maintain public services in the prior decade, and then moving on to casual fatalism, a preference for the private sector and an ideology that put the economy before the health of the population. The report of the People's Covid Inquiry accuses the government of misconduct in public office and the case it makes is strong. Those in charge of the pandemic response got things badly wrong and it will be up to voters (and history) to pass judgement.

The pandemic has reminded us of the vital importance of maintaining properly resourced public services but it has uncovered something more profoundly rotten. Covid has laid bare the discrimination and the social and health inequalities in our society and we now have the opportunity to do something about them. Professor Sir Michael Marmot has called for the government to Build Back Fairer. That includes addressing the dire state of public services and will require a fully funded and properly staffed NHS, along with appropriate recognition of those frontline workers who kept the NHS afloat even while our politicians failed them.

'It shouldn't have happened, needn't have happened, and should never happen again.'
Jan Shortt, National Pensioners Convention, to the People's Covid Inquiry

You may choose to look the other way but you can never say again that you did not know.
William Wilberforce

1   https://www.bmj.com/content/372/bmj.n352
2   https://www.bmj.com/content/375/bmj.n3132
3   https://www.bmj.com/content/369/bmj.m2052
4   https://www.bmj.com/content/373/bmj.n1374
5   Sir Michael Marmot to the People's Covid Inquiry
6   https://www.health.org.uk/sites/default/files/upload/publications/2020/
     Build-back-fairer-the-COVID-19-Marmot-review.pdf
7   https://www.theguardian.com/politics/2021/nov/30/most-deprived-
     schools-hit-hardest-by-education-cuts-in-england-ifs-says
8   https://www.bmj.com/content/371/bmj.m4499
9   https://www.theguardian.com/world/2020/may/07/revealed-the-secret-
     report-that-gave-ministers-warning-of-care-home-coronavirus-crisis
10   https://www.bmj.com/content/375/bmj.n2485
11   https://www.bmj.com/content/375/bmj.n2992
12   https://www.theguardian.com/world/2020/apr/19/michael-gove-fails-to-
     deny-pm-missed-five-coronavirus-cobra-meetings
13   Ibid
14   https://news.sky.com/story/dominic-cummings-claims-boris-johnson-was-
     writing-shakespeare-book-instead-of-dealing-with-covid-12467178
15   https://www.youtube.com/watch?v=n3NAx3tsy-k
16   https://www.bmj.com/content/373/bmj.n1374
17   https://www.irishtimes.com/news/world/uk/unflappable-confidence-of-uk-
     s-health-establishment-about-to-be-tested-1.4214245
18   https://www.theguardian.com/politics/video/2020/mar/12/coronavirus-
     johnson-warns-many-more-families-are-going-to-lose-loved-ones-video
19   Evidence to the PCI (para 8.2.13-15)
20   https://www.bmj.com/content/373/bmj.n1432
21   https://www.bmj.com/content/375/bmj.n2606
22   Professor Martin McKee to the People's Covid Inquiry
23   https://www.manchestereveningnews.co.uk/news/uk-news/health-chief-
     says-local-tracing-18737956
24   https://www.pharmatimes.com/news/randox_recalls_coronavirus_test_kits_
     after_safety_concerns_1346729
25   https://www.channel4.com/press/news/dispatches-uncovers-serious-
     failings-one-uks-largest-covid-testing-labs
26   ibid
27   https://www.theguardian.com/politics/2022/feb/04/owen-patersons-
     randox-lobbying-texts-to-matt-hancock-released
28   https://www.theguardian.com/world/2020/apr/23/hospitals-sound-alarm-
     over-privately-run-test-centre-in-surrey
29   https://www.bmj.com/content/369/bmj.m2484

30   https://www.bmj.com/content/370/bmj.m3552

31   https://www.bmj.com/content/369/bmj.m2522

32   https://unitetheunion.org/media/3331/9199_biomed-scientists_survey_
      summer2020_final-digital.pdf

33   Ibid

34   https://www.newstatesman.com/chart-of-the-day/2021/12/uk-sick-pay-
      remains-among-the-lowest-in-europe

35   https://committees.parliament.uk/committee/127/public-accounts-
      committee/news/158262/muddled-overstated-eyewateringly-expensive-
      pac-damning-on-test-trace-that-has-failed-on-main-objectives/

36   ibid

37   https://weownit.org.uk/privatised-and-unprepared-nhs-supply-chain

38   https://www.bmj.com/content/375/bmj.n2849

39   https://newseu.cgtn.com/news/2020-04-19/UK-government-defends-
      sending-protective-equipment-to-China-PPejh72hoI/share_amp.html

40   https://www.bbc.co.uk/news/health-52145140

41   https://www.bmj.com/company/newsroom/health-workers-and-their-
      families-account-for-1-in-6-hospital-covid-19-cases/.

42   https://www.ons.gov.uk/file?uri=%2fpeoplepopulationandcommuni-
      ty%2fhealthandsocialcare%2fcausesofdeath%2fdatasets%2fcoronavirus-
      covid19relateddeathsbyoccupationenglandandwales%2fcurrent/reftables-
      final.xlsx

43   Lobby Akinola, evidence to the People's Covid Inquiry

44   https://www.bmj.com/content/372/bmj.n438

45   https://www.bmj.com/content/372/bmj.n442

46   https://www.theguardian.com/world/2021/feb/23/hancock-criticised-for-
      claim-there-was-no-national-covid-ppe-shortage

47   Dr Michelle Dawson, evidence to the People's Covid Inquiry

48   https://lowdownnhs.info/news/nhs-funds-siphoned-off-as-beds-stand-
      empty/

49   https://chpi.org.uk/blog/smoke-and-mirrors-nhs-englands-totally-
      transparent-multi-billion-pound-deal-with-the-private-hospital-industry/

50   ibid

51   https://www.theguardian.com/society/2021/sep/18/private-hospitals-profit-
      from-nhs-waiting-lists-as-people-without-insurance-pay-out

52   https://lowdownnhs.info/private-providers/10bn-spend-on-private-
      hospitals-to-bridge-gap-in-nhs-capacity/

53   ttps://www.theguardian.com/society/2022/jan/13/sajid-javid-nhs-en-
      gland-private-hospitals-omicron

54   https://www.huffingtonpost.co.uk/entry/nightingale-hospitals-government-
      secrecy-costs_uk_5ed11b62c5b6228cdfe1b5cb?utm_campaign=share_
      email&ncid=other_email_o63gt2jcad4

55   https://www.kingsfund.org.uk/blog/2021/04/nhs-nightingale-hospitals-

worth-money?utm_source=email&utm_medium=email&utm_
term=socialshare
56   https://www.bbc.co.uk/news/uk-politics-57254915
57   https://www.standard.co.uk/business/government-covid-private-contracts-
30-billion-pwc-deloitte-british-airways-b933081.html
58   https://goodlawproject.org/news/special-procurement-channels/
59   https://www.theguardian.com/politics/2021/nov/16/michael-gove-backer-
won-164m-in-ppe-contracts-after-vip-lane-referral
60   https://www.theguardian.com/world/2022/jan/06/tory-peer-michelle-
mone-involved-ppe-medpro-government-contracts
61   https://www.opendemocracy.net/en/dark-money-investigations/
revealed-key-cummings-ally-given-840000-covid-contract-without-
competition/?utm_source=em
62   https://www.theguardian.com/politics/2021/dec/01/matt-hancock-says-
labours-covid-contract-claims-rubbish
63   https://www.theguardian.com/politics/2021/may/28/matt-hancock-broke-
ministerial-code-over-family-firm-given-nhs-contract
64   https://www.transparency.org.uk/COVID-contracts-conflict-2020-2021-
year-corruption-took-centre-stage
65   https://goodlawproject.org/case/saiger-case/
66   https://www.bbc.co.uk/news/uk-54974373
67   https://www.theguardian.com/world/2020/may/07/government-confirms-
400000-turkish-gowns-are-useless-for-nhs
68   https://www.bbc.co.uk/news/uk-53672841
69   https://goodlawproject.org/update/more-money-to-pestfix/
70   Dr Michelle Dawson to the People's Covid Inquiry (7.8)
71   Dr David Wrigley to the People's Covid Inquiry (7.8)
72   http://www.nao.org.uk/work-in-progress/government-procurement-during-
the-covid-19-pandemic
73   https://goodlawproject.org/update/high-court-vip-lane-ppe-unlawful/
74   https://www.theguardian.com/sport/2020/jun/16/horse-racing-tory-
donations-and-a-swift-return-from-lockdown-matt-hancock
75   https://www.bmj.com/content/376/bmj.o391.full
76   https://assets.publishing.service.gov.uk/government/uploads/system/
uploads/attachment_data/file/1051381/DHSC-Annual-Report-and-
Accounts-2020-21.pdf
77   https://www.bmj.com/content/372/bmj.n602
78   https://www.bmj.com/content/374/bmj.n1858
79   https://www.bmj.com/content/373/bmj.n1543
80   https://www.bmj.com/content/373/bmj.n1594
81   https://www.bmj.com/content/373/bmj.n1543
82   https://www.bmj.com/content/372/bmj.n703
83   https://blogs.bmj.com/bmj/2021/06/11/david-wrigley-dont-call-us-resilient/

84   https://publications.parliament.uk/pa/cm5802/cmselect/cmhealth/22/2202.htm
85   https://www.bmj.com/content/372/bmj.n602
86   https://www.bmj.com/content/375/bmj.n2528
87   https://www.manchestereveningnews.co.uk/news/greater-manchester-news/nhs-attacks-boris-johnson-appointments-21659730
88   https://www.bma.org.uk/news-and-opinion/fighting-back-the-struggle-with-anti-vaxxers
89   https://blogs.bmj.com/bmj/2021/06/11/david-wrigley-dont-call-us-resilient/
90   https://www.theguardian.com/society/2022/feb/13/nhs-backlog-poses-existential-risk-boris-johnson-government
91   Unjum Mirza, ASLEF, to the People's Covid Inquiry
92   Evidence to People's Covid Inquiry, section 5.7, 5.8 and 5.9
93   https://www.bmj.com/content/373/bmj.n1508
94   https://www.bmj.com/content/373/bmj.n1246
95   Personal communication
96   https://www.bmj.com/content/373/bmj.n1256
97   https://www.dailymail.co.uk/news/article-10090001/The-new-face-face-revolution-Sajid-Javid-launches-overhaul-GP-access.html
98   https://www.mirror.co.uk/news/politics/gps-named-shamed-fail-see-25210866
99   https://www.manchestereveningnews.co.uk/news/greater-manchester-news/nhs-attacks-boris-johnson-appointments-21659730
100 https://www.theguardian.com/world/2021/may/24/up-to-8700-patients-died-after-catching-covid-in-english-hospitals
101 Ibid
102 https://www.health.org.uk/news-and-comment/charts-and-infographics/visits-to-a-e-departments-in-england-in-april-2020-fell-by-57
103 https://www.theguardian.com/society/2021/sep/24/nhs-on-the-edge-with-some-patients-waiting-48-hours-for-a-bed
104 Ibid
105 https://www.theguardian.com/commentisfree/2021/nov/15/people-dying-ambulances-javid-health-secretary
106 https://fullfact.org/health/coronavirus-care-homes-discharge/
107 https://www.independent.co.uk/news/uk/care-england-university-of-oxford-london-school-of-hygiene-and-tropical-medicine-europe-b1990936.html
108 Press conference 15 May 2020
109 https://www.bmj.com/content/374/bmj.n1701
110 Clare Phillips, Operations Manager for Supported Living Services for Adults with disabled Disabilities, to People's Covid Inquiry (4.21.3)
111 Alia Yule, Migrants Organise, to People's Covid Inquiry (6.10)
112 Ibid

113 https://www.bma.org.uk/advice-and-support/covid-19/your-health/covid-19-the-risk-to-bame-doctors

114 See chapters by Neena Modi and Kevin Courtney

115 https://www.bmj.com/content/372/bmj.n258

116 https://wbg.org.uk/analysis/reports/lessons-learned-where-women-stand-at-the-start-of-2021/

117 https://www.bmj.com/content/374/bmj.n1926

118 https://committees.parliament.uk/work/1003/covid19-supporting-the-vulnerable-during-lockdown/news/154620/centralcommand-system-failed-to-reach-around-800k-clinically-extremely-vulnerable-people-before-hundreds-of-thousands-added-to-local-lists/

119 People's Covid Inquiry (2.4)

120 Ibid (5.8)

121 Ibid (4.7)

122 https://www.bmj.com/content/376/bmj.o254

123 People's Covid Inquiry (2.4.3)

124 https://www.theguardian.com/business/2020/oct/30/treasury-rejects-theory-eat-out-to-help-out-caused-rise-in-covid

125 https://www.pulsetoday.co.uk/news/coronavirus/gp-practices-threatened-with-legal-action-for-asking-patients-to-wear-a-face-covering/

126 https://www.bbc.co.uk/news/uk-northern-ireland-58222366

127 Jan Shortt, Gen Secretary National Pensioners' Convention to the People's Covid Inquiry

128 People's Covid Inquiry (4.2.4)

129 https://www.bmj.com/content/372/bmj.n259

130 Peoples Covid Inquiry (4.7)

131 https://www.theguardian.com/politics/video/2020/may/25/dominic-cummings-says-he-drove-to-barnard-castle-to-test-his-eyesight-video

132 https://www.youtube.com/watch?v=74C9g8530cE

133 https://www.standard.co.uk/insider/downing-street-parties-boris-johnson-birthday-carrie-covid-lockdown-b970616.html

134 https://www.bmj.com/content/373/bmj.n1505

135 https://www.bmj.com/content/373/bmj.n1504

136 https://committees.parliament.uk/publications/7496/documents/78687/default/

137 https://www.bma.org.uk/news-and-opinion/austerity-covid-s-little-helper

138 https://www.health.org.uk/publications/reports/the-marmot-review-10-years-on

139 https://www.bma.org.uk/news-and-opinion/austerity-covid-s-little-helper

140 https://www.theguardian.com/world/2020/jul/01/experts-say-ministers-are-blaming-public-health-england-over-covid-19-errors

141 https://www.telegraph.co.uk/politics/2020/08/15/hancock-axes-failing-public-health-england/

142 https://www.independent.co.uk/news/uk/politics/boris-johnson-public-health-england-coronavirus-data-leicester-iain-duncan-smith-a9595176.html.

143 https://www.thesun.co.uk/news/12419722/sun-says-phe-chop-covid-mayhem/

144 https://www.bmj.com/content/371/bmj.m4476

145 https://www.bmj.com/content/374/bmj.n2323

146 https://www.england.nhs.uk/contact-us/privacy-notice/how-we-use-your-information/covid-19-response/nhs-covid-19-data-store/

147 https://www.foxglove.org.uk/2021/04/01/success-uk-government-concedes-lawsuit-over-23m-nhs-data-deal-with-controversial-us-tech-corporation-palantir/

148 https://commonslibrary.parliament.uk/research-briefings/cbp-9309/

149 https://www.thetimes.co.uk/article/how-the-government-wasted-200-million-on-a-covid-vaccine-that-never-arrived-khwzhvvgd

150 https://www.theguardian.com/world/2021/may/12/boris-johnson-inquiry-into-handling-of-covid-crisis-will-start-spring-2022

151 See Johns chapter

152 www.peoplescovidinquiry.com

153 https://committees.parliament.uk/publications/7496/documents/78687/default/

154 https://www.theguardian.com/world/video/2021/oct/12/barclay-refuses-to-apologise-for-governments-covid-handling-video?CMP=share_btn_link

155 https://www.theguardian.com/world/2022/feb/25/government-has-abandoned-its-own-covid-health-advice-leak-reveals

156 https://www.theguardian.com/world/2022/feb/19/england-plan-to-scrap-covid-self-isolation-unwise-experts-warn

157 https://www.facebook.com/matthancockofficial/videos/the-first-responsibility-of-any-government-is-to-protect-its-citizens-the-threat/739366256910744/

158 See Michael Mansfield chapter

159 https://www.bmj.com/content/372/bmj.n31 https://www.bmj.com/content/372/bmj.n438 - staff bullied over PPE

160 https://www.theguardian.com/politics/2022/jan/30/we-got-the-big-calls-right-said-boris-johnson-but-did-he-really

161 https://www.mirror.co.uk/news/politics/no-boris-johnson-not-get-26047673

Chapter 3

Austerity into the 2020s

John Lister

This chapter covers the escalation of the crisis in the NHS as efforts began to chart a path of recovery after Covid from as early as July 2020, while performance on all fronts has fallen back.

It begins by looking at the succession of guidance documents published by NHS England, setting increasingly impossible targets and objectives. In July 2020 the focus was on speeding discharge of patients from acute hospital beds, and the so-called 'discharge to assess' policy that has been exposed as effectively 'discharge regardless'. By Christmas 2020 the focus had shifted to greater use of private hospitals and providers. The Christmas 2021 guidance set out no less than ten 'priorities', but made no mention of the thousands of NHS beds still out of use since the pandemic hit, or staff shortages. By February 2022 a new Delivery Plan focused heavily on 'partnership' with the private sector – and ignored emergency services, mental health and primary care, while accepting waiting lists will increase and long waits persist until 2025.

The budget statements since March 2021 have scaled back, and now ended any extra funding for Covid. After a big fanfare for the 3-year "Health and Care Levy" in September 2021 with its completely inadequate increase in funding for NHS and social care, austerity has been reimposed in the 2021 spending review and 2022 spring statement. They give no additional funding even for booster jabs to combat new variants of Covid. A new decade of austerity and decline seems to be under way.

The record summer pressures on A&E and ambulance services in 2021 continued into a grim autumn and a wretched winter, with the NHS expected to cope with up to 25% of its acute bed capacity either left empty or filled with Covid patients, and 110,000 staff vacancies Waiting lists are still rising above 6 million. Cancer, mental health and maternity services are all facing major problems, lacking staff, beds and funding. While NHS services decline, and backlog maintenance bills have risen above £9bn, the promised new hospital projects are at a standstill for lack of funding: but the prospects are rosy for private hospitals, which are profiting both from self-pay patients and from the NHS.

* * *

Glimpses of the scope and scale of the problems facing the NHS as the UK haltingly emerged from the peak of the Covid crisis began to appear as early as the summer and autumn of 2020, as the first premature moves were made to ease the lockdown.

Tough new guidance: summer

At the end of July 2020 a 13-page letter from NHS England[1] demanded local health leaders draw up a series of plans to tight timescales despite the peak holiday period. This made it impossible for there to be any local consultation or genuine involvement in producing them. There were no extra resources on offer, and staffing was already under a tremendous strain.

For the most significant of these plans trusts were given just the month of August to draw up *and implement* delivery plans to restore full operation of cancer services. This depended upon the rapid roll-out of a new network of 'Community Diagnostic Hubs' – which had not yet secured funding.

In the absence of necessary NHS capacity, trusts were told to turn to the private sector, ensuring sufficient diagnostic capacity was in place in 'Covid19-secure environments', including use of 'independent sector' facilities. The diagnostic hubs were supposed to run for '12 to 14 hours a day seven days a week', although where the staff were to be found to work these hours was not discussed. They had to offer a range of diagnostic services including 'CT, MRI, ultrasound, etc. …'. Through these new, in most cases still non-existent, hubs local systems were told to 'very swiftly return to at least 90% of their last year's levels of MRI/CT and endoscopy procedures, with an ambition to reach 100% by October'.

Three weeks later, in the peak holiday month of August, new Department of Health and Social Care (DHSC) guidance to hospital trusts announced that the additional government funding that had been provided to support out of hospital 'post discharge recovery and support services' during the peak of the pandemic would cease … six weeks after patients had been discharged.[2]

Trusts were instructed to operate twice-daily ward rounds to check that each patient fitted at least one of the 9 categories on a checklist: if not, then, regardless of their social circumstances, the patient had to be discharged as soon as possible, and dispatched to home or social care. Hospitals would have to explain any delays to this whistle-stop discharge process.

The guidance claimed (with no supporting evidence) that 50% of people could simply be discharged home from hospital (assuming relatives or neighbours would take the strain) with no further support from NHS or social care; 45% would need some support from health and/or social care to recover at home; 4% would need rehabilitation or short-term care in a 24-hour bed-based setting; and just 1% would need ongoing 24-hour nursing care. Senior geriatricians warned in vain that the guidance could prompt an increase in 'urgent readmissions', 'permanent disability' and 'excess mortality', while charities said families could be left with 'unsustainable caring responsibilities' because of the new rules.[3]

Despite this system being branded as 'discharge to assess' it soon became clear that it was basically 'discharge regardless'. In many areas assessments were delayed, or resources were lacking to provide for the patients' assessed needs. A year later, the Association of Directors of Adult Social Services (ADASS) published a survey of almost all 152 social services councils in England, revealing a backlog of 75,000 disabled and older people waiting for help with their care and support. Almost 7,000 had been waiting more than six months for assessment, while more than 19,000 who had been assessed and deemed eligible were waiting for a service or direct payment to arrange their own care and support.[4]

But far from being able to allocate any necessary extra resources to clear this backlog, councils were being forced to plan for further cuts of £600m in social services spending, after cumulative cutbacks totalling more than £8bn since the austerity regime first kicked in under George Osborne in 2010.[5]

Tough new guidance: winter

On 23 December 2020 NHS England's traditional complex and burdensome pre-Christmas letter to NHS leaders[6] required all systems to aim for 'top quartile performance in productivity' on ophthalmology, cardiac services and musculoskeletal/orthopaedics – effectively demanding the impossible feat of every system performing above average.

NHS England bureaucrats themselves had not yet worked out how to spend 'an additional £1bn of funding for elective recovery in 2021/22', but promised: 'In the new year we will set out more details of how we will target this funding.' It was clear a major share of this extra money was set to go to private hospitals. The letter stressed the importance of 'maximising use of the independent sector' (coyly referred to as 'IS'). There was no corresponding focus on maximising use of NHS beds.

Trusts and commissioners were told NHS England had extended the national arrangement with the independent sector through to the end of March, 'to guarantee significant access to 14 of the major IS providers'. Further private capacity could also be arranged.

Trusts were also urged to aim for 'Timely and safe discharge … making full use of hospices'. Only two months earlier, two thirds of hospices had been facing financial crisis and redundancies, and were pleading in vain for extra government funding.[7]

More tough guidance

Nine months later, in September 2021 NHS England published a Ten Point Action Plan[8] focused largely on urgent and emergency care (UEC). This was subsequently passed off by Sajid Javid as a 'recovery plan' for emergency care.[9] However it did not address the shortages of beds and staff, and did not deliver any significant improvement in performance.

As ambulance unions and trust bosses raised increasing concerns in October 2021 about chronic delays in handing over emergency patients to swamped A&E departments, NHE England responded … by simply ordering hospital trusts somehow to sort it out.[10]

NHS England's 40-page circular for Christmas 2021 listed no fewer than TEN implausible 'priorities' for 2022-23.[11,12] NHS England boss Amanda Pritchard, in the midst of the surge of Omicron, and with 5,000 NHS beds still out of action since the spring of 2020, told an exhausted NHS the new objectives were based on an (imaginary) scenario 'where COVID-19 returns to a low level and we are able to make significant progress in the first part of next year'. The priorities for 2022-23 included tackling the elective backlogs 'through a combination of expanding capacity, prioritising treatment and transforming delivery of services'. How this could be done without either the staff or the capital required was not explained.

Managers were told they had only a few weeks to ensure that every system had developed an elective care recovery plan for 2022/23, setting out how the first full year of longer-term recovery plans will be achieved. Again, the private sector was seen as central. NHS England demanded local independent sector capacity had to be 'incorporated as a core element' to deliver improved outcomes for patients and 'reduce waiting times sustainably'. The ambition was for depleted systems somehow to deliver over 10% more elective activity in 2022/23 than before the pandemic.

Far from reopening its own empty beds, NHS England was looking instead to increase the capacity of the NHS 'by *the equivalent of* at least 5,000 general and acute beds'. These were not hospital beds, but patients being monitored and/or cared for at home, who were regarded as part of 'virtual wards'[13] or 'hospital at home'[14] projects, often run jointly with private companies.[15,16] But by no means all professionals are huge fans of 'virtual wards': the *HSJ* reports that both the Society for Acute Medicine and the Royal College of Physicians have raised concerns about the huge increase in the use of virtual wards, in which patients are supposed to be remotely monitored by clinical staff. Doctors are worried about the speed and timing of the rollout and argue there is a lack of evidence the approach is safe.[17]

NHS England also expected trusts to minimise handover delays between ambulances and hospitals, and reduce 12-hour waits in Emergency Departments 'towards zero' and no more than 2%.

Delivering ... income for the private sector

In similar vein to previous circulars, the NHS England 'Delivery Plan' to tackle the growing backlog of waiting list treatment, announced on 8 February 2022,[18] is not a plan at all. It lacks sufficient investment and – most important of all – a workforce plan, without which none of the promised improvements will happen.

The 50-page document only covers elective care, with nothing to say about mental health, GP services or urgent and emergency care, all of which are facing dire and worsening problems after more than a decade of underfunding, compounded by the 2-year pandemic.

The Royal College of Emergency Medicine soon signalled its disappointment at the absence of any more developed plan for both elective and emergency services. In a Press Release flagging up worsening performance data[19] the RCEM warned that for as long as NHS England delayed addressing the problem

> … patients are coming to real harm with those waiting the longest facing a risk of death. … Elective care is not isolated from Urgent and Emergency Care, this … must be carefully incorporated into any recovery plan. Any credible recovery plan must detail the workforce required.

Instead, leaving around 5,000 NHS front line acute beds still out of use, the Delivery Plan proposes to pump even more NHS cash into private hospitals and private sector providers. Once again a major emphasis of the document is on 'Making effective use of independent sector capacity'.

This has been the one consistent area of increased spending in recent years. The Delivery Plan was unveiled just after the Department of Health and Social Care's Annual Report[20] had confirmed the huge £2.5bn (25.6%) increase in NHS spending on private providers that took place during 2020, clearly linked to the disastrous contract for use of private hospital beds that delivered such poor value for money (as discussed in Chapter 2).[21] Similarly high levels of spending on private providers have continued in the 4-year £10bn 'Framework contract' with private hospitals, even as the level of additional 'Covid' funding has fallen back.[22]

For cancer patients, despite increased use of private hospitals and contractors, the Delivery Plan only promises that numbers waiting over 62 days from an urgent referral will be reduced 'to pre-pandemic levels by March 2023'. This target will give no confidence to patients or staff; even before the pandemic the 62-day target to start cancer treatment had not been hit for six years, and more than one in five waited more than two months for their first treatment.[23]

The Delivery Plan also admits waits of over a year for non-cancer treatment will not be eliminated until 2025 – after the next election.

Meanwhile numbers waiting are expected to rise until 2024 – perhaps as high as 9 million.[24] Without reopening the 5,000 or so acute beds closed at the start of the pandemic, and investment to restore and expand NHS capacity, it's clear that even increased spending will deliver only limited results if most of it is funnelled unproductively through private providers.

Budget blow to both NHS and social care

A year into the Covid pandemic, Rishi Sunak's March 2021 budget said next to nothing about the NHS, and nothing about social care, delivering a kick in the teeth for NHS England and all the organisations that had pressed hard for spending increases to put the NHS back on its feet, tackle backlog maintenance and reward staff for their extraordinary efforts coping with Covid.[25]

Despite Covid deaths still averaging 1,500 or so per week, and the fears of the global spread of the new Brazilian strain of the virus, the Chancellor slashed Covid funding to NHS England by £15bn to just £3bn for 2021-22.[26] This was a far cry from the request of NHS Providers,[27] and even Office of Budget Responsibility chair Richard Hughes warned that Sunak's allocation of funding took no account of NHS costs to tackle backlog waiting lists, vaccination programmes and test and trace.[28]

Health Foundation boss Anita Charlesworth pointed out that the planned cut to public spending meant that, in real terms, per capita funding for the day-to-day running costs of public services would 'still be 6 per cent below 2010 levels by the middle of this decade'.[29]

Nor did the budget include any new capital investment to tackle the massive bill for backlog maintenance in England's NHS – which had risen almost 40% in 2019-20 to £9bn (almost as large as the whole of the DHSC capital budget, and more than double the 2013/14 total).[30] In 2020, after 45% of NHS trust leaders had reported their estate was in poor or very poor condition, Chris Hopson, chief executive of NHS Providers, said:

> It shows how rapidly our very old NHS estate is falling into disrepair, putting patient lives at greater risk and making it much more difficult for frontline staff to provide the right quality of care. More worrying

still, over half of this is for work of 'high' or 'significant' risk. In short, this problem poses an increasing threat to safety. It's also impacting directly on the response to the pandemic.[31]

Without additional money for investment there was no realistic prospect of remodelling many hospitals to adapt to the post-Covid need for social distancing and improved infection control, reopening closed beds and restoring the capacity to treat routine and emergency patients as well as Covid. In December 2021 a speech by NHS England's Director of NHS Estates Simon Corben made no mention of any plan or aspiration to restore the clinical capacity that had been lost in the pandemic.[32]

£36bn 'levy' – too little, too late, taxing the wrong people

September 2021 brought whirlwind efforts by the Johnson government to push through a £36bn 3-year package of tax increases[33] that will fall most heavily on the lowest-paid workers. This was to spend more on the NHS and social care from April 2022 while not taxing billionaires or businesses. The extra spending appeared to represent a major change of policy from Chancellor Rishi Sunak, who had warned colleagues that Covid-19 handouts 'can't go on forever'.[34] £36bn was nowhere near enough to do all the things ministers claimed it would do. £6bn of it was to go to devolved governments (Wales, Scotland and Northern Ireland), and less than half the money, just £15.6bn, was earmarked for NHS England … spread over three years.

The NHS share of what Johnson named the 'health and care levy' fell well short of the £10bn extra for 2022-3 that had been called for by NHS Providers and the NHS Confederation, whose joint response warned:

> No one should be in any doubt that this extra funding is welcome. But the government promised to give the NHS whatever it needed to deal with the pandemic, and, while it makes a start on tackling backlogs, this announcement unfortunately hasn't gone nearly far enough. Health and care leaders are now faced with an impossible set of choices about where and how to prioritise care for patients.[35]

The Treasury Red Book[36] listed how the money was supposed to be spent:

- £4.2bn by 2025 'to make progress on building 40 new hospitals by 2030 ... and to upgrade more than 70 hospitals'. But everybody knew £4.2bn was nowhere near enough.
- £2.3bn by 2025 to 'transform diagnostic services, with at least 100 community diagnostic centres ...'. The first such 'community' diagnostics centre, opened in Somerset, turned out to be yet another project reliant on the private sector, run by Rutherford Diagnostics Limited, 'in partnership' with Somerset NHS Foundation Trust. Most if not all of the new centres will also rely on private companies.
- £2.1bn by 2025 for 'innovative use of digital technology' – i.e. more expensive, chaotic whizz-kiddery, unproven apps and systems that ignore millions of people who are digitally excluded.
- £1.5bn (just over £3m per year per acute trust) by 2025 for 'new surgical hubs, increased bed capacity and equipment'. Where will the staff be found?
- Just £450m over three years for projects in England's 54 mental health trusts – again a pathetically inadequate amount to pay for the changes proposed.

There was also far too little extra cash for social care, for which funding had been cut year after year since 2010. In September 2021 a survey of 95% of providers told ITV news they were unable to take on all the new clients in need of their help, while many more were unable fulfil their contracts for lack of staff.[37] A report from the Association of Directors of Adult Social Services showed nearly 300,000 people were awaiting social care assessments, care and support, or reviews of their needs – up by just over a quarter (26%) over the previous three months.[38] Yet just £5.4bn (£1.8bn per year) was allocated from the 'levy' to social care.

The new formula for means testing charges for social care and 'capping' personal spending at the eye-watering level of £86,000 has also raised more problems that it answered, offering most benefit to wealthier middle-class families with higher-priced houses in the south at the expense of the less well-off and families in the Midlands and north, where property prices are lower.[39]

Sunak warning: 'booster jabs will mean cuts'

By December 2021 Rishi Sunak was further tightening the financial straitjacket on the NHS. Estimates suggested that six-monthly vaccinations could cost an extra £5bn a year; but no such extra cost had been factored into Sunak's tight-fisted allocations to the NHS up to 2025. According to a *Daily Mail* report, the Chancellor warned health secretary Sajid Javid and health officials that the limited NHS budget would not cover the extra costs of booster jabs to tackle the latest variant of Coronavirus, and no more money would be raised because 'people would feel the effects of [any additional extra] spending in NHS and household budgets'.[40]

The Chancellor had changed his tune from early promises that the NHS would get 'whatever it needed' to fight Covid-19. According to a *Spectator* report,[41] Sunak was leading a cabal of cabinet ministers who were critical of the NHS itself, while the *Financial Times* reported he had also had meetings with US health corporation bosses on a trip to California.[42]

Starving the NHS of the funding it needs to restore and expand capacity has emerged in recent years as the main driver of privatisation. It forces desperate NHS managers to turn to private hospitals to supply extra beds, private contractors to supply cataract and other routine operations, imaging services, laboratory services and mental health care. The extra costs and inefficiencies of this fragmented system pile further pressures back on the NHS – while the private sector, which trains no staff, can only expand by recruiting from the limited pool of NHS-trained staff.

Sunak and the Treasury, eager to recoup the government's £200m investment in the highly successful Vaccine Manufacturing Innovation Centre at Harwell near Oxford, also appeared to be driving the efforts to sell it off to a private corporation, jeopardising its potential future role in pioneering new vaccines and saving lives.[43]

The spending gap widens

February 2022 figures from the King's Fund, calculating the progress of funding for the NHS and social care since the banking crash of 2007-8, indicate how dramatically the brakes were applied from 2010 when David Cameron's government embarked on a decade of austerity.[44]

It's widely accepted that for the NHS to cope with inflation, demographic change (a rising population and an increasing proportion of it in the more costly older age groups), technological change and other cost pressures, real spending needs to increase by around 4% each year, and from 1958 to 2010 that was more or less the average (3.9%). Since the Tory-led coalition took office in 2010, however, the rate of increase has remained consistently below this level, leading to a growing shortfall in funding, and this is set to continue.

Calculating from the King's Fund's figures we can see that if the Department of Health and Social Care had received an annual increase of 4% from 2010 its core budget would have been £189bn by 2021-22; £33bn higher than the actual figure. The cumulative gap between pre-2010 average levels of increase and post-2010 levels of funding has now exceeded £200bn. Rishi Sunak's spending review allocations do not prevent this gap widening further, at least to 2025, while inflation is now eroding the value of any 'extra' funding.

By contrast, when retired banker Sir Derek Wanless examined the long-term funding of the NHS for the New Labour government in 2002, he found that, compared with the European average, UK health spending had fallen behind by £267bn over the previous 25 years.[45]

The Health Foundation, working on the much lower assumption that 3.5% real terms increase per year would be sufficient for recovery from the pandemic, estimates that much larger increases in spending than offered by last autumn's spending review are needed between now and 2030 to restore NHS performance.[46]

The deep and rapid financial squeeze since 2010, now compounded by the ongoing impact on capacity from the pandemic and the renewed austerity that has followed from it, has made all the difference between an NHS that could sustain sufficient beds and staff, keep up with maintenance and invest in precautionary stocks of PPE, and today's conditions of constant crisis.

Covid caseload and NHS capacity

In January 2021, as the NHS was first being asked to plan for post-pandemic recovery, the *HSJ* reported that the number of hospital patients being treated for Covid19 had risen above 30,000 for the first time, to 32,070 – 62% higher than the previous peak in spring 2020. According to the *HSJ* this was 'just under a third of the total beds available'.[47]

This, like many other discussions of NHS capacity since the spring of 2020, under-estimated the number of frontline beds that have been closed or left unused since the pandemic struck.

NHS daily winter 'sitrep' reports showed that on 30 December 2019, prior to the pandemic, 98,000 frontline general and acute beds were available in England, of which 94% (92,000) were occupied.[48] But one year later the total of general and acute beds available had fallen to 91,000 – a reduction of almost 7,000. And of these beds only 80,000 (88%) were occupied. In other words, numbers of beds in use had fallen by almost 12,000 (13%) – more than one in eight since spring 2020.[49]

So, with up to 32,000 (40%) of the remaining beds in use filled with Covid patients, capacity to treat emergencies and waiting list patients was severely limited. The scale of reduced capacity has been seldom, if ever, discussed in the mainstream news media, but the numbers of patients admitted for routine treatment halved in January and February 2021 compared with the previous year – down 54% in January and 47% in February – and waiting times for treatment had lengthened again. Mental health services had also been hit, with a reduction of almost 11% in beds occupied.[50]

However, as Chapter 1 has shown, it's important to recognise Covid did not cause the waiting list crisis. Even before the pandemic struck waiting lists had reached 4.4 million; almost double the 2.5 million in 2010 when David Cameron took office.[51] The target for 92% of patients to begin treatment within 18 weeks of referral from their GP had not been hit for five years. Waiting lists initially FELL in the early part of 2020 as patients stayed away from hospitals, before rising again more sharply in 2021 as more people were vaccinated, and the tide of Covid patients and the lockdown appeared to ease.

Trust bosses reveal a service under strain

By November 2021 the *HSJ* was reporting desperate trust managers breaking the usual silence and speaking out about their fears for their trust's ability to cope with growing pressures.[52] An NHS Confederation survey found almost 90% of trust bosses believed the pressures on their organisation had become 'unsustainable', putting patient safety at risk, and that the NHS was at a 'tipping point', directly refuting Health Secretary Sajid Javid's complacent claims.[53]

Even though COVID-19 cases had fallen well below their January 2021 peak, with 5,800 Covid patients in English hospital beds, a November 2021 survey of trust leaders by NHS Providers found trusts were still 'beyond full stretch'.

- 87% were extremely concerned about the impact of winter on their trust and local area, (compared with 56% when asked the same question in 2020, ahead of what proved to be one of the toughest winters in the history of the NHS.)
- 84% were worried about their trusts having the capacity to meet demand for services.
- 85% were worried that insufficient investment was being made in social care in their area.
- 94% were concerned about staff burnout.[54]

Chris Hopson, chief executive of NHS Providers, argued the government should seriously consider introducing some kind of emergency support for the social care workforce: 'One option is a retention bonus of a minimum of £500 each for the 1.5 million social care staff in England, similar to the schemes now operating in Scotland and Wales'. His blog concluded:

Longer term, trust leaders are clear that this is a completely unsustainable position for the NHS and social care to be in, and we have to address the underlying causes – a broken workforce model, insufficient capacity to match growing demand, inadequate funding and a social care system in crisis – which COVID-19 has significantly exacerbated.[55]

Campaigners warned of the danger that delays, failures and gaps in care would mean growing numbers of patients and the wider public – and large numbers of staff – would lose confidence in the NHS. More patients in pain who could afford it would opt to 'self-pay', and others would look to health insurance to cover future need for elective care. This would leave the large majority who could not afford it, or would simply be excluded from such options by their pre-existing health problems, along with all the people needing emergency care or more complex treatment, queueing to use an increasingly run-down service.

Emergency care: a summer crisis

In June 2021 extraordinarily high numbers (1.44 million patients) attended more specialised Type 1 accident and emergency units – the highest ever figure since records began. The larger numbers brought more delays, with only 73% treated or discharged within 4 hours, by far the worst June performance on record.[56]

July 2021 was the busiest-ever July for ambulance services, while the number of patients waiting over 12 hours in corridors on trolleys for admission also increased to a record high. Union leaders wrote to ambulance employers, Sajid Javid and Health Select Committee chair Jeremy Hunt seeking investment in an expanded workforce to tackle the crisis.[57]

Royal College of Emergency Medicine (RCEM) President Dr Katherine Henderson called for a transparent discussion about how the whole of the health service deals with the current levels of demand, warning that: 'Emergency care does not happen in a vacuum but is often the canary of the system'. Bed numbers had declined continuously since 2010. The RCEM calculated that, depending upon the scale of the winter pressures, the NHS needed to reopen between 5,000 and 16,000 of the currently unused beds, which would also need extra staff.[58]

The Lowdown warned that it was vital for campaigners to force a major government U-turn, and secure capital investment to reopen NHS capacity. If not, by the end of the 4-year £10bn 'framework contract' for the use of private hospital beds for NHS patients, the NHS would have become institutionally dependent upon private sector beds to maintain its elective caseload. If this happened, the biggest-ever privatisation of clinical services would have been carried through without any systematic protest.[59]

Billions would be routinely flowing out of meagre NHS budgets into the coffers of private hospital corporations, leaving frontline NHS services starved of resources. Meanwhile scarce NHS nursing and medical staff would have to be split up, with teams having to work away from the main hospital sites in small private hospitals, making them unavailable to assist teams coping with emergencies and complex operations.

999 crisis triggers no emergency response

By November 2021 every ambulance service in England was on the highest level 'black alert' as they struggled to cope with the impact of rising demand. A&E departments were operating at full capacity, but with insufficient beds available, causing crews to be held up for hours waiting to do handovers. One patient died in the back of an ambulance while waiting outside Addenbrooke's Hospital in Cambridge. In Oxfordshire a pensioner was left on the floor of his house for more than five hours waiting for an ambulance: a second call to 999, after an hour, had to be diverted to a call centre in Yorkshire because the local service was too busy.[60]

Urgent and Emergency Care statistics showed that in November 2021 almost a quarter (24%) of over 500,000 patients admitted as emergencies had to wait over 4 hours on trolleys for beds to become available, and almost 11,000 waited over 12 hours. But more shocking was the number of A&E departments taking the most serious Type 1 patients that not only failed to hit the NHS Constitution target of treating and discharging or admitting 95% patients within 4 hours, but failed massively. The England average in November for Type 1 patients within 4 hours was just 62%, with the worst of all being Barking Havering and Redbridge with just 29.5%.[61]

A damning report on delays in handing over emergency patients to the care of hospitals published by the Association of Ambulance Chief Executives (AACE) found 'unacceptable levels of preventable harm are being caused to patients'.[62] West Midlands Ambulance Service (WMAS) nursing director Mark Docherty told the Trust's board that 'we know patients are coming to harm' because of delays, and that some patients were 'dying before we get to them'.[63] One WMAS crew waited 13 hours to hand over a patient at the Royal Shrewsbury Hospital in October, and the service lost almost 17,000 hours due to handover delays in September, nearly three times as many as a year earlier.

Another RCEM report, 'Crowding and its Consequences', found that at least 4,519 patients had died as a result of dangerous crowding in Emergency Departments in England in 2020-2021.[64]

January 2022 saw a massive 27% increase in the numbers of patients waiting over 12 hours on trolleys after a decision to admit (up from just under 13,000 in December to 16,500).[65] The RCEM pointed out that this poor performance was still an under-estimate of the real problem, and had come about despite relatively low numbers of A&E attendances, and a reduction of the most recent peak of Covid admissions.

Longer NHS delays mean bigger private profits

By September 2021 1.4 million more patients were waiting for procedures such as a hip or knee replacement or cataract removal than when the pandemic struck.[66] The total of 5.6m people waiting was the highest since records began in August 2007, and NHS Providers and the NHS Confederation warned it could take up to seven years to clear the backlog.[67]

Private hospital firms were set to profit as waiting lists grew. Demand for self-pay surgery for anything from hip replacements to heart operations had soared, with more patients choosing to go private 'as a last resort' after waiting (or being told they would have to wait) for months. Some took out loans or sought help from family members. Others used money they might otherwise have spent on holidays abroad.

October data from the Private Healthcare Information Network showed the significant increase in numbers of patients paying up front to use private hospitals to escape growing NHS waiting lists: 65,000 patients resorted to self-pay operations between April and June 2021, up 30% from the same period in 2019.[68]

Research commissioned by the *Financial Times* showed that for the first time ever more patients were getting hip and knee operations in private rather than NHS hospitals. 56% of these joint replacements in the first eight months of 2021 had been performed in private hospitals, compared with 40% over the same period in 2019. The proportion of these patients funded by the NHS had fallen by a third, from 27% to 18%.[69]

US-owned private hospital group HCA told the *Daily Mail* there had been an increase in 'higher acuity care' since the start of the pandemic, including a 20% increase in 'self-funded cardiothoracic inpatient procedures' costing upwards of £17,500. There had also been a 30% increase in self-funded neurosurgery, such as on the spinal cord and brain.[70] Desperate patients facing long delays to access NHS treatment were also increasingly willing to pay for cancer care.

Nuffield Health reported rising demand from self-paying patients, as did the largest private hospital chain, BMI Hospitals (taken over by Circle, which in turn has now been taken over by US health insurer Centene).[71]

Two more major American hospital chains, the Mayo Clinic and the Cleveland Clinic, were expanding in the UK. The Mayo had opened a new London clinic in partnership with Oxford University Hospitals FT, charging £670 for a consultation. The Cleveland was planning to directly employ 60% of its doctors and 100 health professionals in a break with the model used by the rest of the private hospital sector, and would therefore contribute to NHS staff shortages.[72]

Independent think tank Centre for Health and the Public Interest (CHPI) revealed that despite the secretive deal to block-book the entire capacity of all 7,956 beds in England's 187 private hospitals along with their almost 20,000 staff, private hospitals had carried out 43% FEWER operations than usual on NHS patients during 2020.[73]

Labour MP Meg Hillier, who chairs the Commons public accounts committee, told the Guardian: 'Taxpayers have covered an entire year of private hospitals' costs in return for less treatment and care than before, and many of them now feel forced to pay those same private hospitals over again in the face of an NHS beset with lengthy backlogs.'[74]

Deadly rise in delayed cancer treatment

NHS England data revealed there had been a catastrophic drop in numbers of cancer patients referred for hospital treatment during the pandemic, with numbers referred between March 2020 and January 2021 down by 350,000, equivalent to nearly one in six, on the previous year's figures.[75]

In September 2021 an IPPR report 'Building Back Cancer Services in England' showed a reduction from 44% to 41% in the proportion of cancers caught early enough to be highly curable, and warned that up to 20,000 cancer diagnoses could have been missed during the pandemic. IRRP research fellow Chris Thomas told the *Times*: 'This will undo at least eight years of colorectal cancer survival rate progress, six years in breast cancer survival rates, and two years in lung cancer survival progress.' There had also been a 25% drop in urgent referrals for urological cancer, 23% fewer for brain cancer patients, and 21% fewer child cancer patients referred.[76]

A blog by cancer specialist Lucy Gossage revealed that cancer treatment in Nottingham University Hospitals NHS Trust was having to be rationed for lack of staff, with some patients denied continuing care. Patients had to be selected for treatment on the basis of how likely they were to survive and recover, meaning that palliative care was being cut back.[77]

In the year following the first lockdown, 369,000 (15%) fewer people than expected had been referred to a specialist with suspected cancer. The Royal College of Radiologists, appealing for extra funding from the coming Comprehensive Spending Review, pointed to the dire shortage of radiologists (short-staffed by 33%) and the need for at least another 1,939 consultants, as well as funding and equipment.[78]

In October NHS England figures showed more than 55,000 people had to wait for more than four weeks after their initial urgent referral to find out whether or not they had cancer. Figures published by NHS England, and analysed by Macmillan for the *Guardian*, estimated that the NHS in England would need to work at 110% capacity for 17 months to catch up on missing cancer diagnoses, and for 13 months to clear the cancer treatment backlog.[79]

To make matters worse Macmillan's research found that more than one in five people diagnosed with cancer in the UK were either unable to get support from a specialist cancer nurse during their diagnosis or treatment or said the support they received was not enough. Macmillan called for governments across the UK to invest a total of around £170 million to fund the training costs of creating nearly 4,000 additional cancer nurses required by 2030.[80]

Maternity safety concerns

Amid rising concerns over the safety of a number of maternity units, a report from the House of Commons Health Committee in June 2021 concluded that an increase in funding of £200- £350 million per year was urgently needed to resolve the endemic problems of understaffing.[81] Professor Ted Baker, the Care Quality Commission's chief inspector of hospitals, told the committee that its inspections had found that 38% of NHS maternity services 'require improvement for safety'.

Although staff numbers had increased in some areas, there were still gaps in all maternity professions – midwives, obstetricians, and anaesthetists. And despite large strides in improving safety, a culture of blame is preventing the NHS from improving still further. Health Education England calculated that the NHS remained short of 1,932 midwives[82] and a Royal College of Midwives survey indicated that 8 out of 10 midwives did not believe that there were enough staff on their shift to be able to provide a safe service.[83] NHS Providers estimated that an extra 496 consultants were also needed to work in Obstetrics and Gynaecology.[84]

Mental health: promises broken

2021 was the year by which Jeremy Hunt had promised to have redressed the 'historic imbalance' between physical and mental health, and ended the scandal of mental health patients being treated miles from home. In 2017 Hunt had also committed to create an extra 21,000 new posts, treating an extra million patients a year, to help deliver Theresa May's promised 'revolution' in mental health.[85] But four years later Hunt, May and their promises had all been overtaken by history.

In January 2021 the Royal College of Psychiatrists issued a grimly familiar warning that mental health trusts were struggling on with too few beds, too few staff and too little funding. 85% of the 320 psychiatrists who had responded to an RCPsych survey said there was more pressure on beds than a year earlier, and 92% estimated that fewer than one bed in twenty was available for urgent admissions. More than a third said lack of resources meant they would have to look for beds outside their area, and a quarter said they would need to delay admission and treat patients in the community.[86]

RCP President Dr Adrian James said: 'The historic problem of shameful mental health bed shortages that government pledged to end in 2021 is only getting worse. More and more people are in mental health crisis as a result of the pandemic and instead of being able to treat them, psychiatrists are forced to send them miles from home or ask them to wait for months on end to get help.'

In October 2021 the RCPsych, which had already called for six new mental health hospitals, outlined a plan that called for £3bn capital and another £5bn over 3 years in to equip mental health services to cope with the increased demands since the pandemic and expand services for adults and children.[87]

NHS England figures showed that up to 1.5 million people may have been waiting for mental health treatment but were yet to receive it.[88] Shocking survey figures from NHS Digital also showed a significant deterioration in mental health for children and young people since 2017. Almost 40% of 6 to 16s had suffered a drop in their mental health, compared with 53% of 17-year-olds. The proportion of 6 to 16-year-old children with eating disorders had almost doubled from 6 to 13%, while the proportion of 17-19 year olds had risen by a third from almost 45% to over 58%.[89]

At the end of December 2021 a report in the *Independent* revealed the desperate situation facing mental health services after more than a decade of austerity.[90] Based on leaked data, Rebecca Thomas reported hundreds of patients with serious mental health problems were winding up in A&E, with many waiting over 12 hours for treatment, because mental health hospitals across the country were full to overflowing. Almost all mental health hospitals in London were at 'black alert' during October and November, meaning their beds were nearly 100% full.[91]

Research by the House of Commons Library found referrals to mental health crisis services had increased by 75% since Spring 2020, but the number of people in contact with services in 2020/21 was 75,000 lower in than the previous year, a fall of 2.7%.[92]

Leaked data showing bed availability in London revealed just ten children's mental health beds out of 140 were available in mid-October, and sources in the east of England told *The Independent* that almost 150 children's mental health beds were closed, causing huge pressures.[93]

The Commons Library also revealed gaps and inequalities in treatment for psychosis, with targets not being met in 20 of the 95 CCGs for whom data was available.

128 bids to be one of eight new hospital projects

By the end of January a staggering 128 trusts – almost two thirds of all trusts in England – had submitted bids to become one of just eight additional new hospital projects. The added eight, to be announced in spring 2022, would bring the total of new hospitals promised by the Johnson government to 48.[94]

Well over 90% of the trusts submitting bids will inevitably see their hopes dashed, with no foreseeable prospect under a Tory government of another funding round this decade. Among those turned down are likely to be proposals to replace some hospitals built in the 1970s with defective structural concrete planks and now increasingly unsafe.[95] Several of these are now either included in larger schemes or submitted separately among the bids that have flooded in as trusts recognise the danger of missing the boat on funding. Mid Cheshire Hospitals Foundation Trust has submitted a £663m plan to replace Leighton Hospital in Crewe, which is one of the endangered hospitals, while Queen Elizabeth Hospital in Kings

Lynn, with over 200 props holding up its roof, is also seeking £679m for a new hospital, and estimates it would cost £554m just to keep the decaying building from falling down.[96] Another concrete nightmare is in Frimley Health Foundation Trust in Surrey, which has set out plans for a complete £1.26bn rebuild to transform it into a 'state-of-the-art net-zero hospital'.[97] Another is Airedale Hospital in Steeton, and replacing it is included in the hugely optimistic plan for THREE new hospitals costing £1.7bn, submitted by the 'Act as One' health and care partnership that covers Bradford District and Craven.[98]

Many if not most of the 128 new plans call for levels of spending that are most unlikely to be agreed. All eight of the government's top priority plans for new hospitals were instructed in 2021 by the New Hospitals Programme to submit cheaper plans costing no more than £400m apiece, along with their favoured (more costly) plans. Since then all of the schemes have been at a standstill.[99] It is widely assumed that £400m will be the maximum funding on the table, so many, if not most, schemes will need to be cut back to fit.

Kettering hospital chiefs have submitted a case for investment of 'up to £765m to fund 'the first three phases' of a £1bn-plus 5-phase scheme.[100] Other grandiose plans not linked to collapsing buildings include the trusts in Lincolnshire integrated care system, which have together submitted bids with a total value of £1.2bn.[101] In London, Imperial College Healthcare has submitted its Strategic Outline Case for rebuilding St Mary's Hospital in Paddington, including 840 beds, at an estimated £1.2-£1.7bn net, 'once receipts from the sale of surplus land are taken into account'.[102]

Even some smaller plans are still coming in above £400m, including the £500m plan to replace Stockport's Stepping Hill Hospital, which has a £95m backlog maintenance bill.[103] The £400m limit is also likely to be a problem for Shropshire's much-delayed and still-stymied 'Future Fit' plan to centralise acute services on a rebuilt Shrewsbury Hospital – for which £312m in capital funding was potentially promised, while the cost has now reportedly exceeded £500m.[104]

Private hospitals set to profit again from new NHS contract

In January 2022 an NHS England press release announced they had been directed by Sajid Javid to sign a 'three-month agreement with multiple independent healthcare organisations'. No details were given on how, if at all, the contract had been advertised, how much above the NHS tariff it was costing to persuade private hospitals to treat NHS patients rather than lucrative 'self-pay' private patients, or how the ten private hospital firms had been selected.[105] The new contract was in addition to the £10bn 4-year 'framework contract', through which the NHS has planned to use private hospitals to help clear the rising waiting list.

The contract put the private hospitals' staff and facilities 'on standby to support the NHS' should the Omicron variant lead to 'unsustainable levels of hospitalisations or staff absences'. This short term and unsatisfactory 'fix' proved clearly that ministers and NHS England have learned no lessons from the huge sums of money wasted on unused private hospital capacity in 2020. Nor have they yet recognised that private hospitals can only take on additional NHS patients by poaching additional staff trained, and often largely employed, by the NHS.

The real problem is that the decade-plus of real terms cuts has reduced the NHS to fewer beds, doctors and nursing staff than almost any comparable European country, and the privatised and dysfunctional social care system has also been run down. Latest figures (9 March 2022) show over 9,000 Covid patients occupying more than 10% of the general and acute beds in use. Almost 26,000 patients, many of them fit for discharge, had also spent more than 14 days in NHS frontline beds on 13 February, for lack of social care.[106]

Diverting some of the least complex elective caseload, and even some NHS cancer patients, to small, off-site private hospitals is a much less efficient way of working than reopening and expanding capacity in NHS hospitals. It may mean a few lucky patients get their operation more quickly, but in the long run it leaves the NHS weakened and chronically dependent on the private sector and puts more patients at risk. It will delight private hospital bosses and their shareholders but does nothing to equip the NHS for the next decade.

More millions wasted on useless 'Nightingale' hubs

The Omicron variant of Covid-19 that took hold late in 2021 was widely dismissed as relatively mild, but it has proved to be extremely infectious; that's why, despite smaller percentages requiring hospital treatment, this still means large numbers of patients.

But once more, instead of prioritising moves to reopen 5,000 unused NHS beds, the Department of Health and Social Care repeated its errors of 2020 and opted to throw even more money into erecting temporary 'mini-Nightingale' surge hubs.[107]

The first eight of these were announced by the DHSC on 30 December; a fortnight later the Bristol unit had been erected in the car park of Southmead Hospital, and was ready to be kitted out, while NHS bosses dodged hard questions on where the staff were to be found to run it.[108]

The one thing trust management seemed willing to say was that they hoped the new facility would 'never be needed'. Not being needed has turned out to be the common factor in almost all of the Nightingale hospitals since the start of the pandemic.[109] Hardly any of them properly opened, and few of their beds were ever used, because any hospital sending covid patients to them had to also send the staff to look after them, and none of the hospitals under the greatest pressure had any staff to spare.

An even worse folly of the Nightingales has since been revealed: that hundreds of the beds procured for the first round of Nightingale hospitals were of inferior specification and are not suitable for use on regular NHS wards, meaning £13m has been wasted buying them and storing them.[110]

In January, trust leaders at East Kent Hospitals flagged up safety concerns about the surge hub that was constructed in the car park of William Harvey Hospital in Ashford,[111] The Trust's board papers include a recommendation that the hub should be included on the trust's risk register, on the basis of concerns including 'inability to comply with building and IPC [infection prevention and control] regulations; digital services unavailability; and staffing requirements'.[112] The chair's report recognised that the hub had 'created additional problems for parking at the hospital for both patients and staff', and questioned 'whether and how' the temporary facility could be safely used for anything.

Despite such pointless and wasteful extravagances, the first half of the 2020s seems doomed to be subject to a new austerity regime as bad as or worse than the dire decade before. NHS staff will be further buffeted not only by the pressures of an under-funded, under-staffed NHS but also by a resurgence of inflation forcing up the cost of living and eroding pay. There will be continued limitations on capacity for elective and emergency services as the Covid pandemic continues to infect significant numbers and fill hospital beds, while the extra funding to cover Covid-related costs ceased from 1 April.[113]

Worse, there is no sign that, despite the warnings from NHS Providers and health professionals, a complacent Sajid Javid has grasped or acknowledged the scale of the problems that staff face day in and day out. His most recent announcement of plans for 'reforms' as this chapter is finalised makes no reference to investment or any steps to reopen or expand NHS capacity, but is focused instead on long-term reliance on private hospitals.

It's clear not just on Covid that ministers have proved themselves incapable of learning lessons and doggedly committed to strengthening the private sector rather than the NHS.

NOTES

1   https://www.england.nhs.uk/coronavirus/wp-content/uploads/sites/52/2020/07/Phase-3-letter-July-31-2020.pdf
2   https://assets.publishing.service.gov.uk/government/uploads/system/uploads/attachment_data/file/1026672/hospital-discharge-and-community-support-policy-and-operating-model-oct-2021.pdf
3   https://www.hsj.co.uk/commissioning/discharge-guidance-could-lead-to-increased-death-and-disability-warn-senior-clinicians/7028402.article
4   https://www.adass.org.uk/adass-spring-survey-21
5   https://www.communitycare.co.uk/2021/03/11/budget-cuts-planned-so-cial-care-councils-count-cost-pandemic-public-spending-watchdog-finds/
6   https://www.england.nhs.uk/coronavirus/wp-content/uploads/sites/52/2020/12/important-for-action-operational-priorities-winter-and-2021-22-sent-23-december-2020.pdf
7   https://www.itv.com/news/2020-10-19/covid-two-thirds-of-hospices-facing-redundancies-as-government-help-runs-out
8   https://www.england.nhs.uk/publication/uec-recovery-10-point-action-plan-implementation-guide/
9   https://www.theguardian.com/world/live/2022/feb/17/covid-news-live-hong-kong-battles-surge-in-cases-canada-warns-truck-drivers-over-block-ade

10   https://www.hsj.co.uk/quality-and-performance/nhse-tells-trusts-to-immediately-stop-all-ambulance-handover-delays/7031210.article
11   https://healthcampaignstogether.com/pdf/NewsBulletin-15.pdf page 6
12   https://www.england.nhs.uk/wp-content/uploads/2022/02/20211223-B1160-2022-23-priorities-and-operational-planning-guidance-v3.2.pdf
13   https://www.nhsx.nhs.uk/key-tools-and-info/data-saves-lives/improving-individual-care-and-patient-safety/virtual-wards-relieving-pressure-on-the-nhs-while-caring-for-patients-at-home/
14   https://www.google.com/url?sa=t&rct=j&q=&esrc=s&-source=web&cd=&ved=2ahUKEwjWoPOCwbv2AhXLTcAKHYDUDpE-QFnoECCwQAQ&url=https%3A%2F%2Fwww.rcplondon.ac.uk%2F-file%2F5578%2Fdownload&usg=AOvVaw1GzYhgPPMjeLE-L_C1fgFC
15   https://homelinkhealthcare.co.uk/virtual-wards/?gclid=CjwKCAiA4KaRBhB dEiwAZi1zztARENdg6c9yk9Hf2aQf3lRXf6218lJaSaPhaj4egBC_3UIkDc6M PBoCZvwQAvD_BwE
16   https://www.doccla.com/?gclid=CjwKCAiA4KaRBhBdEiwAZi1zziXDf4G-J6FWMWrHIfA4DHgxW7lj3ZZcyqkoGjOCY5SFVSfuwV0DYYhoCrH-QQAvD_BwE
17   https://www.hsj.co.uk/quality-and-performance/patients-at-risk-from-hastily-rolled-out-virtual-wards/7031648.article
18   https://www.england.nhs.uk/coronavirus/wp-content/uploads/sites/52/2022/02/C1466-delivery-plan-for-tackling-the-covid-19-backlog-of-elective-care.pdf
19   https://rcem.ac.uk/recovery-must-not-be-isolated-to-elective-care-rcem-says/
20   https://rcem.ac.uk/there-must-be-a-meaningful-recovery-plan-for-urgent-and-emergency-care-rcem-says/
21   https://assets.publishing.service.gov.uk/government/uploads/system/uploads/attachment_data/file/1052421/dhsc-annual-report-and-accounts-2020-2021-web-accessible..pdf
22   https://lowdownnhs.info/private-providers/10bn-spend-on-private-hospitals-to-bridge-gap-in-nhs-capacity/
23   https://www.nuffieldtrust.org.uk/resource/cancer-waiting-time-targets#background
24   https://www.spectator.co.uk/article/exclusive-leaked-nhs-report-shows-waiting-list-hitting-9-2-million
25   https://www.independent.co.uk/news/uk/politics/nhs-funds-coronavirus-hancock-b1819032.html?r=13961
26   https://lowdownnhs.info/news/budget-letdown-nhs-faces-record-waiting-lists-and-staff-exodus/
27   https://lowdownnhs.info/funding/whatever-it-takes/
28   https://www.standard.co.uk/news/uk/obr-rishi-sunak-budget-mps-government-b922925.html
29   https://www.health.org.uk/news-and-comment/blogs/the-chancellors-squeeze-on-public-spending-signals-a-long-and-deep-period
30   https://digital.nhs.uk/data-and-information/publications/statistical/estates-returns-information-collection/england-2019-20

31 https://nhsproviders.org/news-blogs/news/alarming-increase-in-nhs-maintenance-backlog-bill

32 https://www.youtube.com/watch?v=5wmHc-VLXwc

33 https://www.gov.uk/government/publications/build-back-better-our-plan-for-health-and-social-care

34 https://www.telegraph.co.uk/politics/2021/01/22/rishi-sunak-warns-mps-covid-handouts-cant-go-forever/

35 https://www.nhsconfed.org/sites/default/files/2021-09/A-reckoning-continuing-cost-of-COVID-19.pdf

36 https://lowdownnhs.info/analysis/when-record-spending-is-nowhere-near-enough/

37 https://www.itv.com/news/2021-09-02/care-sector-facing-its-worst-ever-staffing-crisis-survey-for-itv-news-finds

38 https://www.adass.org.uk/adass-new-rapid-survey-findings

39 https://lowdownnhs.info/funding/why-the-36bn-extra-is-still-not-enough/

40 https://www.dailymail.co.uk/news/article-10309481/Rishi-Sunak-warned-officials-cost-regular-booster-jabs.html

41 https://www.spectator.co.uk/article/hospital-pass-the-nhs-is-on-life-support

42 https://www.ft.com/content/7a86ef6a-19c7-4626-a879-37f29325c4ea

43 https://www.ft.com/content/d312c4cb-201d-4ce6-a98f-715b20d77998

44 https://www.kingsfund.org.uk/projects/nhs-in-a-nutshell/nhs-budget

45 https://www.theguardian.com/uk/2002/apr/18/budget2002.economy

46 https://health.org.uk/publications/health-and-social-care-funding-projections-2021

47 https://www.hsj.co.uk/coronavirus/31-jan-update-london-and-south-east-set-to-see-low-levels-of-covid-hospital-admissions-by-end-of-feb/7029235.article

48 https://www.england.nhs.uk/statistics/statistical-work-areas/winter-daily-sitreps/winter-daily-sitrep-2019-20-data/

49 UEC-Daily-SitRep-Acute-Web-File-28-December-03-January-2021.xlsx (live.com)

50 https://news.sky.com/story/boris-johnson-has-no-doubt-record-4-7m-nhs-treatment-list-backlog-can-be-tackled-12276297

51 https://www.bma.org.uk/advice-and-support/nhs-delivery-and-workforce/pressures/nhs-backlog-data-analysis

52 https://www.hsj.co.uk/comment/this-is-far-worse-than-january-the-vaccine-hasnt-saved-us-this-time/7031273.article

53 https://nursingnotes.co.uk/news/politics/we-dont-believe-the-pressures-on-the-nhs-are-unsustainable-proclaims-javid/#.YioWtUDP2bg

54 https://nhsproviders.org/state-of-the-provider-sector-2021-survey-findings/key-findings

55 https://www.thecarehomeenvironment.com/story/37055/nhs-providers-calls-for-500-bonus-to-retain-recruit-care-home-staff

56 https://rcem.ac.uk/RCEM/News/News_2021/RCEM_serious_problem_in_Emergency_Care.aspx

57 https://healthcampaignstogether.com/pdf/NewsBulletin-13.pdf

58   https://rcem.ac.uk/rcem-16000-additional-beds-might-be-needed-for-the-nhs-to-cope-this-winter/
59   https://lowdownnhs.info/news/summer-crisis-for-depleted-nhs-hospitals/
60   https://lowdownnhs.info/emergency-care/ambulance-crisis-who-is-rushing-to-help/
61   https://www.england.nhs.uk/statistics/statistical-work-areas/ae-waiting-times-and-activity/ae-attendances-and-emergency-admissions-2021-22/
62   https://www.independent.co.uk/news/health/ambulance-delays-safety-nhs-hospitals-b1957219.html
63   https://www.hsj.co.uk/emergency-care/trust-declares-it-is-causing-catastrophic-harm-to-patients/7031207.article
64   https://rcem.ac.uk/wp-content/uploads/2021/11/RCEM_Why_Emergency_Department_Crowding_Matters.pdf
65   https://www.england.nhs.uk/statistics/statistical-work-areas/uec-sitrep/urgent-and-emergency-care-daily-situation-reports-2021-22/
66   https://www.theguardian.com/society/2021/sep/09/record-56m-people-in-england-waiting-for-routine-hospital-treatment
67   https://nhsproviders.org/news-blogs/news/patients-in-peril-as-nhs-future-funding-finalised
68   https://lowdownnhs.info/safety/as-waiting-lists-push-people-to-the-independent-sector-safety-comes-under-scrutiny/
69   https://healthcampaignstogether.com/flip/NB12/NewsBulletin-12.html
70   https://lowdownnhs.info/analysis/thousands-go-private-many-more-forced-to-wait/
71   https://lowdownnhs.info/news/centenes-investment-shake-up-could-mean-nhs-u-turn/
72   https://clevelandcliniclondon.uk/professionals/how-we-work-with-doctors
73   https://chpi.org.uk/blog/smoke-and-mirrors-nhs-englands-totally-transparent-multi-billion-pound-deal-with-the-private-hospital-industry/
74   https://www.theguardian.com/world/2021/oct/07/private-hospitals-treated-eight-covid-patients-a-day-during-pandemic-says-report
75   https://news.sky.com/story/boris-johnson-has-no-doubt-record-4-7m-nhs-treatment-list-backlog-can-be-tackled-12276297
76   https://www.ippr.org/files/2021-09/building-back-cancer-services.pdf
77   https://www.telegraph.co.uk/news/2021/09/24/chemotherapy-nhs-cancer-patients-stopped-amid-shortage-staff/
78   https://www.rcr.ac.uk/sites/default/files/royal_college_of_radiologists_comprehensive_spending_review_submission_2021.pdf
79   https://www.theguardian.com/society/2021/nov/26/late-diagnosis-of-breast-cancer-rises-as-nhs-struggles-in-covid-crisis
80   https://healthcampaignstogether.com/flip/NB13/NewsBulletin-13.html back page
81   https://committees.parliament.uk/publications/6578/documents/73151/default/
82   https://lowdownnhs.info/news/maternity-safety-compromised-in-a-third-of-nhs-trusts

83   https://publications.parliament.uk/pa/cm5802/cmselect/cmhealth/19/1905. htm
84   https://nhsproviders.org/media/690988/202103-1.pdf
85   https://www.conservativehome.com/frontpage/2017/07/newslinks-for-monday-31st-july-2017.html
86   https://lowdownnhs.info/comment/mental-health-services-still-waiting-on-promised-improvements/
87   https://www.rcpsych.ac.uk/docs/default-source/improving-care/better-mh-policy/policy/rcpsych-spending-review-2021-representation---final---redacted-version-12102021.pdf?sfvrsn=7a15537_4
88   https://www.england.nhs.uk/wp-content/uploads/2021/09/C1400-2122-priorites-and-operational-planning-guidance-oct21-march21.pdf
89   https://digital.nhs.uk/data-and-information/publications/statistical/mental-health-of-children and-young-people-in-england/2021-follow-up-to-the-2017-survey
90   https://www.independent.co.uk/news/health/mental-health-nhs-covid-pressure-b1964693.html
91   https://www.independent.co.uk/news/health/mental-health-nhs-covid-pressure-b1964693.html
92   https://researchbriefings.files.parliament.uk/documents/SN06988/SN06988.pdf
93   https://www.independent.co.uk/news/health/mental-health-nhs-covid-pressure-b1964693.html
94   https://lowdownnhs.info/news/stampede-of-bids-for-new-hospital-funding/
95   https://www.buildingbetterhealthcare.com/news/article_page/A_ticking_time_bomb/178629
96   https://www.itv.com/news/anglia/2021-10-06/more-props-needed-to-stop-norfolk-hospital-roof-collapsing
97   https://www.bbc.co.uk/news/uk-england-surrey-60024571
98   https://www.nationalhealthexecutive.com/articles/plans-new-hospitals-bradford-worth-17bn-%20NHS
99   https://lowdownnhs.info/news/48-new-hospitals-only-one-by-2025/
100 https://www.kgh.nhs.uk/building-a-better-kgh-271120/
101 https://www.hsj.co.uk/more-than-100-trusts-bid-for-massively-oversubscribed-new-hospitals-programme/7031801.article
102 https://www.imperial.nhs.uk/about-us/news/key-milestone-for-the-redevelopment-of-st-marys-hospital
103 https://www.nationalhealthexecutive.com/articles/stockport-nhs-ft-40-new-hospitals
104 https://www.bbc.co.uk/news/uk-england-shropshire-60061178
105 https://lowdownnhs.info/analysis/surge-deal-good-for-business-bad-for-the-nhs/
106 26,000 patients, many of them fit for discharge
107 https://www.hsj.co.uk/coronavirus/first-eight-new-nightingales-revealed/7031621.article
108 https://www.bristolpost.co.uk/news/bristol-news/bristols-nightingale-surge-hub-ready-6485914

109 https://lowdownnhs.info/coronavirus/from-nightingale-to-nightmare-how-journalists-undermined-a-pr-stunt/

110 https://www.thetimes.co.uk/article/0cb6435a-86d0-11ec-83a3-cc7abcec4f36?shareToken=5a85a6beecd4644ddd6fd49df9922188

111 https://www.hsj.co.uk/coronavirus/trust-unsure-whether-and-how-its-mini-nightingale-might-be-used/7031809.article

112 https://www.ekhuft.nhs.uk/patients-and-visitors/about-us/boards-and-committees/the-board-of-directors/board-meetings-archive/

113 https://healthcampaignstogether.com/NHS_scrape_covid_beds.php

Chapter 4

Plans and guidance – the politics and policies of austerity

John Lister

This chapter looks in more detail at some of the policy shifts, political decisions and guidance documents that have emerged since the Health and Care Act took effect in 2013.

It therefore analyses some of the key content of the Five Year Forward View in 2014 – and the extent that any of the main proposals were implemented. It looks in more detail at the process of establishing the 'footprint' areas for Sustainability and Transformation Plans in 2016, but also at the extent to which campaigners at local level and the major demonstration in March 2017 called by Health Campaigns Together created conditions in which STPs themselves and their proposals became increasingly toxic.

It goes on to discuss the resultant proposals for 'integrated care systems' and the Long Term Plan published in January 2019, with its call for major revisions in the law to give statutory powers to the bodies that had been set up ad hoc to run integrated care. A year later on the eve of the pandemic NHS England's 'Operational Planning and Contracting Guidance 2020/21' insisted waiting lists had somehow to be reduced and waits of more than a year eliminated.

In August 2020, in the midst of the pandemic that had shown the need for a better-resourced and more effective body, it was announced Public Health England was to be scrapped, and only partially replaced, while private consultants and contractors continued to fail to deliver test, track and trace.

In July 2021 the Health and Care Bill began what has proved to be a lengthy process through Parliament, with ministers sticking very much to their initial demand for sweeping new central powers, and no corresponding guarantee of any local accountability. In November 2021 MPs voted to add on a new clause in the Bill that would cap costs of social care at £86,000.

The chapter ends with discussion of NHS England's Delivery Plan published in January 2022 (which outlines another major lurch towards increased and long term reliance on private hospitals and private contractors for clinical care), and health secretary Sajid Javid's March 6 policy speech, reviving old and unhelpful ideas.

* * *

The narrative in the core chapters in this book is focused on charting and documenting the ways in which the NHS before, during, and as it emerges from the Covid pandemic has been degraded by over a decade of austerity and a consistent drive towards outsourcing and private providers.

To allow this narrative to flow more easily, there has only been minimal discussion of the various policies and guidance that have been developed by NHS England, including the more recent legislation still going through parliament at the time of writing, to work around, and potentially now reverse, some of the provisions of the 2012 Health and Social Care Act.

The 2012 Act and its implications were explored at some length in two previous books[1,2] as well as shorter, more polemical leaflets and analysis.[3] This chapter will not go back over that ground, but will attempt briefly to sketch an outline of the subsequent evolving policies, which have been shaped by a number of factors including

- NHS England's frustration at the clumsy and fragmented structure which the 2012 Act imposed on the NHS – especially the complexity of driving through unpopular changes at local level;
- the influence of models for 'integrated care' and other methods devised by US health insurers to minimise use of costly hospital services;
- the over-arching pressure from budgets that were each year further reduced in real terms while the population and demand for care increased;
- Growing recognition by senior management of the failure and expense of the competitive/compulsory tendering model imposed by the Act.

Five Year Forward View

The first substantial attempt to work around Andrew Lansley's massive root and branch restructuring of the NHS was the Five Year Forward View, (FYFV)[4] published in October 2014. Simon Stevens, a former Labour councillor and advisor to Tony Blair's government, had taken over as CEO of NHS England six months earlier, after working for nine years as a vice president of US health insurance giant UnitedHealth.[5]

Looking back at the 44-page FYFV is like stepping into a museum; most of the key commitments have long ago been dropped, side-lined or reduced to token gestures, not least the insistence that:

> The future health of millions of children, the sustainability of the NHS, and the economic prosperity of Britain all now depend on a radical upgrade in prevention and public health.

The upgrade never happened. Instead, since 2014, we have seen year after year of cuts to public health budgets which are supposed to fund schemes to help tackle obesity and reduce consumption of alcohol, drugs, and tobacco.[6] This was the result of ministerial decisions, but Stevens should not have relied on such unrealistic assumptions.

Many of the main FYFV ideas, whether people agreed with them or not, have also remained little more than words. For instance, it called for patients to be given control over 'shared budgets' for health and social care – a controversial idea with many campaigners,[7] and one which lacks sound evidence that it can work in the NHS. Nonetheless, in a speech in July 2014 Stevens suggested that 'north of five million such personal budgets might be operational by 2018, sharing £5bn between them.[8]

But this apparently bold proposal, if funded at that level, would have meant average payments of just £1,000 per year, £20 per week. This amount would be well short of the amount required to secure any meaningful care package for any but the most minor health needs, even if the services required were available, and the patient/client was confident enough and able to sort out their own care.

The vision was unrealistic on almost every level: the number of personal health budgets has apparently been rising each year since they launched in 2014, but there were fewer than 23,000 people receiving one in the first nine months of 2017/18, a long way short of 5 million[9]. By 2021 the number had risen to only 100,000.[10]

Carers, too, were promised new support by the FYFV. Yet the plight of carers has remained desperate, with increased misery for many of them as they have been hit by the succession of welfare cuts and the nightmare of universal credit.

According to the FYFV, barriers between GPs and hospitals, physical and mental health services and health and social care were going to be broken down. A 'Forward View' for GPs was published, but there was also supposed to be a shift of investment from secondary care into primary care, which has not happened (how many times have governments proposed that since the 1980s?).[11] In reality, overworked, under-staffed GPs have faced ever-increasing demands, with no sign of the promised increase in numbers or resources.

There were bold promises to invest in more staff and improved services for mental health. Neither of these happened. Mental health staffing and resources remain chronic, unresolved problems, with private sector providers dominating whole sectors, and NHS performance on almost every measure as bad or worse than 2014.

The FYFV also went on to propose new 'models of care', unwisely comparing these with a completely random collection of examples of 'Accountable Care Organisations' which it argued were emerging 'in Spain, the United States, Singapore, and a number of other countries'. Given Stevens' previous employment, this understandably led to widespread fears of 'Americanisation', with all its horrors; despite the fact that the FYFV, in contrast to the 2012 Act, made no reference at all to working with the private sector, or to competition, let alone private insurance and charges for treatment.

Sustainability and Transformation Plans

The next major attempt to reorganise the NHS on a de facto basis (without seeking new legislation) also contained references to Accountable Care Organisations. An instruction to local NHS leaders to come together with local authorities to establish fewer, new, 'footprints', each covering a 'local health economy' that would draw up 'Sustainability and Transformation Plans', (STPs) was unveiled three days before Christmas in 2015 and rolled out during 2016.[12]

By March, England's NHS had been carved up into 44 'footprint' areas, in which commissioners and providers were supposed to collaborate.[13] In order to achieve this, the 200 or so Clinical Commissioning Groups (CCGs) had to be lumped together into far fewer, much larger and less locally accountable CCGs.

That might have appeared to be good news if the complex, costly and divisive competitive market system entrenched by Andrew Lansley's Health & Social Care Act were in fact being swept away, and a new, re-integrated NHS empowered to work together again with local people to improve services. But that was very much NOT the case. Instead the main task in each 'footprint' area was to balance the books of the 'local health economy' and to take drastic steps where necessary to cut spending and eliminate deficits.

Each area had to draw up a 5-year Sustainability & Transformation Plan (STP), to be vetted by NHS England. But while they did so, all of the legislation compelling local CCGs to open up services to 'any qualified provider' or put them out to tender remained in full force. The private sector was still snapping up contracts.

The new drive for STPs was led by Simon Stevens – the man who had urged Tony Blair's government to experiment with private sector providers for the NHS. There were good reasons to mistrust what this would lead to.

By the end of 2016, when most STPs had finally been grudgingly published, this author summed up:

> STPs won't do what they say on the tin: they are not sustainable, there's no capital to finance any serious transformation, and many of them plainly don't add up. But they are seen as the future of England's NHS. Just 38 of England's 44 STPs have been published, in varying states of completion. Some are June drafts, some October; some contain financial, workforce and other essential appendices, some don't. Some have radically increased targets for savings just months after first estimates.

But all STPs have one thing in common: just weeks before they are scheduled to begin implementation, none of them has been subject to any serious public engagement or consultation.[14]

Each of the plans centred on an estimate of the size of the funding deficits by 2021 if no changes were made – the so-called 'do nothing' deficit. The idea was to scare people into accepting cuts that would otherwise have been rejected out of hand. A survey of all 44 plans added up these exaggerated projections of hypothetical funding gaps: the total was £23 billion by 2021, £19bn of it down to the NHS. The remainder was for social care, for which not one STP had any tangible plan or proposal.[15]

In response, half of the STPs proposed to close beds, 18 of them proposed cuts or downgrades in A&E services, and 32 echoed the Five Year Forward View aspiration to establish 'Accountable Care Organisations'. However, the schemes that were proposed carried a cost: in total the proposals in the 44 STPs required additional capital funding totalling £14bn, but there was no hope of securing anything like that much.

Mission Impossible

In March 2017 a huge demonstration marched through London to defend the NHS, demanding No Cuts; No Closures; No Privatisation. It had been initiated by Health Campaigns Together, working with Keep Our NHS Public and Peoples Assembly, and it showed the potential of this new alliance of health and other trade unions and campaigners.[16]

That same month NHS Providers published a devastating report 'Mission Impossible?',[17] banging home the point that the ministers who had decided to impose austerity cuts on NHS spending had to be forced to face the actual consequences, and take responsibility for the resulting chaos. Its CEO Chris Hopson summed up:

NHS Providers has analysed what NHS trusts have to deliver from 1 April 2017 and compared it to the available funding. The result is an unbridgeable gap, with worrying implications for patients and staff.

Toxic terms

Throughout 2016 campaigners, many of them working with Health Campaigns Together, made it impossible for NHS England to carry through their original plan for Sustainability and Transformation Plans, and made the very term 'STP' politically toxic by popularising the parody version, 'Slash, Trash and Privatise'. Attempts to switch the focus to 'Accountable Care' in the summer and autumn of 2017 triggered two Judicial Reviews and increasing public rejection of any even notionally 'American' model, with even the King's Fund warning the ACO concept was 'deeply unpopular' with the public.[18]

By February 2018, the pressure from local campaigning against anything called 'Accountable Care Organisations' forced NHS England to discard that US-inspired term and rebrand the same projects as 'integrated care organisations' instead.[19] Pressure to halt the dash towards 'accountable care' models had been increased by the Chair of the Commons Health Committee Sarah Wollaston urging health secretary Jeremy Hunt to put the process of establishing ACOs – and any new regulations that would be required to empower them – on pause, pending a committee review.[20]

The June 2017 election had not given Theresa May a big enough parliamentary majority to change the law to give any powers to the ad hoc local 'integrated care' bodies that had been set up.

Private sector companies also made it clear that they did not expect to be winning contracts to run the new systems, as many people had feared. Indeed, the only big contracts that had been awarded had gone to existing NHS providers, not multinational corporations, not least because of the pitifully low levels of funding that were available for the new contracts.

A National Audit Office Report also pointed out the embarrassing fact that few, if any, of the new models of care and new ways of working favoured by NHS England had any evidence to support them. One of the key factors in the various plans to remodel services was the need to expand community services to care for people outside hospital. But there was no new money to invest in it, and the idea of a 'Forward View' for community services had been abandoned.[21]

In many areas campaigns were waged against the preparatory steps to establish 'integrated care systems' (ICSs) by merging clinical commissioning groups into far fewer and even less locally accountable organisations. Three of the initial 44 STP areas had also been merged, to leave an NHS England plan for just 42 ICSs covering England, including one giant ICS spanning coast to coast in the North of England, from Newcastle and Durham to Carlisle and Cumbria.

Long-Term Plan

In January 2019 NHS England attempted to shift the discussion and win over some critics with a Long-Term Plan[22] that included a catalogue of worthy, if empty, aspirations to improve some services and tackle inequalities. It also pressed government for legislation to repeal Section 75 of the 2012 Act and the linked regulations that compelled competitive tendering for clinical services. Its focus was on forcing local NHS and council leaders to work together in 'integrated care systems', even though these still lacked any legal basis or authority.

But it would be a mistake to read the Plan as proposing any end to, or even reduction in private contracts. Unlike the Five Year Forward View, it explicitly proposed greater use of private hospitals and clinics to treat NHS patients. At no point did it even hint at rolling back existing private contracts when they expire.

Indeed, the proposal to make competitive tendering the exception rather than the rule could easily result in contracts being rolled over … to existing private sector providers. The Plan also specifically called for new 'pathology and imaging networks' to be established, involving 'partnership' with private companies.

Another key weakness was that the Plan was not linked to any workforce plan (we now know from a House of Lords speech by Simon, now Lord, Stevens[23] that this was because of Treasury resistance to any spending commitments). Many vital issues were either ignored completely or blithely brushed aside in the 136-page Plan. These included:

- the declining actual performance of trusts;
- the inexorable rise in emergency caseload;
- insufficient capacity and bed shortages in acute hospital services;
- the disastrous financial plight of most acute trusts;
- the £8bn and rising bill for backlog maintenance;
- the cuts inflicted and lack of capacity in mental health and community services;
- the impact of repeated cuts in public health budgets;
- the widening gap in society between rich and poor and the resultant inequalities in health – exacerbated by austerity and reactionary government policies on housing, welfare,

education, and local government;

- and of course the gathering crisis of a dysfunctional social care system, for which the long-promised Green Paper had again been postponed.

To make matters worse there was clearly not enough money in the pot to pay for all the new ideas. Theresa May's famous 70th "birthday present" of £20.5bn real terms 'extra' funding over five years[24] was barely enough to stabilise the NHS and keep the lights on.

2020 vision

A year later, just before the pandemic struck, NHS England published new 'Operational Planning and Contracting Guidance 2020/21', which was only 40 pages long, but densely packed, with each page studded with extra demands on local health bosses.[25]

Again, the common factor running through all the demands on local commissioners and providers was NHS England's determination to force them into 'Integrated Care Systems' with little if any public accountability to local communities.

The Lowdown noted that there was no mention of public involvement, engagement – or indeed of the public at all, except as the recipients of services commissioned and decided by local health systems. Instead, the Guidance claimed that the NHS was in a period of 'stability' as a result of the 2018 funding settlement, creating the opportunity to achieve the magical trick of putting the NHS 'on a sustainable financial footing' whilst also somehow 'expanding and improving the services and care it provides patients and the public'.

More magic was required to achieve NHS England's demands for improvements in elective care. Despite shortages of beds, staff and funding, 'the waiting list on 31 January 2021 should be lower than that at 31 January 2020. ...'. Somehow or other, 'Providers should ensure appropriate planning and profiling of elective and non-elective activity throughout the year, taking into consideration expected peaks in non-elective performance over winter months in order to avoid risk of unplanned cancellations. Waits of 52 weeks or more for treatment should be eradicated.'

So easy to say, so hard to do. If it had been that easy it would already have been done.

There were equally fanciful demands for changes to outpatient services, reduced waits for cancer treatment, and an even more unrealistic section on public health, which simply piled on more tasks and targets without discussing the current state of play, the cuts in funding that had been made, or identifying any additional resources.[26]

Public Health England scrapped

In August 2020 came news that Public Health England (PHE), which had been set up in 2013 as part of Andrew Lansley's reorganisation of the NHS, was to be scrapped and replaced by a new National Institute for Health Protection.[27] Matt Hancock went on to announce – in what has since been ruled a breach of the law[28] – that he was appointing Tory Baroness, jockey and crony Dido Harding, a McKinsey alumnus who had, without any health credentials, chaired NHS Improvement since 2017, to chair the new body.

The decision to axe PHE, which was an executive agency of the Department of Health and Social Care and therefore under the control of Hancock and his team, was widely derided as a cynical device to divert blame for the government's own failures in its establishment of the costly but ineffective privatised test and trace system, grotesquely misnamed as 'NHS Test and Trace'.[29]

PHE was far from perfect in its performance: it had only a limited budget and was further limited in its scope by the fact that the bulk of the public health grant was controlled by local authorities, and that too was cut back from 2014. By 2018 the Health Foundation was warning that real terms cuts of almost 25% in per capita public health budgets were having the greatest impact on the poorest households and communities. Then, ahead of the pandemic, PHE's budget for 2020 was cut by almost 25% to just £300m per year.[30]

The new Institute was not to be responsible for public health issues. It was formed by merging part of PHE with the newly-formed 'NHS Test and Trace' and the Joint Biosecurity Centre, which was set up from scratch in 2020 to provide data and advice on Covid-19 infection outbreaks, but lacked either a permanent base or any organisational structure.

As they brushed aside a barrage of objections and pushed through the abolition of PHE to take effect from October 2021, ministers admitted they had no plans for what would happen to PHE's work in tackling obesity, reducing smoking and tackling health inequalities, which their previous behaviour had proved they did not value or understand.[31] The decision made a nonsense of Boris Johnson's announcement only weeks earlier of a drive against obesity (which had in any case been dismissed in the Telegraph as 'nannying' and 'embarrassingly out of touch').[32]

In September 2020, over 70 health organisations wrote to the prime minister concerned that plans for the reorganisation of health protection in the UK paid 'insufficient attention to the vital health improvement and other wider functions of Public Health England'. They added that there was a 'real risk that some of the critical functions of PHE will be ignored'.[33]

Ministers had had no immediate answers to these concerns. The Department of Health and Social Care (DHSC)'s February 2021 paper on legislative proposals for a Health and Care Bill, said proposals for the future design of the public health system would be published 'in due course'.[34]

In March came the announcement of a new Office for Health Promotion, to 'combine Public Health England's health improvement expertise with existing DHSC health policy capabilities, in order to promote and deliver better health to communities nationwide'. The Office is to 'sit within the DHSC, and ... lead work across government to promote good health and prevent illness which shortens lives and costs the NHS billions every year'.[35]

However there has been no extra funding for the new Office to facilitate the apparently ambitious agenda it has been set. Jo Bibby, Director of Health at the Health Foundation think tank, told i-news: 'The recognition of the critical role of Directors of Public Health is welcome but there is no indication that the historic cuts to local budgets will be restored.'[36]

Health and Care Bill

The Health and Care Bill[37] which was tabled in July 2021, in the midst of the ongoing pandemic, is remarkable above all for its lack of any reference to the major pressure points on the NHS – the chronic workforce crisis, for which no strategy has yet been developed, the desperate shortage of capacity to match the size and health needs of the population, and the under-funding that has grown in cumulative impact each year since 2010.

The main selling point of the government's Bill (which was tabled in July 2021 and is still going through the House of Lords report stage as this book is completed) is that it repeals a highly controversial section of the 2012 Health and Social Care Act – Section 75 – which requires services above an annual cost of £600,000 to be put out to competitive tender. NHS England summed up what it wanted to change in the 2012 Act:

> The main reason that the current procurement rules are so unhelpful in the NHS is that, combined with other policies and provisions [...] they can sometimes create an expectation that nearly all contracts for NHS services should be advertised and awarded following a competitive tendering exercise. This can create continual uncertainty, upheaval and disruption among providers.
>
> As we move away from this model, we want to make it straight-forward for the system to continue with existing service provision where the arrangements are working well and there is no value in seeking an alternative provider.[38]

This aspect of the Bill, removing a section of the 2012 Act that attracted some of the fiercest opposition, has been widely welcomed, although it does not stop privatisation, and the possibility of simply renewing contracts without any competitive process could also apply to private sector providers. In practice Section 75 itself has for years been increasingly widely ignored; it is estimated that as few as 2% of clinical contracts go through a full competitive tendering process.[39] The Bill only ends the requirement to put *clinical* contracts out to competitive tender, leaving hospital support services to be tendered as before.

Since 2014 NHS England has devised numerous work-arounds to avoid competitive tendering, while still handing out large contracts to private companies. These include use of 'framework contracts', which establish lists of pre-approved providers who can be awarded contracts without any formal tender. Moreover, ministers could, had they wished to, easily have amended or simply scrapped the regulations on tendering without any need for a new Bill.

The Bill as published contains much more, not least giving statutory powers to the Integrated Care Systems (some of which have functioned for some time in a shadow capacity without any actual power to take or enforce decisions). It establishes new Boards (ICBs) which will be the main 'local' decision-making bodies allocating resources and planning services. With just 42 ICBs covering the whole of England, this would leave the lowest-ever number of "local" bodies in 50 years – and the weakest-ever local voice for patients, the public and health workers defending against cuts and pressing for services they need.

The Bill states that chairs of the ICBs will be appointed centrally by NHS England – and answerable only to them. They can only be removed by agreement of the Health Secretary. Chairs will have extensive powers and be involved in choosing the ICB directors and chief executive. The government has resisted attempts in the Lords to require ICBs to include representatives of mental health, and also to enforce clarity on levels of mental health spending, and thus potentially limit the domination of large acute trusts.[40]

And while the original Bill left room for private sector participation in ICBs, health ministers were forced into concessions in the Commons Committee stage to exclude this,[41] and another important Lords amendment goes further, and virtually excludes the 'conflict of interest' that would arise from private sector participation in any ICB decision-making at Board or committee level.[42]

As drafted, the Bill would have given 138 new powers to the Secretary of State, including controversial powers to intervene at any stage in, or even to initiate, local plans to close or reorganise hospital services. In response the Lords passed an amendment to remove Clause 40 which gave sweeping new powers for local intervention.

The Bill was drafted with only limited commitment to monitor staffing levels 'at least every five years'; and ministers have continued to resist amendments seeking to make this more rigorous and frequent, and rejected the amendment passed on this by the Lords with all-party support.

Another issue challenged in the Lords has been Clause 80 of the Bill, through which the government proposed to repeal the legislation that requires each patient's needs to be assessed before they are discharged from hospital. Ministers argue that a system of 'discharge to assess' is better for patients, while the Lords have pressed for safeguards..

Opponents of the government proposal point out that special provisions were made to speed discharge of patients as the pandemic took hold, and a few local pilot schemes around the country have deployed additional resources to facilitate this new system. However, the general picture outside hospitals is one of grossly inadequate community health, primary care and social care services, and in many areas there are already long delays in assessing patients' needs, and longer delays in meeting them.[43]

The National Audit Office warned back in 2017 that there was little or no evidence to support claims that 'integrating' services, which remain severely under-funded and under-staffed, would bring improved outcomes for patients.[44] Five years later there still is no evidence. Research last year by the Centre for Policy Studies found failures in most areas, and major problems in two of the biggest early ICSs: a sharp rise in delayed transfers of care in Greater Manchester, and an increase in emergency readmissions within 30 days of discharge in West Yorkshire.[45,46]

Capping care costs – at £86,000

Last November MPs also bolted on to the bill clause 155, highly controversial proposals to cap the amount anyone in England will have to spend on their personal care over their lifetime to £86,000. The government has resisted an all-party Lords amendment that would effectively remove this clause.

The plans are widely seen as flawed. The claimed benefits of the legislation, in preventing care costs eating away a large portion of an older person's estate, most commonly in the form of a family home, will apply in a profoundly unequal way. £86,000 is a relatively small fraction of the average house price in the wealthier, mainly southern areas, but a much larger fraction in more deprived parts of the country, so paying out £86,000 could virtually wipe out the assets of home-owners in the north, but protect a major share of assets in London and the home counties.

The government also wants the costs of the 'cap' to be covered by a regressive tax (an increase in National Insurance, the so-called 'health and care levy'). This would hit the lowest-paid hardest but has only marginal impact on the highest-paid; and would not affect many people living on unearned income at all.[47]

Spending on daily living costs (commonly referred to as 'hotel costs') in a care home is not included.[48] The Health Foundation is among the critics who have pointed out that because only people's *personal contribution* to their care costs will count towards the cap:

> There will be no difference in the length of time it will take wealthy individuals, who can fund the entirety of own care, to hit the cap. But for less wealthy individuals, who receive means-tested support to help them meet their care costs, it will take longer to hit the cap.[49]

Many social care service users will die well before the cap is reached, leaving their family to pay the full cost of their care as well as forking out now for the increase in National Insurance. Caroline Abrahams, charity director at Age UK, which urged peers to vote against, said:

> The government's social care cap scheme was supposed to provide it [a cap on care costs] for everyone but, if this change goes through, huge numbers of ordinary older people can kiss that sense of relief goodbye – as, it should be noted, can most disabled people of working age who use social care too.[50,51]

Plan to deliver … for private sector[52]

As the Bill was grinding its way through the parliamentary process, NHS England's 'Delivery Plan' to tackle the growing backlog of waiting list treatment was revealed on 8 February 2022. It is focused on long-term reliance on the 'capacity' of the private sector.[53]

It admits from the outset that it doesn't cover mental health, GP services or urgent and emergency care, all of which are facing dire and worsening problems after a decade of underfunding compounded by the 2-year pandemic. It lacks sufficient investment and, most important of all, a workforce plan, without which none of the promised improvements will happen.

And while it talks in abstract terms about expanding the NHS workforce and 'physical capacity' it does not even discuss ways of reopening the 5,000 or so NHS beds which closed in March 2020 as part of the pandemic preparation. These are still not being used and cannot be reopened because the NHS lacks the capital investment required to reorganise space within hospitals and refurbish buildings to allow social distancing and infection control.

Insofar as there is any plan at all for expanding capacity it is based on a long-term 'partnership' with this same private sector, effectively institutionalising NHS dependence on costly and inefficient private sector hospitals and beds (despite the evidence, discussed in other Chapters, that private hospitals and private sector providers have shown themselves during the pandemic to be dreadful value for money.)

A 2-page section of the Delivery Plan is focused on 'Making effective use of independent sector capacity'. It makes it quite clear that the need for the private sector is due to the lack of adequate NHS capacity, and goes on to insist that:

> Systems will include local independent sector capacity as part of elective recovery plans, and will work in partnership with independent sector partners to maximise activity to reduce waiting times sustainably.

Except of course the reliance on private beds and services means that the NHS itself will NOT have sustainable capacity to run as a coherent and comprehensive public service. Despite all the rhetoric about 'integration' it will have to rely on profit-seeking private companies.

The 3-month deal signed in January 2022 with private hospitals[54] recognises that the private sector can make more money selling operations to 'self-pay' private patients seeking to skip over long NHS waiting lists than from treating NHS patients at normal NHS tariff prices.[55] To use the private sector as additional capacity therefore means the NHS paying over the odds to make it profitable for them – and leaves a lop-sided 'partnership' with companies who have a very different agenda from the NHS, since they benefit either way from a lengthening NHS waiting list.

NHSE chief executive Amanda Pritchard eventually signed off on the three-month contract, having covered her back by requesting 'ministerial direction' on the matter. Her letter to Sajid Javid warned that the deal would leave the health service 'exposed financially' and that it represented 'a material risk that the NHS pays for activity that is not performed'. She pointed out that 'On a per bed basis this is significantly more expensive than the equivalent costs of an NHS site with much less certainty on the potential staffed capacity'.[56]

Using private hospital beds as extra capacity also means dividing up the already over-stretched NHS workforce to send teams from major hospitals to deliver operations in small-scale private hospitals miles away.

Private hospitals are not evenly distributed across the country but concentrated in London, the south-east and more prosperous populations.[57] Many more deprived areas which are supposedly to be 'levelled up' have no significant access to private hospitals, and will be further deprived by this aspect of the Plan.

Where private hospitals are available as 'partners' it is clear that the NHS would be confined to a role of providing emergency services, medical care and more costly, complex treatments that the private sector has always avoided ('such as cardiac, vascular and neurosurgery ....') while transferring 'high volume and low complexity conditions, as well as some cancer pathways and diagnostics, to the independent sector'.

Meanwhile the promises in the Delivery Plan are meagre. Cancer patients are promised that numbers waiting more than 62 days from an urgent referral will be reduced 'to pre-pandemic levels by March 2023 (by which time many will have died waiting). But even before the pandemic the 62-day target to start cancer treatment had not been met for almost five years (since August 2015),[58] and more than one in five cancer patients waited more than two months for their first treatment.

The Delivery Plan admits that waits of over a year for non-cancer treatment won't be eliminated until 2025 – after the next election. Numbers waiting are expected to go on rising, perhaps as high as 9 million,[59] until 2024.

So while the plan will be welcomed by private sector hospitals and providers, it offers no real hope to patients or stressed out NHS staff. Instead it threatens to consolidate the biggest-ever expansion of spending on private providers as a permanent feature of the NHS going forward.

The threat of more 'reforms'

On 6 March Sajid Javid told the *Times* of his 'vision' for more reforms to hospital services and primary care.[60,61] His 8 March speech to the Royal College of Physicians started from what Javid claims is 'a crossroads: a point where we must choose between endlessly putting in more and more money, or reforming how we do healthcare'.

He now says he wants to expand the number of people benefiting from 'personalised care'. But without additional staff and services, this just amounts to more online 'do it yourself' manuals in the form of apps and websites, and leaves millions of digitally excluded people on the outside looking in.

His proposal to expand the use of personal budgets raises the question of why so little has happened on this since Simon Stevens first floated the idea back in 2014.

He also talked about an enhanced 'right to choose' a healthcare provider for elective care. This right already exists in the NHS Constitution.[62] And it is cold comfort to an older patient faced with losing their mobility while languishing, for example, in Birmingham on the country's longest waiting lists,[63] to be told they can compete with millions of other patients who are also facing long delays, for the chance of securing a quicker operation at Guy's and St Thomas's in London, where the delays are shorter.

If this renewed focus on the 'right to choose' ever happens it will inevitably increase costs, create organisational nightmares for pre-operative tests and discharge arrangements, demoralise more NHS staff, and of course offer no relief or hope to NHS hospitals with long waiting times.

'Patient choice' was Tony Blair's big thing from 2000. It was a deception even then, when budgets were increasing year by year, and effectively only served as a smokescreen for greater use of private providers.

In 2022 it would mean encouraging patients to scour the country for NHS or private hospitals with shorter waiting times (Javid suggests perhaps offering funding to cover 'travel costs, maybe accommodation costs, including maybe for someone to go with them to support them'). It dumps the problem back on to the individual patient, or their GP.[64]

This bizarre notion of trying once more to use a chaotic and under-funded market system to reduce waiting times is reminiscent of the first shambolic days of the 'internal market' system under John Major's Tory government in 1991.[65]

Javid appears unaware that given a real choice patients want timely access to good quality care where they are.

They don't want a system that requires them to spend weeks trawling the internet, then join a bunfight with other desperate patients to get on another operating list, and then have to trek long distances to and from a distant operating theatre.

That's not choice: that's a nightmare, and without massive additional spending to reopen closed beds and expand capacity it does nothing to expand capacity.

In short ministers, NHS England and more local NHS leaders have spent more than a decade on 'reorganisations' that have fragmented and undermined the NHS, and making 'plans', not one of which has addressed the real problems. All they have done is line the pockets of management consultants and distract the people who should actually be trying to plan and run healthcare based on the needs of local people.

As this chapter has been finalised fresh reports from the *Health Service Journal* indicate the Chancellor Rishi Sunak has arbitrarily doubled the target for efficiency savings from 1.1% per year to 2.2%, claiming this would 'save' £4.75bn per year,[66] but taking no account of what would have to be sacrificed to make such savings. Even before this the *HSJ* was warning that some trusts were already facing impossible targets of up to 5% efficiency savings in a year, something 'never delivered before by NHS'.[67]

If anyone doubted it before, these revelations make it clear that austerity is back in the NHS, and the impact will be more damage, more suffering, more lives shortened ... and more demoralisation of staff who cannot give patients the quality of care they were trained to provide.

No plan will work without funding for revenue costs and investment on the one hand, and a strategy to recruit, train and retain the workforce on the other. And the diversion of billions from the NHS core budget to buy treatment for patients in private hospitals and contract out imaging and pathology will always be less efficient and effective than investing in adequate capacity in NHS hospitals. Austerity has driven NHS leaders into acceptance of self-defeating plans that head to a spiral of decline.

It's left up to campaigners to challenge the plans, the logic of austerity, and the mythology of markets, and fight for the restoration of the NHS as a unified, coherent public service centred on patients and their needs rather than the imperative of tax cuts and profits.

NOTES

1   Davis, J., Tallis, R (2013) *NHS SOS*, OneWorld, London
2   Davis, J., Lister, J., Wrigley, D. (2015) *NHS For Sale*, Merlin, London
3   https://healthemergency.org.uk/bill.php
4   https://www.england.nhs.uk/wp-content/uploads/2014/10/5yfv-web.pdf
5   https://lowdownnhs.info/analysis/simon-stevens-five-years-of-failure-that-have-plunged-nhs-into-growing-chaos/

6   https://www.ippr.org/blog/public-health-cuts

7   https://www.pulsetoday.co.uk/views/debate/are-personal-health-budgets-a-good-idea/

8   NHS chief announces plan to give patients cash to fund their own care | NHS | The Guardian

9   https://www.pulsetoday.co.uk/news/politics/more-people-to-access-personal-health-budgets-under-government-plans/

10   https://digital.nhs.uk/data-and-information/publications/statistical/personal-health-budgets/2021-22-q3/personal-health-budgets-q3-2021-22

11   https://www.england.nhs.uk/wp-content/uploads/2016/04/gpfv.pdf

12   https://healthcampaignstogether.com/pdf/planning-guid-16-17-20-21.pdf

13   https://healthcampaignstogether.com/pdf/Resource%20pack.pdf

14   https://flickread.com/edition/html/index.php?pdf=584fc5291fcd1#64

15   https://healthcampaignstogether.com/pdf/sustainability-and-transformation-plans-critical-review.pdf

16   https://healthcampaignstogether.com/pdf/HCTNo6.pdf

17   https://nhsproviders.org/media/2727/mission-impossible-report.pdf?utm_source=resourcepage&utm_medium=link&utm_campaign=missionimpossible&utm_content=report%20pdf

18   https://www.nationalhealthexecutive.com/Public-Health/move-to-us-style-healthcare-through-acos-deeply-unpopular-with-public/192938

19   https://healthcampaignstogether.com/pdf/HCTNo10.pdf

20   https://pharmaceutical-journal.com/article/news/select-committee-chair-calls-for-delay-in-new-model-of-care-contract

21   https://www.nao.org.uk/wp-content/uploads/2017/02/Health-and-social-care-integration.pdf

22   https://www.longtermplan.nhs.uk/wp-content/uploads/2019/08/nhs-long-term-plan-version-1.2.pdf

23   https://hansard.parliament.uk/lords/2022-01-24/debates/AB5351C6-2935-446D-847E-CB3C193CDE45/HealthAndCareBill#contribution-DF9AA920-86D6-4DC8-B6C0-CF6EEDB953F1

24   https://www.bbc.co.uk/news/health-44495598

25   https://www.england.nhs.uk/wp-content/uploads/2020/01/2020-21-NHS-Operational-Planning-Contracting-Guidance.pdf

26   https://lowdownnhs.info/analysis/public-health-cuts-expose-hollow-claims-of-one-nation-approach/

27   https://www.theguardian.com/politics/2020/aug/18/matt-hancock-unveils-national-institute-for-health-protection

28   https://goodlawproject.org/update/dido-harding-mike-coupe-unlawful/

29   https://www.gov.uk/guidance/nhs-test-and-trace-how-it-works

30   https://www.health.org.uk/publications/taking-our-health-for-granted

31   https://www.theguardian.com/commentisfree/2020/aug/18/the-guardian-view-on-scrapping-public-health-england-not-just-wrong-but-highly-risky

32   https://www.telegraph.co.uk/women/politics/boris-johnsons-nannying-obesity-drive-embarrassingly-touch/

33   https://www.theguardian.com/politics/2020/sep/02/health-leaders-warn-boris-johnson-over-axing-of-public-health-england

34   https://assets.publishing.service.gov.uk/government/uploads/system/
      uploads/attachment_data/file/960548/integration-and-innovation-working-
      together-to-improve-health-and-social-care-for-all-web-version.pdf

35   https://www.gov.uk/government/news/new-office-for-health-promotion-to-
      drive-improvement-of-nations-health

36   https://inews.co.uk/news/analysis/office-for-health-promotion-launch-
      the-governments-new-health-plan-will-only-work-with-proper-
      investment-933754

37   https://healthcampaignstogether.com/pdf/H&CbillBriefing.pdf

38   https://www.england.nhs.uk/wp-content/uploads/2021/02/B0135-provider-
      selection-regime-consultation.pdf

39   https://lowdownnhs.info/analysis/private-sector-unfazed-by-white-paper/

40   https://hansard.parliament.uk/lords/2022-03-01/debates/1CBD4FA4-0922-
      4E2F-A727-1DE4FF5A8E45/HealthAndCareBill

41   https://lowdownnhs.info/health-and-care-bill/no-private-firms-to-sit-on-
      integrated-care-boards-2/

42   https://hansard.parliament.uk//lords/2022-03-01/debates/1CBD4FA4-0922-
      4E2F-A727-1DE4FF5A8E45/HealthAndCareBill#contribution-AA7DFA54-
      1EF0-461E-BFF4-42803217E192

43   https://www.ageuk.org.uk/globalassets/age-uk/documents/reports-and-
      publications/reports-and-briefings/health-and-care-bill---lords-report-stage-
      briefing---february-2022.pdf

44   https://www.nao.org.uk/wp-content/uploads/2017/02/Health-and-social-
      care-integration.pdf

45   https://drive.google.com/file/d/1ENxbdaqcSdnYR9TIJlijj2NpK8_JWfLD/
      view

46   https://lowdownnhs.info/analysis/long-read/more-flaws-exposed-in-
      integrated-care/

47   https://www.resolutionfoundation.org/publications/nationally-insured/

48   https://www.resolutionfoundation.org/publications/nationally-insured/

49   https://www.health.org.uk/news-and-comment/blogs/the-care-act-
      amendment-who-is-set-to-lose-out

50   https://www.thetimes.co.uk/article/poorer-pensionsers-would-be-worse-
      off-under-social-care-cap-g87nkpgc7

51   https://www.ageuk.org.uk/globalassets/age-uk/documents/reports-and-
      publications/reports-and-briefings/health-and-care-bill---lords-report-stage-
      briefing---february-2022.pdf

52   This section extracted from Lowdown article https://lowdownnhs.info/
      comment/plan-to-tackle-nhs-queues-lacks-funding-for-staff-but-favours-
      private-sector/

53   https://www.england.nhs.uk/coronavirus/wp-content/uploads/
      sites/52/2022/02/C1466-delivery-plan-for-tackling-the-covid-19-backlog-
      of-elective-care.pdf

54   https://lowdownnhs.info/analysis/surge-deal-good-for-business-bad-for-the-
      nhs/

55   https://www.ft.com/content/771d3df9-3602-4573-b737-6d6e4927257b

56 https://www.gov.uk/government/publications/coronavirus-covid-19-ministerial-direction-on-independent-sector-contracting/request-for-direction-on-independent-sector-contracting-from-nhs-england-chief-executive-officer-to-secretary-of-state-for-health-and-social-care

57 https://ifs.org.uk/uploads/publications/wps/WP201715.pdf

58 https://www.bma.org.uk/news-and-opinion/a-long-wait-to-get-better

59 https://www.spectator.co.uk/article/exclusive-leaked-nhs-report-shows-waiting-list-hitting-9-2-million

60 https://www.thetimes.co.uk/article/delayed-nhs-patients-will-be-able-to-choose-private-ops-online-t93zlmsvv?shareToken=c8a84cfc2990584fd5d16f1005aa8d73

61 https://lowdownnhs.info/topics/gp-surgeries/javid-pushes-ahead-with-changes-to-primary-care/

62 https://www.gov.uk/government/publications/the-nhs-constitution-for-england/the-nhs-constitution-for-england#patients-and-the-public-your-rights-and-the-nhs-pledges-to-you

63 https://www.birminghammail.co.uk/news/midlands-news/health-ministers-asked-birmingham-hospital-23252048

64 https://www.thetimes.co.uk/article/delayed-nhs-patients-will-be-able-to-choose-private-ops-online-t93zlmsvv?shareToken=c8a84cfc2990584fd5d16f1005aa8d73

65 https://lowdownnhs.info/analysis/long-read/a-history-nhs-privatisation-part-3/

66 https://www.hsj.co.uk/finance-and-efficiency/chancellor-doubles-nhs-efficiency-target/7032120.article

67 https://www.hsj.co.uk/finance-and-efficiency/trusts-told-to-make-savings-never-delivered-before-by-nhs/7032088.article?storyCode=7032088

Chapter 5

Privatisation – no answer, but a growing problem

John Lister

This chapter explains why the British experience confirms that in health care at least the private sector has proved itself not an answer, but a problem. Initial moves to bring in private sector providers – beginning with the Thatcher government's drive to outsource hospital support services in the 1980s, Tony Blair's government's efforts to bring in private provision of elective clinical care in the 2000s and Andrew Lansley's massive reorganisation to entrench competition and a market system from 2012 – were all driven by ideology, despite the evidence.

More recent privatisation has been based more on the lack of NHS capacity after a decade of real terms cuts and lack of capital for the NHS to invest in a public sector option.

The private sector share of NHS spending on clinical care has risen in cash terms from almost nothing in 1997 when Tony Blair took office, and rose over 25% to £12bn in 2020-21 as the NHS with thousands of beds closed turned to private hospitals for extra capacity, and seem set to remain at this much higher level for some years at least.

The chapter looks at the pattern of contracts and contracting since 2012, noting that in clinical care the private sector has mainly picked up smaller-scale community service contracts.

A look at the performance of private contractors shows a continuing catalogue of failures, including Hinchingbrooke Hospital, and the collapse of Carillion early in 2018, and with it the use of PFI for new hospital projects. However the turn to 'integrated care' is bringing new openings for private contractors, not least in the provision of back office and data services as part of the 'Health Systems Support Framework'.

The chapter also includes a substantial section on the biggest area of private sector domination, mental health, where one in every eight inpatient beds in England was provided by American companies in 2019, and 44% of Child and Adolescent mental health services.

Both the decade of austerity and the pandemic have proved awfully fertile ground for the growth of private providers seeking to pick up a growing slice of the NHS budget.

The pandemic has helped to underline one important fact in relation both to the NHS in Britain and healthcare systems all over the world: the private sector is not the answer to any of the big problems. Rather, it is part of the problem.

The origins and early history of privatisation in the NHS have been documented and discussed in various studies by this author.[1,2] The impact of the 2012 Act in deepening and widening the division between commissioners and providers of healthcare into a full-scale NHS market,[3] and its immediate aftermath[4], have also been examined in some detail. We will not repeat that information here, but focus on more recent events; however, a brief historical overview is useful to understand what's different in today's situation.

Driven by ideology

The drive to carve up the NHS and create contracts for private companies did not begin until 35 years after it was founded as a largely publicly owned and publicly funded service.

The Thatcher government had already begun privatising whole publicly-owned utilities and turning them into private, shareholder-owned corporations.[5] However, despite Thatcher's own ambition to switch to a system of compulsory private health insurance, her cabinet saw the need to tread much more carefully with the NHS, and her personal views were only revealed in the public domain in 2016.[6]

Privatisation (initially limited to 'outsourcing', or 'contracting out' of services that previously and properly should be part of the NHS) was based from the outset on political ideology rather than on any evidence. From 1983 onwards ministers began the process by salami-slicing off low-profile but potentially profitable services, starting with non-clinical support ("ancillary") services, primarily cleaning, catering and laundry.

At first ministers claimed that their objective was 'efficiency'. In fact the process ticked four boxes on the Thatcherite agenda:

- it reinforced the free-market ideology later known as 'neoliberalism';

- it started the process of whittling down a major public service, delivering some short-term cash savings at the expense of quality;
- it offered contracts for the Tories' mates in the private sector;
- and, no less important, it undermined the power of the NHS unions, which were most strongly organised and most combative in these sectors of the workforce.

Where services had been contracted out, the support workers were no longer NHS employees, and, especially after anti-union laws had been passed, this meant the possibility of combined strike action of support staff and professionals over pay and conditions (as had happened in the 1970s and 1982) would be largely eliminated. Even though the health unions have changed since then, with a greater unionisation of professional staff, the long-term damage this split inflicted on them is still exposed each time the issue of action over pay is discussed.

Tony Blair's government notoriously refused to repeal all of Thatcher's anti-union laws, and similar neoliberal ideology underpinned New Labour's increasingly irresponsible experiments with the use of private finance for hospital building projects from 1997, and using private providers for clinical services from 2000.

Blair's party shared the belief that the power of competition (or in New Labour-speak 'contestability') could improve quality and increase efficiency in healthcare. That's why, with extra money to spend, New Labour ministers chose not to invest directly in expanding the NHS, but also to invest in developing new, private providers and a competitive market. They even set targets for a growing share of NHS operations to be delivered, at higher cost, by the private sector.[7]

And when David Cameron's ConDem coalition took office in 2010, it was ideology, in defiance of the growing body of evidence, that drove Andrew Lansley's Health and Social Care Act. This restructured and fragmented the NHS, to create and institutionalise a competitive market in clinical and non-clinical services at considerable cost, but with no detectable benefit other than to private providers.

Lack of investment and capacity

Ideology is still certainly a factor in the thinking of ministers. The current government's first thought is to turn to the private sector for additional capacity.

However, it has become increasingly obvious, as the years of austerity from 2010 have dragged on, that the main justification for more recent privatisation has become the lack of adequate capacity and investment in the NHS. This has made it possible for ministers to argue (and increasingly force even reluctant NHS managers to agree) that a depleted NHS somehow 'needs' the resources of private contractors and private hospitals to fill gaps in services[8] and address growing delays.[9]

By 2017 the private sector was boasting that it was providing 'capital, capacity and capability to the NHS to help meet the increasing demands it faces'.[10] The sector was delivering:

- over 22% of all NHS gastroenterology, trauma and orthopaedic services;
- over half a million NHS elective surgical procedures annually;
- almost 10% of all NHS MRI scans; and
- almost half of all NHS community services.

A report by the Institute of Fiscal Studies at the end of 2019 found that the NHS was becoming increasingly reliant upon independent sector provider (ISPs) for some types of elective work:

> For example, in 2017–18, ISPs conducted 30% of all NHS-funded hip replacements, 27% of inguinal hernia repairs and 20% of cataract procedures. Replacing this capacity within NHS providers would therefore require careful planning. [...] 82% of the growth in hip replacements between 2003–04 and 2018–19 was accounted for by ISPs.[11]

By October 2021 research commissioned by the *Financial Times* found the chronic dependency on private hospitals for NHS joint replacements had worsened in the pandemic. More than half (56%) of joint replacement operations had been performed in private hospitals in the first eight months of 2021, compared with 40% over the same period in 2019. The proportion of these patients funded by the NHS had dropped by a third, to just 18%, leaving almost half of them paid for privately, from insurance or out of pocket.[12]

The Covid pandemic further reduced the capacity of NHS hospitals, mental health services and GPs to cope with routine elective treatment and emergencies. The most recent figures as this chapter is completed show almost 14,000 general and acute beds occupied by Covid patients, while over 11,000 beds were 'available' but out of use (unoccupied) in Quarter 3 of 2021-22 – leaving NHS capacity for emergencies and elective cases reduced by 25%. Mental health bed numbers have actually increased slightly in the same period, but the numbers of beds occupied (i.e. people receiving inpatient care) has fallen, leaving more than one bed in eight unused.[13]

Rising share of NHS funds go private

As private sector involvement grew, the amounts siphoned out of public sector budgets to pay private providers began to increase. Department of Health and Social Care (DHSC) *Annual Report* figures show spending by NHS commissioners on private providers of clinical services rose each year, from close to zero in 1997 when John Major's Tory government finally fell,[14] to just over £2bn (2.8%) in 2006, when separate figures were first published[15] and almost £9bn (7.6%) by 2016,[16] and £9.2bn in 2018.

The most substantial jump prior to the Covid pandemic was a 24.7% (£1.6bn) increase in 2013/14 as the 2012 Act took effect.[17] However, the private sector share of spending flat-lined in 2016/17, and declined slightly to 7.3% in 2017/18.

These official figures are for commissioner spending only[18] (in other words they do not include additional contracting out of services by NHS and foundation trusts), so they significantly understate the scale and impact of private sector involvement in the NHS. David Rowland of the Centre for Health and the Public Interest (CHPI) has argued that by including trust spending, all NHS spending on GPs and dentistry, and all spending on social care (almost all of which is privately provided), the real figure could be as high as £29bn in 2018/19. He also argues that the real baseline for calculations should

153

be spending by NHS England, and not the whole Department, bringing the private share as high as 26%.[19]

This author disagrees and has argued that the bulk of NHS primary care and dentistry should not be equated with spending on for-profit corporations. However even by this more cautious and accurate assessment, this means total NHS spending on private providers rose 34% in six years: from £13.5bn (14% of NHS England's budget) in 2013/14, to £18.1bn (16%) in 2018/19.[20] This figure will surprise some people: for some it will seem too high, while those who have an exaggerated view of the scale and strength of the private sector will no doubt feel it may be too low. It certainly shows that there is still a lot of NHS left to fight for.

The latest DHSC Annual Report, just published, shows that after several years of relatively little growth, the official figure for NHS spending on private providers rocketed in 2020-21, to over £12bn,[21] an unprecedented increase of almost £2.5bn (25.6%) in a year. At the centre of this was the massive contract that was signed by NHS England as the pandemic hit in 2020, to block-book beds in private hospitals.[22]

Despite the shockingly poor value of that contract to the NHS,[23,24] a further 4-year, 'framework contract,' worth up to £10bn, was put in place[25] to make it easier for NHS trusts or commissioners to make use of private sector beds as 'additional capacity' until 2024-5. The hope was to find a way of bringing down waiting lists and waiting times without having any more money to invest in the NHS itself.

With no plans or resources in place to reopen the 5,000 or so NHS beds that have remained unused since they were closed in March 2020 (to free up space for Covid patients and enable social distancing),[26] the new higher level of spending – and NHS dependence on private beds – is likely to continue for some years to come.

The DHSC Annual Report shows spending on voluntary sector and non-profit companies also rose in 2020, by a relatively modest (but still very considerable) 9.4%, to just under £1.9bn. Spending on all non-NHS bodies rose by 27.4% in the year.

However, the private sector's share of total DHSC spending

actually fell in 2020/21, from 7.2% in 2019/20 to 6.75%, because the Department's total budget, swollen by one-off Covid-linked payments, also rose dramatically, by 34%. But with so much extra money having changed hands for doing so little, it's hardly surprising the private sector did not complain at this apparent setback.

With additional funding to cover Covid costs scaled down in 2021-22 and ending on 1 April 2022, it's already clear the the proportion of DHSC funds flowing to the private sector is set to increase and stay at a higher level for at least the next few years.

Covid brings a bonanza for private hospitals

The broader use of the private sector – PPE procurement, test and trace, consultancy, etc. – during the pandemic has been outlined in Chapter 2. Here we will focus on the significant drive to make more use of private clinical services.

The first £2.15bn paid out by the NHS to private hospitals in 2020, to cover their costs and ensure capacity would be available, was broken down by *Private Eye* (issue 1561). £468m had been paid to the largest hospital chain Circle Health Holdings (boosting its revenue by more than 50%). Circle, with 54 hospitals and over 2500 beds, was already partly owned by predatory US health corporation Centene, which went on to buy up the remainder of the company.[27] *Private Eye* reports that the NHS payments in 2020 effectively trebled the value of the company.

£430m went to Spire, (39 hospitals and 1,870 beds), helping to almost double the company's share price. Australian-owned Ramsay Health Care UK picked up a cool £385m (equivalent to 76% of its revenue) in the first 13 months of the pandemic for providing capacity in its 29 hospitals with 892 beds.

Both Spire and Ramsay subsequently bragged that the increased NHS waiting list gave them even more lucrative possibilities with self-pay patients. Spire's 2020 Annual Report noted that they were able to keep back beds from the NHS deal to ensure they could continue to treat private patients: 'Q4 saw exceptionally strong growth in self-pay revenue with priority given to more clinically urgent complex cases, which carry a greater average revenue per case.'[28] Spire's Strategic Report also notes income was maintained during the pandemic, thanks to the NHS crisis:

> our self-pay admissions were broadly in line with the same period in 2019. This wave of activity, following the pause between March and August, was largely due to pent up demand and a desire by people to avoid a lengthy wait for treatment in the NHS at a time of increasing NHS waiting lists and times.[29]

NHS England's eagerness to strengthen its ties with Ramsay was underlined in October when NHS England's Director of Clinical Improvement found time to formally open a new Ramsay Hospital in Chorley,[30] an area where the future of NHS acute services remains uncertain.

The private hospitals were happy to accept NHS subsidies to cover their costs during the Covid lockdown, and to fill their otherwise under-used beds with NHS patients as part of the 4-year £10bn 'framework' deal. But despite the lavish payments, nowhere near the full 8,000 private sector acute beds were made available to the NHS, and fewer still were used.[31]

For the NHS to make full use of the beds, either the private hospitals would have to poach more staff from the same limited pool of staff trained by the NHS, increasing the pressures on front-line NHS services, or the trusts would have to split their own clinical workforce to send teams to work off-site in small private hospitals. Any benefit from access to additional beds to speed up elective work would be offset by the greater problems maintaining adequate staffing of emergency services.

Also the private hospital firms themselves would rather treat their own, more profitable, self-pay and insured private patients than fill beds with NHS patients at the lower NHS tariff cost.

In any case, even if it were possible to utilise ALL of the private acute beds on a short or medium term basis, it would still leave the NHS facing a drastic loss of capacity at the end of the contract, compared with 2019. Having squandered billions on short-term deals with private providers, the NHS's own capacity gap would remain, leaving it even more chronically dependent on the private sector.

US corporation not so impressed

The recent boom times in England's puny private hospital sector need to be put in context. As mentioned above, Centene apparently put itself in pole position to cash in on the weakness of the NHS when it paid $700m for complete control of Circle and its 54 hospitals in 2021.[32] The company had also controversially taken a relatively large stake in GP services in England, making them the largest private player in the primary care market, with 1% of GP practices.[33] And the corporation also seems to have established high-level influence with the Johnson government. In 2021 Samantha Jones, then CEO of Operose, Centene's UK subsidiary, was appointed as a senior advisor to Johnson himself, and more recently stepped up to become chief operating officer in Downing Street.[34]

Nonetheless at the end of 2021 Centene revealed that they are contemplating a complete withdrawal from Britain, and from all their international operations (worth around $2 billion per year),[35] to concentrate on their vastly larger ($126bn per year) 'core' business in the US. The corporations' total revenue has been growing, but profitability has been falling.[36]

Centene's apparent willingness to walk away from such recent British investments underlines the fact that the profitability of contracts in a chronically under-funded NHS is not necessarily as high as we might expect. It's almost certainly less than can be extracted from contracts and insurance in the vastly better-funded US healthcare system.

Contracts and contracting since 2012

The private sector has been complaining for some time that they have not reaped the expected reward from the 2012 Health and Social Care Act. In 2019 the Independent Healthcare Providers Network (IHPN) pointed to their findings from Freedom of Information requests[37] which showed the proportion of NHS contracts awarded through competitive tendering had *fallen*, from 12% of all contracts in 2015/16 to just 6% the following year, before a partial recovery to 9% in 2017/18. The value of these contracts had fallen by a third, from 3% to just 2% of CCG spending on clinical services over the same period. Competitive tendering had been largely replaced by 'framework contracts'[38] listing approved providers or extending contracts to existing providers.

A survey by NHS Providers had previously found that the private sector had been very successful in bidding for community health services, securing many more contracts than the NHS, but that most of these were small in value. They estimated NHS trusts had just one in five community contracts, but *more than half* of the contracts by value, ten times the 5% share won by the for-profit private sector.[39]

With regard to basic hospital support services such as cleaning and catering, even 30 years of pressure to contract out had left private contractors well short of full penetration of the market. Research, looking at NHS data for 130 hospital trusts from 2010 to 2014, found that less than half of them – around 40% – had contracted out their cleaning services.[40] 2010 figures suggest similar numbers had opted to contract out catering services.[41]

Outsourcing of support services seems to have been on the decline for some time, following the high profile failures of large-scale contracts in Leicester (Interserve 2016)[42] and Nottingham University Hospitals (Carillion 2017).[43] Prominent trusts, especially in London, have more recently been persuaded to bring support services back in house,[44,45,46] while North West Anglia Trust was persuaded by trade union pressure last November to drop plans for outsourcing catering services at Hinchingbrooke Hospital.[47]

By contrast, spending has been increasing on outsourced clinical services, especially mental health, and more recently elective surgery. However, doubts over the wisdom of contracting out have not been dispelled. In 2017 the BMA attempted to identify doctors' concerns over privatisation, and found the most common fear about independent sector provision was the destabilisation of NHS services, followed by the impact of the fragmentation of NHS services. Two years later these remained the primary issues, closely followed by concern that independent sector provision represented worse value for money for the NHS and that the care they provided was of worse quality.[48]

2015-2019: the best of times and the worst of times for contractors

It's easy to gain a false impression that the private sector, with the backing of successive governments, has been effectively able to call all the shots and endlessly pile up a growing portfolio of contracts. But this would be to ignore the many and repeated contract failures that have been an ever-present feature since the first hospital support services were contracted out in 1984.

Time and again large scale and long-term contracts that appear to open the floodgates to more private sector domination and to offer substantial profits turn out to be more costly or complex than the contractor expected. As a result, their performance falls embarrassingly below specifications, and contracts are wound up years early. A proper reckoning of the true scale of outsourcing and privatisation therefore needs to monitor the progress of contracts after they are first announced, and to make sure the revenue lost when a company pulls out early is deducted from any cumulative total.

There is no room in this chapter to work through all the failed contracts since 2010. The NHS For Sale website has probably the most comprehensive coverage of contracts and what happens to them, and its Snapshot of NHS Outsourcing Failures covers a host of services including diagnostics, GP surgeries, hospitals, mental health, pathology, support services, and patient transport and ambulance services.[49]

However, it is useful here to look at a few of the more significant failures.

Circle

In January 2015 the pro-privatisation lobby suffered a major body blow. Circle, the company that claimed to be a so-called 'John Lewis-style partnership',* finally pulled out of its disastrous contract to run

---

* Theoretically giving each employee part-ownership of the company, a share of its annual profits, and a say in how it is run. Despite the company's claims, not one of these benefits proved to apply to Circle employees, and Circle dropped even the pretence that staff were co-owners in 2013. (https://healthemergency.org.uk/pdf/Smoke%20and%20mirrors.pdf)

Hinchingbrooke Hospital in Cambridgeshire, just three years into a 10-year £1bn management franchise.[50] Its collapse also killed off plans to replicate the Hinchingbrooke model in a growing number of similar contracts that would 'franchise out' the management of NHS hospitals to private companies.

While apologists tried to claim Circle was not to blame for the fiasco,[51] the facts all pointed in that direction. Circle left the Trust saddled with a £7m-plus deficit, despite their implausible promise to generate more than £300m savings in 10 years. From the outset they had rejected any notion of 'partnership' with staff; indeed the company refused time and again to meet with unions, or even allow staff (now clad in 'Circle Hinchingbrooke' uniforms) time to participate in Circle's own 'partnership forums'. Circle departed just after a Care Quality Commission report unveiled the abysmal quality of care in Hinchingbrooke.[52]

In its three years in control, Circle's failure ever to balance the books meant the company made not a penny in profit, and survived only on NHS cash handouts and some of Circle's own money to prop up the budget. By July 2014 Hinchingbrooke was one of 19 seriously indebted trusts referred by the Audit Commission to health secretary Jeremy Hunt for closer scrutiny. Circle's failure to retain staff led to sky-high spending (almost double the average for Foundation Trusts) on 'interim staffing' – locums, bank and agency staff. In the 2013 NHS Staff Satisfaction Survey, Hinchingbrooke came out worse than the NHS average on two thirds (19) of 28 Key Findings and in the lowest 20% of trusts in almost half. It was among NHS trusts where staff were most likely to have experienced bullying or abuse from colleagues. Its staff turnover rate was almost 50% higher than the NHS average.[53]

Capita

Circle was far from the only high-profile failing company. Capita (the firm *Private Eye* calls "Crapita" after serial contract failures) plunged into trouble early in 2016 just six months into a 4-year £1bn contract for primary care support services that was supposed to deliver 'significant savings' for NHS England. According to *Pulse* magazine, stocks of prescription forms ran out, and some practices also ran out of blood vials.[54] In October just 21% of GPs said they were satisfied with the Capita service.[55] Some of the greatest frustration was in trying to get through to the laughingly entitled 'Customer Support Centre'. By the end of 2016 a BMA survey found a staggering 81% of GPs who responded had experienced delays in the delivery of urgently-requested patient records, some of which were delayed by up to three weeks.[56]

GPs were not the first in the NHS to have a less than positive experience of Capita: in June 2014 five of eight Liverpool NHS Trusts who had contracted their payroll and recruitment services to Capita withdrew from the contracts because of concerns about the quality of the service provided.

Lion's share of new funding goes private

In March 2017 a report by the Health Foundation (A year of Plenty?[57]) warned that private providers were growing at the expense of NHS trusts. Because an increased proportion of NHS beds were taken up with emergency cases, more of the potentially profitable elective services were going to private hospitals, forcing the NHS into becoming an 'emergency only' service.

NHS providers had received just £650m out of £2bn of extra funding in 2015, compared with £900m of additional funding that went to pay for care provided by non-NHS bodies. NHS trusts had also found themselves reliant on using private sector beds to avoid falling further behind on elective treatment targets and facing cash penalties. The Financial Times in June 2020 estimated NHS work already accounted for 'more than 80 per cent of Ramsay's revenues, and around 40 per cent for BMI/Circle and Spire'.[58]

'Integrating' the private sector

Also in 2017 Centene first came to public attention, when it was brought in by Capita to support the development of 'a new integrated healthcare model' in Nottinghamshire. Centene offers advice on the 'integration of systems and pathways' based on the experience of its US parent company, which provides 'a portfolio of services to government sponsored healthcare programs, focusing on under-insured and uninsured individuals'. In the US Centene aims to save money by avoiding costly readmissions to hospital, using 'person-centred innovation and technology' to make sure patients who have chronic conditions adhere to their treatment.[59]

This all seemed to fit with the mood music of NHS England's Five Year Forward View.

Centene also has 90% ownership of Ribera Salud, the controversial Public-Private Partnership in Valencia in Spain. Ribera began as a scheme to design, build, operate and deliver clinical services in a new hospital, but expanded to cover the building of several hospitals. It then won a contract to assume all risks for delivering healthcare services for 20% of the Valencia population. It is now a 'health management group operating in both private healthcare, and the fully integrated Accountable Care System sector', and owns and manages the largest private hospital in Spain, Hospital Povisa de Vigo. The company also has 'controlling and noncontrolling interests in primary care, outpatient, hospital and diagnostic centres in Spain, Central Europe, and Latin America'.[60]

In November 2016 the Spanish newspaper *El Pais* reported that Ribera Salud was under police investigation for allegations of fraud, including overcharging, and issues with sub-contracting.[61] And in 2017, when the right wing lost power in Valencia, the new regional government promised to roll back the privatisation.[62] They pointed to significant problems with a lack of oversight of the 'concessions' given to Ribera Salud, with no effective control, nor checks on the quality of its service, nor in any financial matters.[63] From 2018 some of the contracts were ended as they expired.[64]

Nonetheless it was at this very time that, through its links with Ribera Salud (which had recruited fans in the NHS Confederation, who were eagerly searching for ways to reduce spending[65]), Centene was brought in by Capita on a £2.7m contract to advise in Nottinghamshire. This enabled Centene to become one of six contractors initially approved in 2017 by NHS England to help roll out 'integrated care' models across the country.[66,67]

Setbacks for private sector

In the autumn of 2017 a joint campaign** succeeded in halting the proposed sale/privatisation of NHS Professionals, a publicly run staffing agency, which was making a healthy profit and doing useful work for the NHS.[68]

Early in 2018 privatisers suffered a seismic shock when Carillion, the multinational construction and services company, abruptly collapsed after years of mismanagement, handing out excessive dividends to investors, and having run up debts of £7bn, more than its annual sales of £5.2bn.[69] Carillion, a leading player in PFI projects in the NHS and schools, had also run a failed Independent Sector Treatment Centre,[70] and won, and then lost, a major contract with Nottingham University Hospitals for support services.[71,72]

Carillion's collapse halted work on two major PFI hospitals: Royal Liverpool and Midland Metropolitan in Smethwick. In each case the public sector had to step in, take over the contracts, and pick up a hefty additional bill for the remaining work, effectively doubling the initial cost for completing each hospital, neither of which has yet been completed.[73] This fiasco effectively marked the end of PFI, leaving the current hiatus in which promises of public funds to build up to 48 'new hospitals' conflict with the desperate shortage of capital to build or repair anything.[74]

2018 also brought a flurry of frustrated private contractors seeking to sue NHS commissioners for axing their contracts. First Virgin managed to screw an undisclosed settlement out of NHS commissioners in Surrey for not renewing the firm's 3-year contract.[75]

Circle also threatened to sue the NHS, even though the company itself had decided to pull out of bidding for a contract to continue running an 'independent sector treatment centre' in Nottingham. The Greater Nottingham Clinical Commissioning Partnership had put the contract (to run one of the largest elective treatment centres surviving from the New Labour period) out to tender at just £50m per year, a reduction of over 25% on the previous year. In Circle's view

** Supported by We Own It, KONP, Health Campaigns Together, Open Democracy, Doctors for the NHS and others, via a successful petition and the intervention of Justin Madders MP

Nottinghamshire health chiefs were at fault for not offering enough money to guarantee a large enough profit for the private equity fund that had bought up the company.[76]

By the summer of 2019 the company were licking their wounds after failing in their High Court challenge. Circle had claimed Nottingham University Hospitals Trust could not possibly treat NHS patients for less money, and that bringing the contract back in-house would be 'unrealistic' and 'not in patients' interests. The Court disagreed, and decided that the contract should go to the Trust, as originally proposed. This meant that all services at the Treatment Centre would return in-house, ending the stream of profits Circle had enjoyed for the previous eleven years.

The decision also meant that Circle lost the right to run their exclusive private hospital in the same building, which had treated no NHS patients. Mike Scott (Nottingham/Notts Keep Our NHS Public) said: 'It's difficult to understand how Circle could even have taken this to Court in the first place. They seem to believe they have some sort of right to suck money out of the NHS for their own profit.'[77]

The fight to keep staff in the NHS

2018 also marked the beginning of a still-unresolved battle by the main health unions against NHS Trusts seeking to cut costs and dodge VAT by hiving off their non-clinical support staff into so-called 'wholly owned companies' (WOCs) – a new form of privatisation.[78] The staff involved would lose their status as NHS employees and the benefits that went with it.

While trust bosses tried to persuade staff with long-term protection agreements, it was clear that few were convinced. None of the promises for the future could be relied upon, and any subsequent recruitment would be on inferior terms and conditions, creating a two-tier workforce.

After some early setbacks in which a couple of trusts were able to establish WOCs, the unions began to get better organised, and fought together to secure important victories through strike action, notably in Wrightington, Wigan and Leigh[79] and Bradford,[80] and also in some cases the threat of strikes was enough – in Mid Yorkshire Hospitals, in Princess Alexandra Hospital and in Frimley.[81]

Mixed signals – but privatisation continues

January 2019 brought the long-awaited publication of NHS England's Long Term Plan, followed at the end of February by the launch of 'a broad process of engagement' seeking to 'build the case for primary legislative change'. The proposals did indeed seek to remove some of the objectionable elements of the 2012 Act, notably section 75, and the associated regulations which compelled Clinical Commissioning Groups to put services out to competitive tender.[82]

However, removing competition is not necessarily the same as reducing the extent of privatisation. This was underlined by NHS England's insistence on driving through highly contentious large-scale contracting-out and privatisation of services even as they launched their 'engagement process'.

The first of a series of eleven major 7-year contracts for PET-CT scanner services had just been secretly awarded in Oxfordshire by NHS England to a private company, InHealth. This led to immediate, furious opposition from consultants, campaigners, and MPs of all parties.[83] NHS England responded with only the most meaningless concessions, trying to fob off opposition by conceding that the service could be run by the staff at Oxford University Hospitals Trust. At the same time they raised the stakes by threatening legal action against anyone raising concerns about clinical standards and care.[84]

Oxfordshire campaigners reacted angrily to a misguided *Guardian* headline[85] that claimed there had been an NHS England 'U-turn', insisting: 'We believe that the current proposed "deal" will lead to a worsening of service across the region. This is direct privatisation of a part of our NHS. We demand a halt to the process.' They were not alone. Oxfordshire Tory MPs, along with local LibDem and Labour MPs, all wrote to question the decision and the way it had been arrived at. Banbury's Tory MP Victoria Prentis wrote to NHS England chief Simon Stevens expressing 'extreme concern' that patient care would suffer.[86]

But the strongest condemnation of the plan came from Oxford University's Professor of Oncology Dr Adrian Harris, who asked:

If the proposed service is so excellent, why did NHSE mislead the local Oxford CCG ... telling them that they couldn't discuss it and wouldn't review the tender, when there was no reason for it not to be openly discussed?

Professor Harris pointed out that all 'profits' from scans from private patients and funded trials would go to the private company, not to the hospital, where the staff and scanners are, 'so no reinvestment for our benefit from our work'. It also meant a 2-tier system, with patients further away being scanned in hospital car parks 'with poor access machines', whereas Oxford patients would be seen at the Churchill Hospital centre.[87]

Noting that 'doctors in Oxford have made it clear that they do not wish to be involved with this service, which they think has a significant number of potential disadvantages for patients', Prof Harris also asked: 'Where are they going to send the scans, as there are no other PET-CT reporters working in these hospitals.'

In the event NHS England toughed it out and the contract held. There has been no similar resistance elsewhere, possibly because the contractors and trusts have learned from the errors they had made and avoided plans that would trigger a local response, or been more successful in ensuring that any new contracts were pushed through without public awareness and debate.

However, the Oxfordshire experience was no exception: the Long Term Plan specifically called for large-scale networks to provide pathology and imaging services. Both the PET-CT fiasco and the first big pathology network that was tendered in South London and the South-East made it obvious that this strategy involves handing even more major contracts to 'partnerships' with private companies.[88]

And some really big, long-term private contracts were being drawn up: in the Bristol, North Somerset and South Gloucester area NHS commissioners had decided to put all adult community health services out to tender, as a single ten-year, legally binding contract. NHS England did nothing to intervene or question the policy.[89]

In the summer of 2019 work began on building a new £100m 138-bed private hospital on the site of Birmingham's Queen

Elizabeth Hospital as part of a 'partnership' agreement between University Hospitals Birmingham Trust and US hospital giant HCA. HCA financed the construction, planning to use 66 beds for private patients, leasing the rest to the Trust.[90]

The rise and rise of management consultants

As the Lowdown has reported,[91] consultancy firms had a field day in the Covid pandemic, but even before that they had been doing very well from the NHS, with their role behind the scenes increasingly institutionalised.

Management consultants have played a key, and lucrative, role in most of the big reorganisations of the NHS going back at least to 1974.[92] After steering New Labour towards increasing reliance on private providers of clinical care in the 2000s, a major McKinsey report commissioned by New Labour shaped many of the cost-cutting policies of NHS trusts and commissioners which aimed to generate £20bn of 'savings' after the 2008 banking crash.[93]

From 2010 the incoming Tory-led coalition in turn employed McKinsey to help construct Andrew Lansley's large and disastrous Health and Social Care Act.[94]

In 2016-17 the King's Fund found that management consultants were being used to support the drawing up of Sustainability and Transformation Plans in 33 of the 44 areas.[95]

In North-West London firms including McKinsey were employed again and again from 2011 (at a combined cost of over £80m) in the long running fiasco of the 'Shaping a Healthier Future' project before it was finally axed. McKinsey veteran Penny Dash was subsequently installed in 2020 as the chair of NW London's 'integrated care system'.[96]

England's NHS spent an estimated £300m on consultancy in 2018/19, despite evidence that management consultants in health care 'do more harm than good'.[97]

In a blatant example of squandering taxpayers money, NHS England paid PA Consulting over £200,000 in 2019 for a 35-day 'function mapping exercise' … to work out what NHSE itself was responsible for![98]

In 2020 Matt Hancock's department brought in a team from

McKinsey for six weeks, at a cost of £563,000, to help define the 'vision, purpose and narrative' of the new body to replace Public Health England after he had announced it was to be axed.[99]

But the pandemic was a real money-spinner. In August 2020 consultancy.uk reported that 16 consulting firms had been awarded coronavirus contracts worth £56m.[100] By January 2021 Health Minister Helen Whately, herself a former McKinsey employee,[101] admitted that 2,300 management consultants from 73 different companies (more than the number of civil servants in the Treasury) were currently working on the lamentable Test and Trace system, with £375m spent on consultancy for that project alone.[102]

These consultants were costing an average of £1,000 per day. Deloitte alone had 900 employees at work in test and trace, and the *Daily Mail* estimated 2,959 consultants and contractors were advising the government on the pandemic.[103] In October 2020 *Sky News* revealed that a 5-person team from Boston Consulting had been paid £25,000 per day helping to 'mastermind the creation of the contract tracing systems'.[104]

But following through from the pandemic, the Department of health and Social Care's own privatisation unit, Shared Business Services (run as "a unique partnership with digital experts Sopra Steria"[105]) has been working to streamline the recruitment of consultants to work at local NHS trust and commissioner level. In 2018 they set up a 4-year 'Framework agreement' which lists 107 pre-approved companies who can simply be hired, without a tender process, to steer the policies and decisions of NHS commissioners and providers.[106]

At no point has any serious value for money audit been carried out to demonstrate the cost-effectiveness of management consultants. Nor has any assessment been made of the extent to which their increased authority has come at the cost of undermining the confidence and authority of NHS management.

It seems as though the more contracts they win, the more entrenched their power and influence becomes. As the North-West London experience proved, once consultants have been brought in they 'keep getting rehired', despite their failure to complete projects or improve the efficiency or quality of services.

Mental Health: a stronghold of private provision

NHS reliance on private providers of mental health services has for many years been much greater than in acute and community services, with a rapid increase since 2010. Department of Health figures compiled by the Nuffield Trust showed 'Funding for independent sector mental health service providers increased by 15 per cent in real terms between 2011/12 and 2012/13 alone, while funding for NHS-provided mental health services decreased by 1 per cent'. [107]

According to the Competition and Markets Authority the market for mental health services was worth a total of £15.9bn in 2015, 27% of which was for hospital services. The private hospital sector had grown in the previous five years, while NHS capacity had been cut by 23%.[108]

By 2018 Laing & Buisson estimated 30% of England's mental health hospital capacity was in the private sector.[109] Their report notes 'robust revenue growth for independent mental health hospitals in recent years,' though 'pressure on prices had meant some diminution in profit margins'. The main driver was 'the long-term trend towards NHS outsourcing of non-generic mental health hospital treatment, which shows no sign of abating'.

Private sector penetration has been most dramatic in child and adolescent mental health (CAMHS). Figures given in parliament in November 2018 showed that the private sector spend had grown by 27% over 5 years, from £122m to £156m,[110] and the *Guardian* in 2019 revealed that no less than 44% of the £355m NHS spending on CAMHS care was going to private providers.[111]

The private sector domination in mental health is most complete in the provision of 'locked ward rehabilitation', in which a massive 97% of a £304m market was held by private companies in 2015. The largest of these was the now merged Cygnet/Cambian (20-30%), with substantial involvement also of the Priory Group with 10-20% and Huntercombe with 5-10%.[112]

In 2017 the merged Cygnet was operating 2,400 beds across 100 sites, with over 6,000 staff. In the summer of 2018 Cygnet also took over the Danshell Group, operating 25 units with 288 beds for adults with learning difficulties.[113]

The increased proportional spend on private providers has made them even more dependent on funding from the NHS to prop up their balance sheets. The largest private mental health provider, the Priory Group, received 52% of its income of almost £800m from the NHS, and another 38% from social care – a total of 90%. The group has since been sold by US private equity company Acadia to the Dutch private equity company, Waterland, for £1.08bn.[114]

By the end of 2019, the *Financial Times* was highlighting the extent of privatisation of mental health provision, noting that one in every eight (13%) inpatient beds in England was provided by American companies, while in some areas the proportion of US-owned mental healthcare facilities was much higher.

The *FT* quoted research by Candesic, a healthcare consultancy, which showed mental health patients in Manchester had a 50:50 chance of being admitted to a privately owned hospital, and a one in four chance of the bed being provided by an American-owned company. In Bristol, North Somerset and Gloucestershire, no less than 95% of mental healthcare beds were owned by private providers, and three-fifths owned by US companies.[115] The *FT* also quoted Laing Buisson estimates that of the £13.8bn spent by the NHS on mental healthcare in 2018, including non-hospital services, £1.8bn (13%) went to the private sector.

Candesic estimated about a quarter of NHS mental healthcare beds in England were provided by the private sector, with 98% of the private facilities' earnings coming from the health service. But it noted profit margins were under pressure 'owing to funding cuts and a rise in costs — particularly staffing, forcing a reliance on more expensive agency workers'.

The report followed criticism by the Care Quality Commission of the care provided by the Priory's Ellingham Hospital, in Attleborough, Norfolk, finding it 'inadequate' and conditions, which included wards for children and adolescents, 'unacceptable'. Two of the 53 facilities owned by the Priory in England had already been rated inadequate by the CQC and a further six as requiring improvement.[116]

Waiting for mental health care

The increased toll of mental illness during the pandemic, and the continued rundown of NHS beds and capacity have led to a significant crisis. Even NHS England has been forced to acknowledge that 1.4 million people are on the waiting list for care, and estimates an additional eight million people would benefit from care, but do not meet current criteria.[117] Despite being under intense pressure for beds,[118] NHS capacity has remained relatively unchanged over the past two years. As part of a policy to move mental health services into the community, NHS bed numbers had fallen from 23,208 in September 2011 to 18,179 in September 2019, before the pandemic began. During the pandemic, capacity changed little and stood at 18,493 in September 2021.

In December 2021 a shocking report in the *Independent*[119] revealed the 'desperate' situation facing mental health services after more than a decade of austerity. Based on leaked data, Rebecca Thomas reported hundreds of patients with serious mental health problems were winding up in A&E, with many waiting over 12 hours for treatment, because mental health hospitals across the country are full to overflowing. Almost all mental health hospitals in London had been at 'black alert' during October and November 2021, meaning their beds were nearly 100% full. Referrals to mental health crisis services had increased by 75% since Spring 2020.

In May 2021 84% of trust leaders told NHS Providers that the amount of time children and young people were currently having to wait to access treatment for services was increasing compared to waiting times six months ago. 78% of trust bosses said they were extremely (47%) or moderately (31%) concerned about their ability to meet the level of anticipated demand for mental health care amongst children and young people for the next 12-18 months.[120]

Reduced and inadequate NHS capacity meant that the NHS had already been forced to turn to the private sector even before the pandemic began, and the massive increase in need for mental health services and the lack of investment has left the NHS even more reliant on the private sector.

A report in the *Financial Times* in January 2022 noted that, despite a sharp increase in need, the private sector was cutting beds for children, with about 325 beds removed in the past five years, leaving just 1,321 beds for child and adolescent mental health services (CAMHS) in England.[121] The *HSJ* flagged up fears that mental health budgets could fall as a share of NHS spending in 2022-3, and trigger new cutbacks.[122]

The past two years have seen the quality of care in a number of hospitals run by private companies, particularly in the area of CAMHS, castigated by the CQC. The two leading companies, The Priory and Cygnet Healthcare, have both had to close wards as a result of damning CQC reports. St Andrews Healthcare, the leading not-for-profit in the sector, has had severe limitations put on its services due to CQC reports. As a result it has significantly scaled back its CAMHS services, with plans to sell its Mansfield site to Nottinghamshire Healthcare NHS Foundation Trust.[123]

With the NHS so reliant on the private sector, there are fears that any reduction in beds will mean the private providers will charge the NHS higher fees for care, which already costs between £500 and £1,300 per bed per day.

Up to date: plans for long-term privatisation

Integrated private consultancies

As this book is completed, the Health and Care Bill is proceeding through the Lords. Campaigning and lobbying for amendments continues, and some MPs are seeking to throw out the whole Bill, but given the Tory majority in the Commons a version of it is certain to become law. The NHS will therefore be substantially reorganised into 42 local 'integrated care systems' (ICS) each run by an Integrated Care Board from July.

Many feared the Bill would allow private companies to sit on ICBs and shape decisions on the spending of billions. The only actual example suggesting local ICS might consider this appears to have been in Bath and North-East Somerset, Swindon and Wiltshire, where a community services contract led to Virgin Care's local managing director Julia Clarke being listed in 2021 as a member of the 'Partnership Board' running the shadow 'Integrated Care System'.[124]

The danger that such arrangements might become the norm in ICBs with statutory powers may have been averted by government amendments to the Bill. The new chair of the Bath and North-East Somerset, Swindon and Wiltshire ICS has assured local campaigners there will be no private sector representation on that ICB. But the establishment of ICSs will inevitably bring a further expansion of private sector involvement in both the structure and working of the ICBs, and in the Long Term Plan's heavy focus on investment in 'digital' techniques and apps.

The 2017 shortlist of half a dozen companies to advise on technical aspects of creating 'integrated systems' has been massively expanded into a huge catalogue of organisations and (mainly) private companies that are all pre-approved to offer advice under the Health Systems Support Framework (HSSF). This began with a list of around 80 providers[125] and has grown to around 200 companies that have been accredited by NHS England to provide support under dozens of topic headings, many of which concern data and digital transformation.[126] At least 30 of the firms are US-owned, offering expertise drawn from operating the notorious American health insurance market.

> NHS England explains that: the Framework provides a quick and easy route to access support services from innovative third party suppliers at the leading edge of health and care system reform, including advanced analytics, population health management, digital and service transformation.[127]

However, the more money that is spent on dodgy management consultants' whizz kiddery, questionable apps, digital quackery and the US interpretation of 'population health management' the less is left to fund the core NHS business of delivering safe and high quality care for sick patients. Most plans for digital systems still take no serious account of the needs of millions of people who for a wide variety of reasons are 'digitally excluded' from fully utilising the latest ideas.[128]

Virgin sold off to venture capitalists

December 2021 brought the news that one of the most prominent privatising companies was not finding the market conditions in a cash-starved NHS as congenial as they had expected. Virgin Care, Richard Branson's company which set out from 2008 to compete for NHS and social care contracts all over the country, especially in primary care, community health care, children's services, sexual health and urgent care, had been handed over to venture capitalists Twenty20 Capital, and rebranded as the HCRG Care Group.[129]

Virgin Care at one point seemed to be one of the most successful private firms in scooping up contracts after the 2012 Health & Social Care Act, and won £2bn of contracts in five years from 2013-2018.[130] It even felt bold enough to sue a group of Surrey NHS commissioners who had dared to terminate a contract, and won what was later revealed to be £2m in damages.[131]

Virgin boss Richard Branson was widely disbelieved when he claimed the company was not aiming to make profits and would reinvest any surpluses – but there was no such promise from the new owners. The company is aiming big. Virgin Care was Twenty20 Capital's seventh transaction in 2021, and its fourth acquisition in the health and social services sector; the company's website declared ominously that it is looking for 'significant returns in 2-5 years'.[132]

Virgin Care's boss Dr Vivienne McVey, staying on as chief executive under HCRG, may insist that only the owner and name of the company have changed, and 'everything else remains the same', but it's not clear how many commissioners of Virgin Care's contracts will be happy to see health and care services taken over by Twenty20 Capital.[133]

Delivering – for the private sector

The NHS England 'Delivery Plan' to tackle the growing backlog of waiting list treatment, announced on 8 February 2022, lacks sufficient investment and, most important of all, a workforce plan. The 50-page document[134] also admits from the outset that it doesn't cover mental health, GP services or urgent and emergency care, all of which are facing dire and worsening problems after a decade of underfunding compounded by the 2-year pandemic.

It talks in abstract terms about expanding the NHS workforce and 'physical capacity', but it does not even discuss ways of reopening NHS beds. The focus is on long-term reliance on the 'capacity' of the private sector, which means funnelling even more NHS cash into the same private hospitals and private sector providers, which have already shown themselves during the pandemic to be dreadful value for money.

NHS England appears to have learned nothing from the huge, remarkably unproductive effort to block book up to 8,000 private hospital beds in 2020,[135] which resulted in the 27 private hospital companies delivering 43% less NHS-funded healthcare than they did in the in the twelve months before the pandemic.[136]

Insofar as there is any plan at all for expanding capacity it is based on effectively institutionalising NHS dependence on private sector hospitals and beds. A 2-page section of the document is focused on 'Making effective use of independent sector capacity'. It makes clear from the outset that a long-term partnership 'with our independent sector partners' will be 'crucial in providing the capacity we require'.

It goes on to insist that '[Integrated Care] Systems will include local independent sector capacity as part of elective recovery plans, and will work in partnership with independent sector partners to maximise activity to reduce waiting times sustainably'.

In some cases the private providers are overseas: In November 2021, 14% of all scans including X-rays and MRI scans were 'outsourced', owing to a shortage of radiologists in the UK.[137] This shortfall has been highlighted by the Royal College of Radiologists, but resulted in virtually no media or ministerial reaction.[138]

Moreover, the increasing reliance on private beds and services means that, despite all the rhetoric about 'integration', the NHS itself cannot run sustainably as a coherent and comprehensive public service.

Paying more to use private beds

To use the private sector as additional capacity means the NHS paying over the odds to make it profitable for them, leaving a lopsided 'partnership' with companies which benefit either way from a lengthening NHS waiting list. It also means dividing up the already over-stretched NHS workforce to send teams from major hospitals to deliver operations in small-scale private hospitals miles away.

The other problem with this reliance on private hospitals is that they are not evenly distributed across the country, but concentrated in London, the south-east and more prosperous populations. Many more deprived areas which are supposedly to be 'levelled up' have no significant access to private hospitals, and will be left out of this aspect of the Delivery Plan.[139]

Where private hospitals are available as 'partners' this means in the long term the NHS would be confined to a role of providing emergency services, medical care and more costly, complex treatments that the private sector has always avoided.

This would leave the private hospitals their preferred, profitable caseload of 'high volume and low complexity conditions', but also perhaps 'some cancer pathways and diagnostics'. The private hospitals would be free to pick and choose the level of care they see as most profitable and wish to provide.

Another implication of this 'partnership' is that the private sector, which trains no staff, and has always relied on poaching NHS-trained staff, could even be drawn in to designing 'a joint approach on workforce...'.

The Delivery Plan will be welcomed by private sector hospitals and providers. It threatens to consolidate the biggest-ever expansion of spending on private providers as a permanent feature of the NHS.

Both the decade of austerity and the pandemic have proved awfully fertile ground for the growth of private providers seeking to pick up a growing slice of the NHS budget. Long term publicly funded contracts to deliver NHS care offer the private sector stability and guaranteed income.

Even if Rishi Sunak and the Johnson government were willing, and felt able, to deliver a fully privatised US-style system based on health insurance and personal payment, there seems no reason for private providers to prefer it. The new status quo allows them to quietly accumulate profits from the NHS – while HMRC does most of the hard work of collecting in the money on their behalf.

NOTES

1   Lowdown series, https://lowdownnhs.info/?s=history+of+privatisation
2   Lister, J. (2008) The NHS after 60, for patients or profits? Middlesex University Press
3   Davis, J., Tallis, R. (eds) (2013) NHS SOS, One World, London
4   Davis, J., Lister, J., Wrigley, D. (2015) NHS For Sale, Merlin, London
5   https://www.centreforpublicimpact.org/case-study/privatisation-uk-companies-1970s/
6   https://www.theguardian.com/politics/2016/nov/25/margaret-thatcher-pushed-for-breakup-of-welfare state-despite-nhs-pledge
7   https://www.thetimes.co.uk/article/million-nhs-operations-could-be-carried-out-privately-cz6s3fj6qq8
8   https://www.ihpn.org.uk/news/dr-howard-freeman-health-foundation-report-rightly-emphasises-key-role-of-independent-sector-in-providing-capacity/
9   https://www.nhsconfed.org/articles/role-independent-sector-nhs-busting-myths
10 https://www.ihpn.org.uk/wp-content/uploads/2018/03/Acting-without-delay-helping-the-NHS-with-delayed-discharge.pdf
11 https://ifs.org.uk/uploads/BN268-Recent-trends-in-independent-sector-provision-of-NHS-funded-elective-hospital-care-in-England1.pdf
12 https://www.ft.com/content/e9ac6302-f000-4c7a-a7ad-1094c130625a
13 https://www.england.nhs.uk/statistics/wp-content/uploads/sites/2/2021/02/Beds-Timeseries-2010-11-onwards-Q3-2020-21-ADJ-for-missings-DE5WC-1.xls
14 Timmins N (2005) Election 2005: from millions to billions in eight years, Financial Times April 19
15 https://fullfact.org/health/how-much-more-nhs-spending-private-providers/
16 https://questions-statements.parliament.uk/written-questions/detail/2017-03-01/66091
17 https://blogs.lse.ac.uk/politicsandpolicy/nhs-spending-on-the-independent-sector/
18 https://questions-statements.parliament.uk/written-questions/detail/2017-01-23/HL4882
19 https://blogs.lse.ac.uk/politicsandpolicy/nhs-spending-on-the-independent-sector/
20 https://lowdownnhs.info/analysis/pieces-of-the-puzzle-on-privatisation/
21 https://www.hsj.co.uk/coronavirus/revealed-the-private-hospitals-handed-the-largest-covid-19-contracts/7028648.article
22 https://assets.publishing.service.gov.uk/government/uploads/system/uploads/attachment_data/file/1052421/dhsc-annual-report-and-accounts-2020-2021-web-accessible..pdf
23 https://www.hsj.co.uk/finance-and-efficiency/leaks-reveal-two-thirds-of-private-hospital-capacity-went-unused-by-nhs/7029000.article

24 https://www.hsj.co.uk/coronavirus/exclusive-medical-leaders-seek-to-shame-private-hospitals-and-their-staff-into-supporting-nhs/7029276.article

25 https://lowdownnhs.info/private-providers/10bn-spend-on-private-hospitals-to-bridge-gap-in-nhs-capacity/

26 https://lowdownnhs.info/news/nhs-funds-siphoned-off-as-beds-stand-empty/

27 https://lowdownnhs.info/news/centenes-investment-shake-up-could-mean-nhs-u-turn/

28 https://investors.spirehealthcare.com/media/n4gj5ud5/2020-full-annual-report.pdf

29 https://investors.spirehealthcare.com/media/fjklf4bx/strategic-report-2020.pdf

30 https://www.ramsayhealth.co.uk/about/latest-news/ramsay-health-care-uk-celebrates-official-opening-of-buckshaw-hospital

31 https://inews.co.uk/news/health/private-hospitals-provided-average-seven-covid-beds-day-2bn-government-contracts-1015414

32 https://inews.co.uk/news/health/private-hospitals-provided-average-seven-covid-beds-day-2bn-government-contracts-1015414

33 https://www.theguardian.com/society/2021/feb/26/nhs-gp-practice-operator-with-500000-patients-passes-into-hands-of-us-health-insurer

34 https://www.theguardian.com/politics/2022/feb/09/johnson-appoints-former-private-health-executive-as-no-10-head-of-people

35 https://www.healthcaredive.com/news/centene-rethinking-international-business-divest-non-core/611403/

36 https://www.fiercehealthcare.com/payers/centene-posts-599m-profit-q4-2021-year-after-posting-loss-fourth-quarter-2020

37 https://www.ihpn.org.uk/news/new-foi-figures-show-low-levels-of-nhs-competitive-tendering/

38 https://sbs.nhs.uk/proc-framework-agreements-support

39 https://nhsproviders.org/media/4885/state-of-the-provider-sector-0518.pdf

40 https://onlinelibrary.wiley.com/doi/epdf/10.1111/puar.13031

41 https://www.thecaterer.com/news/foodservice/can-outsourcing-buy-more-for-less-in-the-nhs

42 https://www.nationalhealthexecutive.com/News/controversial-leicester-nhs-contract-scrapped-four-years-early

43 https://www.huffingtonpost.co.uk/entry/nottingham-university-hospitals-carillion-contract_uk_5891f523e4b064366c57c9c6.

44 https://lowdownnhs.info/hospitals/7211/

45 https://www.hsj.co.uk/epsom-and-st-helier-university-hospitals-nhs-trust/hospital-brings-cleaning-and-catering-in-house-to-support-minority-ethnic-communities/7030312.article

46 https://lowdownnhs.info/hospitals/unions-win-fight-for-staff-to-move-back-in-house/

47 https://lowdownnhs.info/news/hinchingbrooke-staff-celebrate-as-outsourcing-plan-dropped/

48   https://www.bma.org.uk/media/1984/bma-privatisation-of-the-nhs-in-england-jan-2019.pdf

49   https://www.nhsforsale.info/contract-failure/50-examples-of-nhs-outsourcing-failures/

50   https://healthemergency.org.uk/pdf/Smoke%20and%20mirrors.pdf

51   https://www.theguardian.com/society/2015/jan/20/circle-failure-hinchingbrooke-hospital-poor-nhs-contract

52   https://www.cqc.org.uk/location/RQQ31/reports

53   https://healthemergency.org.uk/pdf/Smoke%20and%20mirrors.pdf

54   https://www.pulsetoday.co.uk/news/technology/gp-practices-suffer-disruption-after-privatisation-of-support-services/

55   https://www.pulsetoday.co.uk/news/practice-personal-finance/gp-satisfaction-with-capita-plunges-to-21-official-survey-shows/

56   https://www.benefitsandwork.co.uk/news/capita-putting-patient-safety-at-risk-claims-bma

57   https://www.health.org.uk/publications/a-year-of-plenty

58   https://www.ft.com/content/61fe9a49-514a-487f-a0c2-3e1f1e2aae3b

59   https://www.centene.com/who-we-are/leadership/brent-layton-president-coo-centene.html

60   https://www.centene.com/content/dam/centenedotcom/investor_docs/Centene-2020-Annual-Review_508.pdf page 8

61   https://elpais.com/ccaa/2016/11/22/valencia/1479834022_535319.html

62   https://elpais.com/ccaa/2017/03/28/valencia/1490687933_974918.html

63   https://elpais.com/ccaa/2016/12/01/valencia/1480592395_059047.html

64   https://www.sciencedirect.com/science/article/pii/S0168851019300223

65   https://www.riberasalud.com/wp-content/uploads/2019/03/Integrated_healthcare_141211.pdf

66   https://www.nottinghampost.com/news/health/controversial-firm-capita-handed-27m-377493

67   https://www.kingsfund.org.uk/sites/default/files/media/Stephen_Shortt_website%20version.pdf

68   https://www.ft.com/content/e5e9b832-93a0-11e7-a9e6-11d2f0ebb7f0

69   https://www.theguardian.com/business/2020/jan/15/carillion-collapse-two-years-on-government-has-learned-nothing#:~:text=The%20demise%20of%20Carillion%20was,sales%20of%20%C2%A35.2bn.

70   https://www.independent.co.uk/life-style/health-and-families/health-news/privatelyrun-hospital-taken-over-by-nhs-after-patient-deaths-following-routine-surgery-8742745.html

71   https://www.bbc.co.uk/news/uk-england-nottinghamshire-38130507

72   https://www.bbc.co.uk/news/business-42666275

73   https://www.theconstructionindex.co.uk/news/view/construction-costs-have-doubled-on-carillions-pfi-hospitals

74   See chapters 3 and 4 above.

75   https://keepournhspublic.com/virgin-threats-net-2m-from-nhs-in-surrey/

76   https://lowdownnhs.info/news/circle-is-broken-by-high-court/

77   https://healthcampaignstogether.com/pdf/HCTNo15.pdf page 7

78   https://healthcampaignstogether.com/pdf/HCTNo11.pdf page 2

79   https://healthcampaignstogether.com/pdf/HCTNo11.pdf page 3

80   https://lowdownnhs.info/news/trade-unions-celebrate-their-successes/

81   https://healthcampaignstogether.com/pdf/Lowdown-issue-04.pdf

82   https://www.longtermplan.nhs.uk/publication/implementing-the-nhs-long-term-plan/

83   https://lowdownnhs.info/news/pet-project-privatised-and-how-many-more/

84   https://lowdownnhs.info/explainers/who-is-inhealth/

85   https://www.theguardian.com/society/2019/mar/27/u-turn-over-plans-to-privatise-cancer-scanning-services-oxford-hospital

86   https://lowdownnhs.info/news/mps-reject-governments-pet-privatisation-project/

87   https://healthcampaignstogether.com/pdf/HCTNo14.pdf page 8

88   https://lowdownnhs.info/comment/se-london-ccg-pathology-outsourcing-set-to-undermine-local-nhs-trust/

89   https://www.nationalhealthexecutive.com/News/nhs-bristol-south-glos-north-somerset-contract

90   https://www.independent-practitioner-today.co.uk/2019/04/birmingham-to-get-new-138-bed-private-hospital

91   Much of this section is drawn from my February 2021 article 'The great consultancy boom – from Covid to ICSs', at https://lowdownnhs.info/coronavirus/the-great-consultancy-boom-from-covid-to-icss/

92   https://www.ncbi.nlm.nih.gov/pmc/articles/PMC6733764/#fnr5

93   https://healthemergency.org.uk/pdf/McKinsey%20report%20on%20efficiency%20in%20NHS.pdf

94   https://www.dailymail.co.uk/news/article-2099940/NHS-health-reforms-Extent-McKinsey--Companys-role-Andrew-Lansleys-proposals.html

95   https://www.ft.com/consultancy-health

96   https://lowdownnhs.info/news/dash-in-to-take-charge-in-nw-london/

97   https://theconversation.com/management-consultants-in-healthcare-do-more-harm-than-good-but-keep-getting-rehired-new-research-155320

98   https://www.hsj.co.uk/policy-and-regulation/nhs-england-hired-consultancy-to-find-out-what-it-is-responsible-for/7025511.article

99   https://www.consultancy.uk/news/25382/16-consulting-firms-awarded-government-coronavirus-contracts

100 https://www.consultancy.uk/news/25382/16-consulting-firms-awarded-government-coronavirus-contracts

101 https://www.favershameye.co.uk/post/future-health-secretary-helen-whately-and-the-firm-that-hijacked-the-nhs

102 https://bylinetimes.com/2021/01/05/government-total-number-private-sector-test-and-trace-consultants/

103 https://www.dailymail.co.uk/news/article-9161125/Test-trace-consultants-earning-average-1-000-DAY.html

104 https://news.sky.com/story/five-person-team-get-25k-a-day-to-work-on-test-and-trace-system-12105042

105 https://www.sbs.nhs.uk/nhs-sbs-about-us

106 https://www.sbs.nhs.uk/fas-consult-18-multidisciplinary-consultancy-services

107 https://www.nuffieldtrust.org.uk/files/2017-01/into-the-red-nhs-finances-web-final.pdf

108 https://assets.publishing.service.gov.uk/media/59e48f8ced915d6aadcdaf0a/cygnet-cambian-final-report.pdf

109 https://www.laingbuisson.com/uncategorised/independent-mental-health-hospitals-buoyant-enjoying-robust-demand/

110 https://questions-statements.parliament.uk/written-questions/detail/2018-11-14/191398

111 https://www.theguardian.com/society/2019/may/11/priory-mental-health-profits-death

112 https://assets.publishing.service.gov.uk/media/59e48f8ced915d6aadcdaf0a/cygnet-cambian-final-report.pdf

113 https://www.cygnethealth.co.uk/content/uploads/2019/05/Quality-Account-17-18-FINAL.pdf

114 https://www.nhsforsale.info/private-providers/the-priory-partnerships-in-care-new/

115 https://www.ft.com/content/4f428fc8-fefe-11e9-b7bc-f3fa4

116 https://lowdownnhs.info/news/american-firms-scooping-up-mental-health-contracts/

117 https://lowdownnhs.info/news/low-nhs-capacity-in-mental-health-leaves-it-beholden-to-private-companies/

118 https://lowdownnhs.info/news/mental-health-data-backs-up-concerns-over-services/

119 https://www.independent.co.uk/news/health/mental-health-nhs-covid-pressure-b1964693.html

120 https://nhsproviders.org/resource-library/surveys/children-and-young-peoples-mental-health-survey

121 https://www.ft.com/content/27818675-ee95-4915-a956-6a387abc599d

122 https://www.hsj.co.uk/mental-health/stevens-intervenes-to-force-transparency-on-funding-amid-fears-of-service-cuts/7031658.article

123 https://lowdownnhs.info/news/low-nhs-capacity-in-mental-health-leaves-it-beholden-to-private-companies/

124 https://lowdownnhs.info/integrated-care/virgin-given-seat-on-ics-board/

125 https://lowdownnhs.info/integrated-care/whos-cashing-in-on-icss/

126 http://www.labournet.net/other/2201/tentacles1.html

127 https://www.england.nhs.uk/hssf/background/

128 https://www.iriss.org.uk/resources/esss-outlines/digital-inclusion-exclusion-and-participation

129 https://www.kentonline.co.uk/sheerness/news/branson-sells-virgin-care-to-twenty20-capital-258405/

130 https://www.theguardian.com/society/2018/aug/05/virgin-awarded-almost-2bn-of-nhs-contracts-in-the-past-five-years

131 https://www.theguardian.com/society/2017/dec/29/richard-branson-virgin-scoops-1bn-pounds-of-nhs-contracts

132 https://twenty20capital.com/how-we-work/

133 https://lowdownnhs.info/integrated-care/virgin-given-seat-on-ics-board/

134 https://www.england.nhs.uk/coronavirus/wp-content/uploads/
     sites/52/2022/02/C1466-delivery-plan-for-tackling-the-covid-19-backlog-
     of-elective-care.pdf
135 https://inews.co.uk/news/health/private-hospitals-provided-average-seven-
     covid-beds-day-2bn-government-contracts-1015414
136 https://chpi.org.uk/blog/smoke-and-mirrors-nhs-englands-totally-
     transparent-multi-billion-pound-deal-with-the-private-hospital-industry/
137 https://www.ft.com/content/e0a69335-9951-4a97-aa17-f3cb3ce60374
138 https://lowdownnhs.info/news/nhs-diagnostics-losing-out-to-the-private-
     sector/
139 https://ifs.org.uk/uploads/publications/wps/WP201715.pdf

Fighting back: a long, honourable tradition

Ways to get involved

Campaigners defending the NHS and fighting for its future have an astonishing history of unbroken resistance running back to the 1970s, making the NHS quite unique among the public services.

Every major cutback or threat to local services has been challenged, and from the very outset in the 1980s each attempt to carve up and contract out services to private companies has been fought by health workers, by campaigners and often by a concerned and angry local public.

The most militant resistance came in a near 10-year wave of 'work-ins', or occupations of hospitals threatened with closure between 1976 and 1985, in which staff took over control and maintained patient care. The first of these was the 3-year 'work-in' at the Elizabeth Garrett Anderson Hospital for Women (EGA) in central London, which began in 1976, with the clinical and support staff taking over the management of the hospital, and exploiting loopholes in the legislation that required staff to be paid as long as they were caring for patients. In 1979, after rumoured intervention by the Queen to Margaret Thatcher, the work-in with a formula that kept the hospital open until 2001. The example of the EGA work-in inspired a wave of occupations between 1976 and 1985, fighting to save smaller hospitals, mainly in in London but spreading to the home counties and Oxfordshire, and as far as Thornton View Hospital near Bradford. In all of the most successful and long-lasting occupations the combination of local community activists and support with the backing of staff and health and other trade unions was key to the success.

The resistance has not been constrained by the politics of the government: while in the 1980s the fightback was amplified by widespread working-class hostility to Margaret Thatcher and her government, the 'internal market' reforms and tight cash limits implemented by John Major's government were also challenged.

And when Tony Blair's government took over in 1997, there was barely a pause before local and national campaigning resumed against cutbacks, centralisation of services, contracting out, the use of the Private Finance Initiative to finance new hospitals, and from 2000 New Labour's preoccupation with building up a new private sector such as Independent Sector Treatment Centres.

From 2010 the Cameron government made it easy to spot the difference, with its immediate imposition of austerity and the unveiling of Andrew Lansley's massive plans to restructure the whole NHS in order to entrench a competitive market. Campaigning has continued ever since, against the various ways in which these policies have emerged, as outlined in Chapter 5.

However, recent campaigns lack the breadth and intensity of the campaigning against Thatcher in the 1980s, not least because of the relative weakening of the trade union movement. A generation of radical younger activists from the 1980s has been followed by a widespread lack of involvement from the next generation, and much cagier policies from Labour as the main opposition party.

Nonetheless the stubborn resistance of campaigners, coupled with the inherent contradictions and weaknesses of some of the most controversial proposals have brought some notable victories, especially at local level, including the defeat/collapse of plans to privatise older people's services in Cambridgeshire, and cancer care in Staffordshire.

A mass campaign, in alliance with local councillors, successfully defended Lewisham Hospital, defeating health secretary Jeremy Hunt twice in court. Persistence paid off when Charing Cross and Ealing Hospitals were also saved from closure, and the disastrous plan to reconfigure services in north-west London was finally thrown out in 2019, after years of campaigning backed by Hammersmith and Fulham and Ealing councils. A long and stubborn campaign also successfully beat back plans to close acute services at Huddersfield Royal Infirmary.

The trade unions have also won some important battles, although up to now they have not been able to mobilise a concerted national fight on pay. Plans to contract out support staff into 'wholly owned companies' have been defeated by strikes, or the threat of strikes, in a number of trusts; and the tide has begun to turn on privatisation, with some large London trusts persuaded to bring support services, and their thousands of staff, back 'in-house' after years of contracting out.

It even seems as if some sections of the Health and Care Bill still grinding through Parliament could also be substantially amended by the House of Lords (see Chapter 4), although this will not be clear until it is returned to the Commons, where the Tory majority is still dominant. There is little sign that many, if any Tory MPs will break ranks on the Bill.

The examples cited above, along with many others, show that despite the prophesies of doom from conspiracy theorists who keep prematurely announcing the demise of the NHS, national and local campaigning has been and continues to be effective. There is still plenty of the NHS to defend and it is vital that we fight on to stop further inroads, as well as trying to push back the privatisation that has so weakened it.

What works?

The stock response of the left to any campaign is to call for trade union action. However, it's clear from experience over five decades that strikes, and the credible threat of strikes, are most likely to take place on trade union issues – pay and conditions; jobs; staffing and safety concerns; discrimination; victimisation of union reps; contracting out and the creation of wholly owned companies, rather than on broader defence of services, cuts, closures and reorganisation.

Moreover, where trade unions do resort to industrial action, they frequently do so without reaching out for support from the wider local public. Quite often local campaigners from outside the NHS have to take the initiative in offering to build broader solidarity in the local communities, support picket lines, and back up the trade union case. Where these links are successfully established (notably in recent strikes against wholly owned companies, pay and conditions disputes with private contractors and seeking to bring outsourced services back in house) the unions clearly recognise the value of such support and have said as much to Health Campaigns Together and Keep Our NHS Public.

By contrast, in almost every sustained campaign against hospital cutbacks and closures, access to care and centralisation of services at the expense of local communities, the lead has been taken not by unions but by NHS campaigners.

Sometimes these campaigns manage to win significant financial, political or organisational support from one or more local health union or other unions, but quite often there is no local tradition of cooperation, or there may even be political friction between union activists and campaigners. This can mean there is no vigorous approach made, or campaigners' appeals for support are unsuccessful. Where this happens, it leaves a problem of trade union members and their local leaders sometimes lagging behind local awareness of problems that will affect their jobs and working conditions, and campaigns weaker than they should be.

The vital core of campaigns

The energy and commitment required to build each of these local campaigns is quite extraordinary and the dedication of the campaigners has been a vital factor in keeping the fight alive. In each campaign a core of a few key activists, often retired or in part-time work, sometimes former health professionals or academics, but often simply people who have worked tirelessly to get on top of complex issues, have taken on the demanding task of analysing and criticising the detailed proposals as they take shape.

They have followed the labyrinthine process of meetings of local CCG governing body meetings, trust and foundation trust boards, local authority scrutiny panels and health and wellbeing boards, and worked in various ways to explain the policies and their implications, as they emerge, to wider groups of campaigners.

Many have produced briefing documents and press releases for local news media; some have developed their own sophisticated printed or online newsletters, websites and social media to continue to widen their reach and convey their concerns to a local public that would otherwise be quite unaware of the threat to their local services.

Without this core of largely self-taught, self-motivated experts, who have popped up time and again when local services have been put at risk, the broader campaigns could not exist. The few people who follow the policies, and then dig through to find the information and the necessary facts and figures to refute the contentious plans, may also themselves develop tactics to fight back. Or they may find local people who can work with them to find ways to convert the hard knowledge into campaigns, develop leaflets, statements, and soundbites that can get the information across. The strongest campaigns over the years have devised an astonishingly wide variety of stunts and photo opportunities and organised larger scale events that reach out on a much more popular level.

In most of the successful campaigns this hard graft results in winning support, or at least more serious coverage, from the local newspaper (some local papers have mounted their own petitions and campaigns and sponsored events) and coverage from local broadcast news.

But strong campaigns can also begin to persuade councillors and MPs that they too could need to take a stand or risk a loss of credibility and electoral support. In some important cases, notably the relatively recent campaigns in north-west London and Lewisham, council leaders have embraced local campaigns and taken advantage of the many ways in which local councils can still, even after all the erosion of their local powers, find ways to lend material as well as political support to campaigns.

Councillors are the local politicians most immediately exposed to such risks, since they stand for election more often, and are most likely to be judged on their performance on local issues. This was vividly illustrated in north-west London, where Labour commitment to defend Charing Cross Hospital, while Tory councillors publicly backed the closure, led to the defeat of a flagship right-wing Tory council in Hammersmith and Fulham in 2014. Labour have since consolidated their control, and gone on to successfully defend the hospital.

The stance of councils on local hospital plans does not necessarily follow party lines. In the last couple of years Telford's Labour council has unsuccessfully sought a judicial review to block plans by Shropshire NHS bosses to centralise emergency services in Shrewsbury: but Medway's Tory council has also supported the unsuccessful legal challenge by campaigners to plans to centralise stroke services in Kent. The possibility of winning even some Tory councils to active opposition to controversial NHS policies underlines the need for campaigners to subordinate their own party political allegiance. Campaigners need to focus first and foremost on hard facts and evidence rather than abstract ideology and knee-jerk political responses if they are to have most impact.

This is also a key factor in persuading Tory MPs to break ranks and stand up for local services, which will only happen when they have been convinced that the concerns raised by campaigners are solidly based, and that the opposition to the local plans is big and broad enough to potentially erode their voter base. The memory of the example of David Lock, elected in 1997 as New Labour MP for Wyre Forest, covering Kidderminster Hospital, still resonates with MPs. Lock unwisely opted to ignore the powerful local campaign defending the hospital and instead supported the plans of Worcestershire Health Authority that stripped out most acute services from Kidderminster in order to centralise them in a PFI hospital in Worcester, 16 miles away. His decision led to Labour losing control of Wyre Forest council and Lock himself famously losing his own seat in 2001 to an independent candidate, Richard Taylor of Hospital Concern. Since then we have seen prominent New Labour and Tory politicians in similar situations publicly siding with local campaigns in their constituency, even while still upholding the policies of their party in government.

While it gives some political satisfaction to trumpet such instances as hypocrisy, the reality is that between general elections the only way to prevent a government-backed policy being carried through is by forcing divisions amongst the government's own MPs.

This reflects the fact that many of the government's own electoral supporters will also be bitterly opposed to this aspect of their policy, not least in the former so-called 'red wall' seats that flipped from Labour to Conservative in 2019. If they want to go beyond the level of propaganda and make a real difference to policies and decisions on the ground, campaigns on national and significant local issues need to aim to build a broad enough support to force such splits and rifts in the ruling party.

National campaigns

For anyone wanting to get involved in campaigning there have been various attempts to link up campaigns into wider coalitions, and we have included a brief listing of the main ones that have been active at national level. None of the campaigns listed here have any party political affiliations, although they may have supporters who are members of any party.

London Health Emergency (LHE): With initial core funding for an office and staff from the Greater London Council, London Health Emergency was formed as an attempt to link up separate borough-based campaigns against closures of hospitals across London in 1983. It became the first organisation to develop 'evidence-based campaigning'[1] on the NHS, and to try to build a coordination of local campaigns at national level. It established a tabloid newspaper, *Health Emergency*, and a separate network of affiliations from local campaigns, pensioners groups, trade union branches and TUCs across the country, as well as working with all four of the main health unions at regional and national level.

LHE publicised and gave practical support to local campaigns on a wide range of issues – from hospital cuts and closures, mental health services, privatisation, and in defence of jobs, services, staffing levels of staff fighting for fair pay. It no longer operates as a separate campaign, having merged its resources into Health Campaigns Together, but an extensive archive of its newspapers and work is still available online at https://healthemergency.org.uk/

NHS Support Federation: In 1989 a new organisation was established with support from the NHS Consultants' Association. The NHS

Support Federation ('the Fed') developed as an independent group of researchers and journalists seeking to ensure universal fair access to high-quality healthcare. Led by Paul Evans, the Fed is a voluntary organisation and funded by supporters including health professionals and the general public, grant-making trusts and the trade unions. It supports the NHS and its staff through evidenced-based campaigns and policy discussions. In 2019 Paul Evans and his team linked up with John Lister from Health Emergency to launch a fortnightly online news bulletin on the NHS and health policy, The Lowdown. https://nhscampaign.org/, https://lowdownnhs.info

Keep Our NHS Public: In 2005 LHE, the Fed and the NHS Consultants' Association were among the founders of a new organisation, Keep Our NHS Public (KONP). This launched as a focal point for campaigners determined to fight PFI and the growing privatisation of clinical services by the New Labour government. It developed a national network of local groups based on individual membership, with decisions taken by a Steering Group and carried out by an Executive Committee, each composed of lay members.

KONP has grown strongly since 2010 to become the dominant membership-based campaign fighting for the NHS. It now has over 70 local groups, some national affiliates and support from some trade unions and organisations focused on other areas of social justice campaigning. KONP has a national office and a number of paid staff, who organise the work and administer the organisation. Its newsletter subscribers have gone up 10-fold, and membership three-fold in the last 3 years. In 2021, as outlined in Chapter 3, KONP had sufficient credibility to initiate the successful and authoritative Peoples Covid Inquiry, chaired by Michael Mansfield QC and calling on expert testimony from dozens of witnesses. https://keepournhspublic.com/

Health Campaigns Together: In the autumn of 2015, a new organisation, based not on individual membership, but an alliance of organisations, was established in an effort to reconnect NHS campaigners with the national health unions. It had initial support from the TUC, Unite and GMB, and was publicly launched as Health Campaigns Together at a lively conference of almost 200 in London in January 2016. It went on to launch a quarterly tabloid newspaper, playing a leading role in the fight to expose NHS England's plans for a new reorganisation of the NHS into 44 Sustainability and Transformation Plans, and linking up with local campaigns across England.

At the end of 2016 Health Campaigns Together, backed by KONP made the call for what proved to be the biggest-ever demonstration for the NHS, in London on 4 March 2017 – an event which was built by a coalition including Peoples Assembly and almost all the major trade unions, and hit headlines in most newspapers and broadcast news. A follow-up Day of Action called at short notice in February 2018 also mobilised many thousands, including a substantial rally in Whitehall.

The alliance has continued to organise events and share information, producing an online monthly news bulletin since September 2020 while circulation of the newspaper was not possible. It has secured dozens of affiliations, including national support from Unite, GMB, UNISON, the pharmacists' union PDA, a number of non-health unions, and has kept close working links with the TUC. https://healthcampaignstogether.com/

SOSNHS: By the end of 2021 it became clear that a new brutal austerity is to follow the pandemic, with a renewed squeeze on NHS finances. Health Campaigns Together and Keep Our NHS Public responded with a fresh initiative, joining with like-minded campaigns and the trade unions to build the broadest possible, high-profile alliance to demand more capital and revenue funding for the NHS.

This has become the successful SOSNHS campaign, which at time of writing has won support of 53 trade unions and campaigns at national level, and mobilised support on the ground in 85 towns and cities for a vibrant Day of Action, and a petition of 175,000-plus signatures demanding 'Emergency funding now!' https://sosnhs.org/

Other useful organisations

Among the many organisations that have rallied to the support of SOSNHS, and offer their own take on the fight for the NHS, but also have a broader range of interests, are:

We Own It. We Own It is an independent organisation, not connected to any political party and mostly funded by individual donations, which campaigns against privatisation of any public services, and for '21st century public ownership'.[2] It argues that 'public services belong to all of us – from the NHS to schools, water to energy, rail to Royal Mail, care work to council services,' and points out 'there are lots of brilliant examples of public ownership we can learn from in the UK and around the world.' On the NHS, We Own It regularly works with KONP and Health Campaigns Together, and was an early supporter of SOSNHS. https://weownit.org.uk/

The People's Assembly Against Austerity was launched in 2013 to bring together campaigns against cuts and privatisation with trade unionists in a movement for social justice. It initially aimed to develop a strategy for resistance to mobilise millions of people against David Cameron's government, but has continued to mobilise, and has been a key ally of Health Campaigns Together and KONP in building a series of successful activities since 2017, including SOSNHS. https://thepeoplesassembly.org.uk/

NHS Million is a non-profit campaign with the aim of creating a 'superteam' of a million people who will love and cherish the NHS and want to celebrate everything that's great about it – even when the chips are down. It was founded in 2016 by Joseph Blunden, an NHS employee who works with hospitals around England to improve the experience of patients and staff, and Dr Katharine Rogerson, a children's doctor based in London. In 2020, they were joined by Dr Samantha Batt-Rawden, an intensive care and air ambulance doctor in the south-east. https://www.nhsmillion.co.uk/

The **National Pensioners Convention** (NPC) was founded by former Transport and General Workers' Union trade union leader Jack Jones in 1979 as the only national campaign group in the country which is run by pensioners for pensioners. It is run through a network of affiliated local groups, who are active in their local areas and regions promoting the NPC's campaigns, and many of these have for years been the mainstay of local campaigning for the NHS. https://www.npcuk.org/

The **Centre for Health and the Public Interest** (CHPI) is 'An independent non-party think tank promoting a vision of health and social care based on accountability and the public interest.' It was founded in 2012 after it became clear that a growing democratic deficit had emerged in the way decisions about health and social care policy were being made.

The aim of the Centre is to subject current policy to careful, evidence-based critical scrutiny; explore alternative solutions to the challenges of providing universal high quality health and social care; promote greater democratic determination and accountability in the organisation and delivery of health and social care; and advocate for probity, integrity and transparency in health policy-making. https://chpi.org.uk/

Medact was formed in 1992 as a merger of two organisations: the Medical Campaign Against Nuclear Weapons (MCANW), and the Medical Association for the Prevention of War (MAPW). The newly-formed Medact recognised the need to adopt a broader global health agenda – incorporating the health threats posed by climate change as well as the structural violence of unjust economic policies and systems. Medact also hosts the **Patients Not Passports** campaign, made up of healthcare workers, migrants, community campaigners, 'and anyone who believes in the universal right to health'. It fights against Hostile Environment immigration policies in the NHS and especially for the end of racist charging policies in the NHS – 'policies which turn health workers into border guards, deter patients from seeking care, delay life-saving treatment, and saddle patients with huge debts they are unable to pay'. https://www.medact.org/

Doctors for the NHS began life in 1976 when the NHS Consultants Association (NHSCA) was formed by medical consultants with a strong commitment to the NHS and its founding principles. The NHSCA founded the NHS Support Federation in 1989 and was one of the organisations that founded Keep Our NHS Public in 2005. In 2014 it decided to broaden its base, and changed its name to Doctors For the NHS, welcoming doctors from primary and secondary care, trainees and Public Health doctors as well as consultants. DFNHS argues that 'service must come before profit: our overriding policy goal is to save the NHS from breaking apart'. https://www.doctorsforthenhs.org.uk/

Disabled People Against Cuts (DPAC) was formed by a group of disabled people after the first mass protest against the austerity cuts and their impact on disabled people in Birmingham in October 2010. DPAC 'is for everyone who believes that disabled people should have full human rights and equality'. It is for everyone that refuses to accept that any country can destroy the lives of people just because they are or become disabled or have chronic health issues. It is for everyone against government austerity measures which target the poor while leaving the wealthy unscathed. https://dpac.uk.net/

As is evident from this list, the number of organisations fighting for the NHS is striking, and it is clear that there is now at least the kernel of a mass movement of people who understand the threats to the NHS and are prepared to campaign to defend it.

You may already be involved. But if you have been moved by reading this book to join us, there are a number of things you can do. You can, for example, join Keep our NHS Public and find out about a local campaign near you: or you can donate on a one off or regular basis to any of the organisations listed above which campaign on a national level.

The NHS is still a hugely important achievement, a vital bastion of social solidarity: its future is crucial for all of us. The essential thing now is to remember and act on the words attributed to its founder, Aneurin Bevan: 'The NHS will last as long as there are folk left with faith to fight for it.'

NOTES

1   https://www.tandfonline.com/doi/full/10.1080/13619462.2018.1525299
2   https://weownit.org.uk/sites/default/files/attachments/When%20We%20 Own%20It%20-%20A%20model%20for%20public%20ownership%20 in%20the%2021st%20century.pdf

Expert contributions

We wanted other voices in the book and the following section contains essays from invited contributors, each with their own area of expertise.

Michael Marmot sets the scene with an account of the austerity which the government imposed on the country in the decade leading up to the pandemic. As a result of these policies we lost a decade in terms of health. The poor got poorer, the vulnerable became more vulnerable and social and economic inequalities increased. The pandemic then exposed and amplified these inequalities, and as a result mortality rates were disproportionately high in the vulnerable groups. He calls for us to address the underlying causes of health inequities and to Build Back Fairer by putting equity of health and well-being at the heart of all policy.

Martin McKee looks at why the UK has had such a very bad pandemic by any measure, including the number of deaths and the economic hit to the country. This is particularly striking when we should have done much better given our top-class scientific establishment, our strong public health community and the universal coverage afforded by the NHS. He points the finger firmly at poor political leadership, and praises NHS staff for doing 'remarkably well'.

Neena Modi and **Kevin Courtney** both look at the effects of the pandemic on children and young people. These include the direct effects of the virus itself including long Covid, and the indirect effects including school closures and consequent interruption of education, social isolation and the pressures on children's support services. They both highlight the fact that many children's services, in particular mental health services, were already in crisis and could not deal with the increased demand brought on by the pandemic. As a consequence there is now a huge unmet need and no sign that the government is preparing to address it. They are both clear that the effects of the pandemic will be long lasting for many children, and reflect years of underinvestment in education and other vital public services.

At the other end of the spectrum **Jan Shortt** examines how the deterioration of elder care in the decade leading up to the pandemic meant that elder services were already in crisis when the pandemic struck. Chronic underfunding of social care and the NHS led to staffing problems, and a policy of marketisation led to care moving into the private sector. These, combined with the pandemic, meant a very high death rate among the elderly, in particular those in care homes. She calls for a National Care Service, publicly owned and free at the point of need.

David Wrigley writes about how primary care was already on its knees before the pandemic, struggling with dwindling resources, workforce burnout and the social consequences of the Tories' decade of austerity. Having rapidly reorganised to deal with the demands of the pandemic, and having been overlooked in the government's outsourcing of vital services such as Test and Trace, GPs were then vilified in a campaign run by the *Daily Mail*, aided and abetted by Sajid Javid.

Lobby Akinnola and **Michael Mansfield** both address the government's refusal to set up a timely inquiry into their failures during the pandemic. Akinnola writes from the heart about what the loss of his father from Covid meant to his family, and invites us to multiply that by the 180,000 Covid deaths since the start of the pandemic. He questions the poor political decisions that led to this shocking figure and demands a comprehensive investigation into why the government presided over so many deaths. Mansfield accuses the government of 'misconduct in public office' and of dragging its feet over setting up an inquiry in time to learn lessons. He cites the People's Covid Inquiry as an example of how it is possible to rapidly identify mistakes in order to rectify them.

Sara Gorton, **Rehana Azam** and **Colenzo Jarrett-Thorpe** examine the many problems of the NHS from the perspective of the health unions. Gorton addresses the malign effects of privatisation, the work-force crisis, the need for fair pay and earnings in solving the problems of recruitment and retention, and the vital role of trade unions in protecting staff and the NHS going forward.

Azam also looks at who the real key workers are, and at the effects of a decade of austerity on their pay. Jarrett-Thorpe points out that staff were already under siege and demoralised before the pandemic and that there is no plan in the unwanted Health and Care Bill to address the workforce issues. He also asks how a workforce which is already stretched beyond its limit is supposed to tackle the government's unrealistic demands going forward.

All deplore the outsourcing of public sector jobs and the market-isation of health care.

Roger Kline looks at the treatment of NHS staff and how a culture of discrimination, bullying and 'a pervasive culture of fear' has affected morale. He highlights the chronic mismatch between demand and resources which has led to pressure on managers and a culture of concealment rather than openness. He too has harsh words for the continuing lack of workforce planning. He calls for inclusive and compassionate leadership to encourage a culture which is safer for patients and staff.

Finally, **Roy Lilley** reminds us that the true purpose of the NHS is to give us all peace of mind, but questions for how much longer. He reminds us that there is an unprecedented mountain of work facing the NHS but no plan to deal with it beyond more unrealistic targets which put yet more pressure on existing staff. Once again the government is accused of having failed the most vital component of the NHS, the workforce.

What is clear from our contributors is that the government had already run public services into the ground in the decade before the pandemic. The pandemic further showed why the NHS and its staff need urgent attention, but all agree that the government has no plan. As Rehana Azam writes – the backbone of the NHS is the immeasurable bravery, compassion and selflessness of its staff. It is not a commodity to be bought and sold. The NHS can't survive on applause alone.

Build Back Fairer and the NHS

Professor Sir Michael Marmot

Institute of Health Equity, University College London

'Why treat people and send them back to the conditions that made them sick? is the opening line of my book, *The Health Gap.*[1] As the present book makes clear, the NHS has been, and is, under threat. Particularly during a pandemic, when the health system is vital, and health workers are selflessly sacrificing their health and comfort, attention turns to health care. I agree that it should. But my focus continues to be on the conditions that make people sick in the first place – the social determinants of health and health equity.

In the 12 months from December 2020 my colleagues and I at the UCL Institute of Heath Equity produced a series of reports, with the title *Build Back Fairer*[2][3]

The rationale of these reports is that the *status quo ante*, before the pandemic, was unacceptable. Coming out of the pandemic, we should be seeking to learn lessons as to how to make the societal changes that would lead to greater health equity, to build back fairer. With a focus on social determinants and health equity, I want to show where we were before the pandemic, the impact of the pandemic on health equity, and what needs to happen next.

Health in England before the pandemic – a decade of austerity.

Health Equity in England: the Marmot Review 10 Years On[4] was published in February 2020 on the 10 year anniversary of *Fair Society Health Lives, the Marmot Review.*[5] The 2020 report examined what had happened to health and health equity in England in the decade from 2010, and to the social determinants of health, as represented by our recommendations as to how to reduce health inequalities.

A word about terminology. Our 2010 Marmot Review was commissioned by the government as a strategic review of health inequalities. Subsequently, we established ourselves as the Institute of Health **Equity**. We followed the WHO lead. Systematic inequalities in health between social groups that are avoidable by reasonable means, and are not avoided, are inequitable. Setting them right is a matter of social justice.

My simple summary of health in England since 2010 is that we lost a decade. Until 2010, life expectancy in England had been increasing about one year every four years for men and for women. After 2010, the rate of improvement slowed dramatically and just about ground to a halt. That slowdown in improvement was more marked in the UK than in any other rich country, except Iceland and the USA. Classify people by where they live and classify where they live by level of deprivation and there is a social gradient in life expectancy. That gradient grew steeper in the decade from 2010. There were, too, important regional differences.

For the least deprived decile, the regional differences were small and life expectancy improved a little in all regions of England. If you're rich it doesn't matter so much in which part of the country you live. For the most deprived decile, the regional differences were much bigger. Life expectancy improved in London but went down in nearly every region outside London. The social gradient in mortality was steeper in Northern Regions than it was in London. An important challenge: the same national index of multiple deprivation has bigger implications for ill-health in the North.

Before the pandemic, then, life expectancy increase had slowed dramatically, health inequalities were increasing, and life expectancy for the poorest people was getting worse. The obvious question is the extent to which this dismal health picture was the result of policies of the government that took office in England in 2010. When we published our *10 Years On* report we were cautious, as academics are, as to whether there was a causal link between policies of austerity and the damage to public health. I have become less cautious. Public expenditure was decreased, child poverty increased in part as a result of fiscal policies – tax and benefits – that were sharply regressive, particularly for families with children: the lower the household income the sharper the reduction in income as a result of fiscal policy changes post-2010. The poor got poorer.

In our 2010 review we coined the phrase proportionate universalism. A typical British approach to welfare of targeting the worst-off may benefit the target group, but it misses the gradient in health. People above the cut-off may have better health than the poorest, but have worse health than those less deprived. A more Nordic approach argues for universalism, policies that include everyone. We proposed combining these two approaches: universal policies with effort proportional to need. The NHS is an example of proportionate universalism. It is universal, available to all free at the point of use, but effort is proportionate to need. Here need is defined clinically. When defined socioeconomically, there is concern at the inverse care law.[6]

Post 2010, we saw a form of inverse care law applied to local authority spending. Spending per person by local authorities was reduced, but the reduction was regressive – the more deprived the local authority the greater the reduction. Reduction in spending per person was 16% in the least deprived quintile of local authorities, going down to a reduction of 32% per person in the most deprived quintile. Such regressive approaches to public spending could indeed have played a role in the increase in health inequalities, and the decline in life expectancy in the poorest areas.

The pandemic exposed and amplified health inequalities

Three striking features of the pandemic are central to the health equity agenda. First, mortality rates from Covid-19 follow the social gradient: the greater the deprivation of the area the higher the Covid mortality. The gradient for mortality from Covid, is similar to the gradient from all causes. Simple observation with profound implications. Government rhetoric has been of the form that now we have vaccines, we need little else to control the pandemic. The evidence shows something quite different. Yes, we need to control the virus, but the pandemic made even clearer that we need to address the underlying causes of health inequities.

Second, race/ethnicity has come to prominence. Covid mortality rates are especially high in people classified as Black African, Black Caribbean, Pakistani, Bangladeshi and, to a lesser extent, Indian. Much of this excess can be attributed to where people live and other socioeconomic characteristics, but not all of it. In the first wave of Covid, for example, a disproportionate number of the doctors who died were from these ethnic groups. We need to take seriously structural racism.

Third, in the first and second waves the UK handled the pandemic really badly. Jeremy Farrar, director of the Wellcome Trust, documents his frustration with the government.[7] The delays in taking preventive action, the money wasted on inadequate test and trace systems, the failure to provide adequate financial support for people expected to self-isolate all contributed. In fact, in the first wave, the UK had the highest excess mortality in the world – i.e. excess total deaths over expected, based on the previous five years.

I wondered at the link between the UK's poor health performance in the decade after 2010, as summarised above, and poor management of the pandemic. My speculation is that the link could work at four levels: poor governance and political culture, increasing social and economic inequalities, disinvestment in public services, and high levels of illness that predispose to greater severity of infection.

Build Back Fairer

In our 2010 report we had six domains of recommendations: give every child the best start in life, education, employment and working conditions, having enough money to lead a healthy life, healthy and sustainable environments in which to live and work, and taking a social determinants approach to prevention.

We have since added two more, addressing racism, discrimination and their consequences; and pursuing strategies to improve health equity and deal with the climate crisis together.

Building back fairer will entail action on all of eight of these recommendations. The question is who should be responsible. I said that we had produced four reports with the title *Build Back Fairer:* for England, the Eastern Mediterranean Region of WHO, Greater Manchester, and Hong Kong. It is our judgement that action can take place at national level, England; at supranational level, the Eastern Mediterranean Region; at city and regional level, Greater Manchester; and at sub-national jurisdictional level, Hong Kong.

At the request of local and regional government, we have been working in England with Greater Manchester, Gateshead, Cheshire and Merseyside, Lancashire and Cumbria, London, Luton, Waltham Forest; and with Gwent in Wales. Some of these requests for help have come from Integrated Care Systems. I started by saying that we need universal access to health care, but my concern was with the conditions that made people sick – the social determinants of health. Working with ICSs we are exploring the ways they can use their resources and actions to address the social determinants of health.

I speculated that there were four mechanisms linking our poor health pre-pandemic with our poor management of the pandemic. Building Back Fairer should address these. In 2010, we were presented with austerity as if it were the only choice. At the beginning of the pandemic, the government said: 'whatever it takes'. It turns out that austerity was not some kind of economic necessity but was a policy choice. The decision should not be tax good or bad; not public expenditure desirable or non-desirable; but what is necessary to meet the needs of the population.

Second, the increase in economic and social inequality needs to be reversed. With a cost of living crisis, the incomes of the poorest are set to fall alarmingly with consequent damage to health. Third, reducing public services for the poorest communities is depriving them of vital services that will again damage health and increase health inequalities. There must be reversal of these regressive cuts. Fourth, improving the health of the population is a public good, quite apart from helping people to resist the ravages of a pandemic.

The mission of the whole of society should be similar to the mission of the NHS: to put equity of health and well-being at the heart of all policy.

NOTES

1. Marmot M. The Health Gap. London: Bloomsbury; 2015.
2. Marmot M, Allen, J., Goldblatt, P., Herd, E., Morrison, J. Build Back

Fairer: The COVID-19 Marmot Review. The Pandemic, Socioeconomic and Health Inequalities in England. London: Institute of Health Equity; 2020.

3. Marmot M, Allen, J., Boyce, T., Goldblatt, P., Morrison, J. . Build Back Fairer in Greater Manchester: Health Equity and Dignified Lives. London: Institute of Health Equity; 2021.

4. Marmot M, Allen J, Boyce T, Goldblatt P, Morrison J. Health Equity in England: The Marmot Review 10 Years On. London UK: Institute of Health Equity, UCL; 2020.

5. Marmot M. Fair society, healthy lives : the Marmot review ; strategic review of health inequalities in England post-2010: [S.l.] : The Marmot Review; 2010.

6. Hart JT. The inverse care law. Lancet. 1971;i:405-12.

7. Farrar J, Ahuja, A. . Spike: The Virus vs. The People - the Inside Story. London: Profile Books; 2021.

Why the UK failed the Covid-19 test

Martin McKee

Professor of European Health at the London School of Hygiene and Tropical Medicine

If you look at the number of deaths that have been attributed to Covid-19 you can see that the UK has done very badly, especially since the end of the first wave of the pandemic.

Our death toll is not absolutely at the top in Europe, because Spain and Italy did very badly in the first wave, but it is not where we might expect given our scientific excellence.

Of course we need to be careful with comparisons. Take excess mortality, widely seen as the gold standard. But remember that the UK has not seen the improvements in the historic death rates that form the baseline for this measure; in 2015 for example, we had a very high death rate during the flu epidemic. So, in a way, to look at the last five years almost rewards the country with highest levels of winter mortality, and the UK has much higher rates than most European countries.

Clearly in economic terms, too, we took the biggest hit among the G7 countries. Although the prime minister keeps saying that we're growing fast, we need to remember that is only because we deteriorated more to begin with and, unlike most other European countries, we are still far below where we were.

So on any measure we've done badly. But the key point to remember in all of this is that we should have done really well, because we have a top-class scientific establishment. We've got a strong public health community. And we've got universal coverage in the NHS. On paper, as we can see from the 2019 Global Health Security Index which measures technical preparedness, we were second best prepared in the world, and yet that didn't manifest itself in good outcomes.

My assessment is that NHS staff did remarkably well in repurposing things and finding new ways of working, although of course they experienced diversions and distractions, like the Nightingale hospitals. But we had a real problem with political leadership. Mr Johnson wasn't at the first five Cobra meetings and was distracted by several other things, including 'getting Brexit done', (something he has yet to achieve, as the people of Northern Ireland know.)

Had we locked down a week earlier, we estimate that he would have saved about half the lives in the first wave.

To pick out one mistake above all, it would be the failure of the UK to learn from East Asia, and in particular to appreciate that Covid 19 is an airborne infection; people in Hong Kong were saying that very early on and we wrote about it too.

After locking down, the UK still had problems because we lagged behind others with our testing capacity. By contracting out test, trace, isolate and support we ended up with a bizarre and ineffective model. The UK had also allowed its stocks of PPE to run down, even exporting some as a donation to China. The NHS also began with lower provision of beds and ventilators than other comparable countries.

Despite Matt Hancock's claims, the government didn't throw a 'protective ring' around care homes, which in our modern economy, like prisons and immigrant detention centres, are a means of monetising the storage of human beings. They are essentially financial vehicles which happen to have people in them. The idea that they're there to look after people is missing the point: they have a different set of objectives. Even though it was known that they were 'institutional amplifiers' and that infection would spread very quickly in them, no proper precautions were taken to prevent that happening, resulting in over 30,000 excess deaths.[1],[2]

Finally, and importantly, the government didn't give meaningful and easy to access support for people to isolate, which meant that the chain of infection wasn't being broken. We don't have the social safety nets in place that other countries have, with their strong social welfare support and much better quality housing. We don't have the degree of food security; in large parts of the UK people are living very precarious existences in multi-generational households, not sure what is going to happen from one week to the next. That is a real weakness.

Of course, a lot of the problem was due to the decade of austerity and the way that they've spent the money during the pandemic. Always turning first to the private sector, despite the repeated failures of some parts of it, has been a major weakness.

The government made a complete mess of procurement; last year's report from the European Commission's expert panel on effective ways of investing in health lists many examples of procurement failures from the UK.[3] A large part of the problem is that the anybody in the NHS or elsewhere, who has the ability to negotiate will be picked out by the private sector and employed on a much higher salary there.

The difficulty is that the private providers can find work in other countries and other sectors, so they will only get involved in health if it is sufficiently profitable, and they will only sign a contract that really exempts them from any risk. What they are doing in essence is transferring risk to the public sector. The risk is nationalised, but the profits are privatised. And I think that's the fundamental problem. I don't have an ideological issue about using the private sector. I just feel that if you're going to use it, then the risks and benefits need to be evenly distributed – and they're not, and they never are, so it's a more of a practical argument rather than an ideological one.

1   https://www.nuffieldtrust.org.uk/news-item/covid-19-and-the-deaths-of-care-home-residents?

2   https://www.health.org.uk/news-and-comment/news/new-analysis-lays-bare-governments-failure-to-protect-social-care-from-covid19

3   https://www.euriphi.eu/news/public-procurement-in-healthcare-systems-opinion-of-the-expert-panel-on-effective-ways-of-investing-in-health/

To sum up on the handling of the pandemic I'll use the analogy of a ship in a storm: you need a captain who knows where they're going, with a map, and a crew that is working together, on a ship that doesn't have holes in the floor that people fall through. At the moment we have a crisis of governance, with lack of accountability, scrutiny, and judicial review. I think that captures my view as to where we went wrong, and the lessons still have not been learned.

Children, the NHS and the Covid-19 pandemic

Neena Modi

BMA president and Professor of Neonatal Medicine at Imperial College, London

What happened to children in the UK during the pandemic

The full extent of the impact of the Covid-19 pandemic on infants, children, and young people will take time to emerge, but it is already clear that these effects have been profound, and for many will be long-lasting. Children have been affected through the direct effects of infection, school closures, and social isolation, but they have also paid a heavy price indirectly through effects on parental mental health and income, the pressures on support services that were already struggling, and the exacerbation by the pandemic of pre-existing health inequalities. The status of children in society, and the extent to which their needs are recognised in biomedical research also merit consideration.

The effects of infection

It soon became apparent that children were less susceptible to severe acute illness from the SARS-CoV-2 virus. This was followed by recognition of a severe inflammatory multi-system syndrome occurring in a small minority of infected children. The incidence is uncertain but has been reported at 3.0-4.5 per 10,000 in the US and UK.[1] These figures may be over-estimates as the number of asymptomatic infections is unknown. Conversely, the true global burden may be far greater as many cases will neither have been recognised nor reported. As the pandemic progressed, reports also began to emerge of what has become known as 'long-Covid', now defined as symptoms that continue or develop after a confirmed diagnosis of Covid-19, affect physical, mental, or social well-being, interfere with some aspect of daily living and persist for at least 12 weeks after first testing positive.

A systematic review of publications describing long-Covid in childhood conducted by the authors of this case-definition, identified a rate ranging from 1–51%,[2] a reflection of the considerable uncertainty around the true prevalence. The overall incidence of infection in children is unknown because neither antigen nor antibody testing has been systematic. As of December 2021, there had been 118 child Covid deaths reported in the UK.[3]

Physical health

The Early Intervention Foundation has highlighted a decrease in physical activity and increase in food insecurity along with an increase in unhealthy food choices as prime effectors of a probable decline in child physical health during the pandemic.[4] Other possible contributors to declining child health are the mixed messages around Covid-19 vaccines, with pregnant and breast-feeding women initially advised against vaccination.[5] This, coupled with a failure to counter vaccine disinformation, and the resulting rise in vaccine hesitancy, are all factors that are likely to have contributed to added breastfeeding challenges against a background of poor UK rates, and a decline in childhood vaccine uptake. Breast-feeding and vaccination against common childhood infections are cornerstones of child public health.

Perhaps the most shocking evidence of deteriorating physical health in children comes from data from the National Child Measurement Programme published in November 2021.[6] This shows a sharp increase in the prevalence of obesity to 14.4% in the reception year and 25.5% in year 6.

The prevalence of obesity in reception had been relatively stable since 2006/07 but rose from 9.9% in 2019/20 to 14.4% in 2020/21. Obesity prevalence is highest in Black children, and over twice as high for children living in the most compared to the least deprived areas. The overwhelming majority of obese children will remain obese as adults, and adult obesity is a major cause of declining longevity and healthy life expectancy. These data thus represent a demographic time bomb that will blight the lives of the affected children forever, and in turn their own children.

Mental health

There is general agreement that on average, the mental health of children and young people has worsened during the pandemic. Girls and those with pre-existing mental health issues experienced more negative impacts.

The mental health of the UK's children and young people was already deteriorating before the pandemic. In September 2021, NHS Digital published data comparing findings from the Mental Health and Young People Surveys in 2017 and 2021.[7] This showed further deterioration with increases in the rates of probable mental disorders from 11.6% to 17.4% in 6- to 16-year-olds and 10.1% to 17.4% in 17- to 19-year-olds.

The proportion of children and young people with possible eating problems also increased, from 6.7% to 13.0% in 11- to 16-year-olds, and 44.6% to 58.2% in 17- to 19-year-olds. Of note, deteriorating mental health is not a uniform occurrence, with a quarter of young people in the 2021 Mental Health and Young People Surveys reporting that their lives had improved during lockdown.

However, the number of children being referred to mental health services increased during the pandemic, and prevalence data must also be set against the longstanding evidence of the inadequacy of children's mental health services. In January 2021, the Children's Commissioner called on the UK government to acknowledge this and increase access to care[8], and in December 2021, the UK Parliamentary Health and Social Care Committee called for 'urgent action to prevent mental health services slipping backwards as a result of additional demand created by the pandemic and the scale of unmet need prior to it'.[9]

There is an inter-relationship between child and parent mental health. The children of those with special educational needs and disabilities, and children and young people from disadvantaged backgrounds are more susceptible to behavioural, emotional and attentional difficulties, compared to those growing up in more favourable circumstances. This speaks to the need for calls for increased service provision to be matched with attention to many of the root causes of mental health difficulties, which lie outside healthcare, in adversity, disadvantage, and widening societal inequities.

Physical and sexual abuse; safeguarding

Increasing numbers of young people were taken into care during the pandemic. The National Society for the Protection against Cruelty to Children reported increased vulnerability of children and young people to online abuse, abuse within the home, and criminal and sexual exploitation, with evidence that normal safeguards to protect children and young people were also reduced.[10] A clinical team from Great Ormond Street Hospital reported a marked increase in the incidence of abusive head trauma, with ten children presenting during the first month of national lockdown, compared to less than one per month in the same period over the previous 3 years, describing this as a 'silent epidemic'.[11]

Referrals of children to social services increased by up to 40% in some parts of England, with reports of foster places in short supply, public sector provisions inadequate, and private care providers charging councils, already struggling with shoe-string budgets, up to £10,000 a week per child. The lead for the independent national review into children's social care is reported as describing the children's services system as a 'tower of Jenga held together by Sellotape'.[12]

Education

There is unequivocal evidence from a number of sources that missing out on education damages children's cognitive development, academic attainment, and long-term productivity. The school closures during the spring and summer of 2020 were followed by substantial drops in attainment across all subjects and year groups. However, younger children showed bigger reductions in attainment than older age groups, as did children eligible for the Pupil Premium, and schools with higher levels of deprivation, situated in the north and midlands, showed greater declines.[13] A report on primary school attainment showed that all year groups struggled to reach age-related expectations due to the pandemic, but the youngest children have been most severely affected. Prior to the pandemic 82%, 79%, and 83% of Year 1 pupils achieved age-related expectations in reading, writing and maths respectively, but by summer 2020 these figures had dropped to 60%, 54%, and 59%.[14]

Getting it right for children in the future

There have been well-documented failings in UK government actions, and it is appropriate to continue to ask for lessons to be learnt. Among these were whether children's needs were adequately considered; were they treated equitably in research; was the strong likelihood of adverse impact though disruption to education by school closures, and social isolation, adequately considered in mitigation strategies; and was the appalling excess impact of the pandemic on children from disadvantaged communities exaggerated by neglect of public health, the NHS, and social care in the preceding decade?

Research

Children could have been better served in research effort. Clinical trials involving children are essential, and the World Health Organisation recommends the inclusion of children and adolescents in health-related research unless there is a good scientific reason to justify their exclusion.[15] However, by July 2021, 18 months after the onset of the pandemic, and 6 months after the licensing of the first vaccines, only a handful had been tested in young people over the age of 12, and in the UK official advice was that only adolescents who are clinically vulnerable, or who live with vulnerable adults, should be vaccinated.[16]

Some arms of the landmark RECOVERY trial evaluating Covid treatments included children,[17] but recent studies such as the

PANORAMIC trial of antivirals excludes all under 18-year-olds.[18] In future, regulators should be more robust in requiring the inclusion of children in clinical trials as the default, unless strong scientific grounds exist for their initial exclusion. If so, they must be proactive in requiring systematic capture of information on safety, efficacy, and pharmacokinetics in children who receive vaccines or medications under emergency use authorisations.

There was also insufficient use of the opportunity to build on one of the UK's greatest assets, the NHS, in establishing long-term surveillance studies in children. SARS-CoV-2 is believed to be a neurotropic virus, hence the effects of infection on the developing brain are of considerable importance. This provides strong justification for systematic, long-term surveillance of infected infants, infants born to infected mothers, and infected children as a component of their normal care.

It is worth questioning why funds were not made available to establish strong and systematic national surveillance programmes that included marginalised groups such as children, pregnant and breastfeeding women, and ethnic minority communities, to identify the short, and long-term impacts of infection, as well as the safety and efficacy of vaccines, as part of a coordinated public health effort.

Public trust and respect

Measures to combat disinformation with powerful, public health messages that are trusted, have been lacking. The loss of trust in the UK government, the breaking of Covid rules by many politicians and policy-makers in a series of now well-documented instances, and the disdain for fundamentally important public health practices such as mask-wearing, will have contributed to the shabby performance of the UK in safeguarding the public.

Trust is also built through compassion and respect. In April 2020, a 13-year-old boy died alone, his family having been refused permission to be with him in hospital.[19] In May 2021 an NHS nurse, Jenny McGee, who had cared for the prime minister when he was in intensive care with Covid, resigned saying she felt the government 'hadn't led very effectively', that there had been 'indecisiveness', 'so many mixed messages', and that nurses were 'not getting the respect we deserve'.[20]

Despite repeated calls, the prime minister refused to meet representatives of the organisation 'Covid-19 Bereaved Families 4 Justice' until September 2021. Trust in, and respect for government has been severely damaged during Covid and will likely have long-lasting effects, especially in relation to public health messaging.

Investing in public services

A hallmark of the UK government's response to the pandemic has been a preference to direct public funds to the private sector instead of using pandemic requirements as an opportunity to provide much needed and long-overdue support to a struggling public sector. This in effect, rubbed salt into the wounds of over a decade of savage austerity in health care, social care, and education.

The shocking waste of public funds on the failed test and trace system, inappropriate procurement of ventilators and Personal Protective Equipment, private hospital capacity that was never used, and Nightingale Hospitals that could never have been staffed given the 100,000 NHS vacancies, are well-documented examples.

However, children have been particularly badly served by stretched social care, safeguarding, and mental health services. The catastrophic failure of the UK test and trace system, outsourced, and placed in the hands of those with little experience, meant that opportunity to gain early information on transmissibility was lost. Hence decisions around social mixing, and reopening of schools and universities were severely hampered by the lack of information on the role of asymptomatic children in transmitting the virus. The government pledge of £3bn to help students catch up on 'lost learning' has been predominantly outsourced to for-profit firms, many of whom have little or no experience, and who siphon off a hefty proportion of the allocated public funds.[21,22] These political and ideological choices have intersected with long-standing disparities, to worsen the impacts of Covid upon the most vulnerable in society, children.

1 Dionne A, Son MB, Randolph AG (2022) An Update on Multisystem Inflammatory Syndrome in Children Related to SARS-CoV-2 Pediatr Infect Dis J 2022; 41(1):e6-e9

2 Stephenson, Pinto Pereira, Shafran et al CLoCk Consortium, Ladhani SN. (2022) Physical and mental health 3 months after SARS-CoV-2 infection (long COVID) among adolescents in England (CLoCk): a national matched cohort study. Lancet Child Adolesc Health. 2022 Feb 7: S2352-4642(22)00022-0

3 https://www.longcovidkids.org/post/child-covid-19-cases-long-covid-hospital-admissions-deaths-11th-december-2021deaths; last accessed 14.02.22

4 https://www.eif.org.uk/; last accessed 14.02.22

5 https://www.bmj.com/content/372/bmj.n4/rapid-responses

6 https://digital.nhs.uk/data-and-information/publications/statistical/national-child-measurement-programme/2020-21-school-year/deprivation; last accessed 14.02.22

7 https://digital.nhs.uk/data-and-information/publications/statistical/mental-health-of-children-and-young-people-in-england/2021-follow-up-to-the-2017-survey; last accessed 14.02.22

8 Children's Commissioner. The state of children's mental health services 2020-21. Jan 2021 https://www.childrenscommissioner.gov.uk/wp-content/uploads/2021/01/cco-the-state-of-childrens-mental-health-services-2020-21.pdf; last accessed 14.02.22

9 https://committees.parliament.uk/committee/81/health-and-social-care-committee/news/159548/mental-health-services-for-children-and-young-people-risk-backward-slide/; last accessed 14.02.22

10 https://learning.nspcc.org.uk/research-resources/2020/social-isolation-risk-child-abuse-during-and-after-coronavirus-pandemic; last accessed 14.02.22

11 Sidpra et al (2021) Rise in the incidence of abusive head trauma during the COVID-19 pandemic Arch Dis Child 2021 Mar;106(3): e14

12 https://www.theguardian.com/society/2021/aug/11/revealed-englands-pandemic-crisis-of-child-abuse-neglect-and-poverty+; last accessed 14.02.22

13 Blainey K, Hiorns C, Assessment from Hodder Education, Timo Hannay, SchoolDash, The impact of lockdown on children's education: a nationwide analysis (2020) https://www.risingstars-uk.com/media/Rising-Stars/Assessment/Whitepapers/RS_Assessment_white_paper_1.pdf; last accessed 14.02.22

14 https://junipereducation.org/resource/press-releases/youngest-pupils-learning-worst-affected-by-covid-19-pandemic-new-report-reveals/; last accessed 14.02.22

15 Council for International Organizations of Medical Sciences (CIOMS) in collaboration with the World Health Organization (WHO) (2016) International ethical guidelines for health-related research involving

humans [online]. Available: https://cioms.ch/wp-content/uploads/2017/01/WEB-CIOMS-EthicalGuidelines.pdf; last accessed 14.02.22

16   https://www.nature.com/articles/d41586-021-01898-9; last accessed 14.02.22

17   https://www.recoverytrial.net/files/recovery-protocol-v21-1-2021-12-19-1.pdf; last accessed 14.02.22

18   https://www.panoramictrial.org/; last accessed 14.02.22

19   https://www.independent.co.uk/news/uk/home-news/coronavirus-boy-death-hospital-london-youngest-uk-ismail-abdulwahab-a9439526.html; last accessed 14.02.22

20   https://www.bbc.co.uk/news/uk-57162428; last accessed 14.02.22

21   https://www.theguardian.com/education/2021/feb/28/englands-catch-up-tutors-are-being-short-changed-by-private-employers; last accessed 14.02.22

22   https://www.theguardian.com/education/2022/feb/13/ive-got-one-word-for-the-tutoring-programme-disastrous; last accessed 14.02.22

The pandemic exposes problems in education

Kevin Courtney

Joint General Secretary, National Education Union (NEU)

Like the NHS, our schools and colleges had to find ways to continue to provide services during the pandemic. Despite two general lockdowns they never completely closed, but stayed open throughout for vulnerable students and children of key workers.

I want to focus on three issues which became more obvious during the pandemic, and which have parallels with the NHS. I also want to explain how we as a trade union have been able to have an impact and force some changes that have saved lives.

Inequality and its impact on children

It is now accepted that poverty is a factor in shaping the health of the population. But there is less recognition of the ways in which poverty and inequalities can limit educational achievement and future options.

Politicians in all political parties talk about 'failing schools', and about poor schools in the north. And the difference is important: kids in schools in Oldham don't get the same GCSE results as kids in Chipping Norton, where David Cameron was the MP.

It's disgraceful, and it's a real mark of something wrong in our country. But it is not because they've got poor schools, it's because of the level of poverty. If you look at life expectancy, you find that, too, is worse in Oldham than in Chipping Norton; politicians don't blame that on poor hospitals, or failing doctors and nurses in the north, that would be too much.

But they do say that about teachers and schools. So it's really important to put the blame where it belongs, not on the teachers, nor on the parents; if you're working three jobs to put food on the table you can't always be there to read to your child.

There's another set of Tory arguments that blames 'failing families' and talks about 'lack of ambition' for their children, but of course high-quality jobs are not evenly distributed across our society.

Inequality was there before the pandemic, but Covid-19 has further exposed the fact that child poverty is on the rise in the UK, with all the consequences that brings for the health, well-being and educational outcomes.

During the pandemic our members actually saw inside children's homes through the zoom links. They saw the differences in children's material circumstances. Some children have their own bedroom, their own laptop, a fast broadband connection. And then there are other children who have to share a bedroom with siblings, share a laptop; you see children sharing a bedroom with a parent who works on night shift and is trying to sleep in that room. You see children who have no bedroom, and who are in short life accommodation.

If you're in a house with a garden, that's a really different situation from somebody on the 20th floor of a tower block with no garden or bedroom of their own. These enormous differences in children's lives have a real impact on their education. Teachers try and do their best to make up the gap but there are limits to what can be done.

As a union we have been looking at publicly available data and dividing all the schools into five equal sized groups based on their proportion of children on free school meals. From the highest number of free school meals to the lowest you see a terrible pattern; schools with most children on free school meals suffered the biggest cuts, had the least experienced teachers, and were most likely to be graded as failing (and the least likely to be graded outstanding) by Ofsted.

This reverses all of the incentives you want to have. You want to encourage people to go and work in those schools, but teachers don't want to go to work somewhere that systematically gets graded as failing. We will be highlighting this as much as we can in the debate about 'levelling up', because lots of those schools with the highest numbers on free school meals are in the former 'red wall' constituencies. We want to point out that children are being badly short changed, and we're going to be pressing for more money for everyday running of schools.

The worry is that government now wants a 'catch up' exercise, based on a model of a child who is an empty vessel, and who hasn't had enough stuff put into them during the lockdown. So we get more people – many of them private sector tutors – to push stuff into children faster, to make them catch up. In that model, there isn't a lot of space for mental health, for socialisation, for children playing.

There is also a racial element in the inequalities of course. It is not acceptable that in 2021, 46% of Black children are growing up trapped in poverty. The causes of poverty must be tackled, and so must the causes of racism.

Lack of investment

In Denmark schools were closed for much less time than in England, at least in the early stages of the pandemic, because Danish class sizes are much smaller. There is also far more outside space in their schools, making it much easier to arrange a socially distanced return at an appropriate time than we could in England. The UK has some of the most crowded school and college buildings of any high-income country. The average secondary school has a 97% occupancy rate.

If we're going to reduce class sizes we need to increase staff; that costs more money. Under David Cameron's coalition government, statutory age education, like the NHS, was 'protected' compared with other public services (although there was no protection for nurseries, anything that wasn't statutory age, or post-16s).

But since 2015, from the time when the Tories were first in government alone, there has been no protection; school spending per pupil in England fell by 9% in real terms between 2009–10 and 2019–20. This is the largest cut in over 40 years.[1] The biggest cuts have hit the more disadvantaged schools, rather than the schools in more prosperous areas. Worsening funding of education has meant class sizes across all years have been creeping up, and staff levels running down, leaving the remaining staff more stressed. None of that was good preparation for the pandemic.

The problem with Covid is that it is airborne, and many of our schools don't have good ventilation in place; we could have done something about this if enough funding had been available. Improved ventilation of schools would not only mitigate Covid, it would also reduce infection from flu and other airborne viruses. And a well-ventilated space that is at the right temperature is good for education. If you have classrooms that have too much CO_2 in them and are too hot, you start to doze off. It's not good.

When it comes to online education, most homes have got some sort of smartphone, but many children don't have access to broadband. A sensible approach would be for schools to give equipment to children who need it, so that all children are using the same as one another. We weren't ready for any of that, so it took a long time to get online learning up and running. The government failed time after time to deliver the laptops that they promised, and to deliver the broadband connections that many children needed.

We should in any case be talking to children in schools about online safety and social media, so again there is a real need to invest in our young people, to do what can be done to tackle inequalities and give them a better introduction to the modern world.

Government reforms that make things worse

Education, like the NHS has been subject to a succession of reforms. The Institute of Government report in February 2022[2] looked at the impact of the academisation of education, running down the role of local authorities and creating Multi Academy Trusts instead. This was another factor which impeded government work in dealing with the pandemic: local authorities that should have been coordinating help had been run down.

Another negative preparation for the pandemic was Michael Gove's tenure as education secretary. He set out to remove teacher assessment from the GCSE systems of assessment. Michael Gove and Nick Gibb, who was schools minister from 2010 to 2012 and again from 2015 to 2021, are really committed to SATs, to terminal exams, and the curriculum being about knowledge, not skills.

The question of mental health and our young people didn't start with the pandemic; it has been worrying us for some time. We think that schooling is part of the problem, as well as potentially part of the solution – in particular, the exams, the SATs system, which put an awful lot of pressure on young people, and are a big cause of stress. The Tory party's current education policy does not work properly for young people – or even fit with the needs of British capital.

So we've set up an independent commission into exams assessment, and it's come up with a set of criticisms of the way we organise GCSE, and a set of proposals for discussions about how to go forward.

Our role as a trade union

In March 2020, the government had created the categories of Clinically Vulnerable and Clinically Extremely Vulnerable but hadn't locked down schools. We put out a video which was seen by at least a million people, in which we said to all our Clinically Vulnerable members that their health and safety did not permit them to be at work and they should report to their head saying they weren't available.

That video had quite a big impact on schools and had a significant effect at a time when the government was trying to open up. We published 'Five Tests for Government before schools can re-open', which said what had to be in place.[3] Many schools that were planning to open on the first of June pushed it back, waiting for case numbers to be a bit lower. So we think our role was significant.

Then, in October 2020, when cases were rising fast in schools, we said schools should teach half the class in person, and half the kids at home. Sixth form colleges were already doing it.

In November 2020 we argued for schools to be included in the lockdown, and got some media attention, as well as pushback from some members who thought we were wrong. The government ignored us, and that lockdown in November had nothing like the effect it would have had if they had told schools to do four weeks online learning. That would have brought the infection base rates down much more before the Christmas holiday, and thousands of people would have been saved.

In early 2021 the alpha variant was spreading fast, but the government insisted they were going to open all the primary schools at the start of term. We knew that that was wrong when we saw SAGE minutes, which said that the case rate was massive and 'R'* would not be below one.

We had an online meeting of 40,000 people, perhaps the largest trade union member meeting in history, in which we advised teachers to avail themselves of Section 44 of the Employment Act 1996[4] and refuse to return to work. Primary schools were opening a fortnight before secondary schools, and tens of thousands of our primary school members sent those letters to their heads – and the vast majority of schools didn't open on that Monday

On the Sunday morning on Andrew Marr's programme, Boris Johnson had argued schools were safe, and parents should send children back to school. By 6pm on the Monday evening there was a complete volte-face. Downing Street announced schools were 'vectors of transmission', and they were closing them. The data hadn't changed between Sunday morning and Monday afternoon, so I think our intervention brought the closure forward. It would have had to happen, probably in that week, but in bringing it forward our trade union action saved thousands of lives.

NOTES

1 https://ifs.org.uk/publications/15150
2 https://www.instituteforgovernment.org.uk/news/latest/government-school-reform
3 https://neu.org.uk/press-releases/5-tests-government-before-schools-can-re-open
4 https://www.tuc.org.uk/blogs/can-i-refuse-work-because-coronavirus-we-explain-your-rights

* R = the number of people that one infected person will pass the virus on to

Elder care: why we need a National Care Service

Jan Shortt

General Secretary, National Pensioners Convention (NPC)

The recent history of elder care

Elder care has changed dramatically over the generations that our members can recall. In the late 1940s a typical household would include the extended family who would look after their parents and grandparents. Women tended to stay at home and formal care was probably not considered as an option for many. Younger members of families were involved with the care too, as one of our members recalls: 'when my other gran and her new husband became ill in the 1970s, there were more options, but my parents still felt it was their role to look after them, which meant us youngsters too.'

Into the 1980s families were more dispersed, women were in the employment market. Formal care through residential and nursing homes became more acceptable and better organised, with respite for family carers and enjoyable activities for those being cared for. Homes had also changed, at least the good ones, with quiet rooms, aromatherapy, lots of activities and helpful ideas. But there were still those using medication as a way of maintaining order. Back then local authorities were much better funded and were able to offer a wide range of services; they ran their own care homes; employed staff on public service contracts, offered meals on wheels to those in need of extra support. Meals on wheels was much more than delivering a hot, nutritional meal – it was a means of making sure that the person was well, could be mobile and, if not, ensuring access to the right sort of assistance.

During the 1990s, many care homes were under real pressure; cleaning had been outsourced; the food was unappealing and communal areas could be whatever space was available in the home. It was an era of increasing funding cuts to local authorities who increasingly found they could not maintain their own care homes, resulting in closures, or homes being taken over by the private sector.

There were still those homes that despite everything offered excellent, caring environments for older people, as one of our members experienced. She says:

My Dad was one of the first residents in an 'extra care' home built in partnership between the local authority and the private sector. He was the first chair of the residents' association, and organised Burns nights and other activities. His flat was roomy, with a Juliette balcony, big bedroom, wet room, plus a modern kitchen and 24/7 care on site.

Elder care in hospital was normally in a geriatric ward, and whilst the nursing levels started off being very good, over time cuts to funding and loss of staff meant that wards (nor just those for older people) could not be staffed adequately. There are still some geriatric wards in hospitals today with a team of doctors, nurses and consultants on hand, although recently the lack of numbers taking the training for this specialism means that the volume of work is high and undertaken by small teams.

Devolved nations are formula-funded from Westminster to provide services to older people and they do it differently from the English parliament. Personal care (on assessment) is free in Scotland; home care is free for over-75's in Northern Ireland; and Wales caps costs at £90 per week for home care services. Legislation in England does not cover the devolved nations and therefore those nations can better serve the needs of the people.

More work, less funding

From 2010 the NHS has been chronically underfunded. Social Care (as it is now termed) was even worse. The dreaded means-test, imposed when long term elder care was switched from the NHS to social services in 1993, had already created the road to inequality in access to care. We are now so far down that road, with post code lotteries and the unfairness of care funding, that it will be very hard to change without a radical rethink. It is surely so unfair that someone suffering with cancer can have all their treatment free on the NHS, yet someone with dementia has to be means-tested and pay for some (if not all) of their care.

Very few councils run care in-house: they have become commissioners of services instead of offering hands-on provision by staff employed on public sector contracts. The services commissioned from the private sector are underfunded, with savings often made at the expense of terms and conditions for staff. The crisis has deepened and local authorities have increasingly only been able to care for those with substantial/critical health conditions.

Legislation, marketisation and deregulation served to open up the care sector to profit-making providers owned by private equity funds, as well as to any business that thought they could provide care on the cheap and give their shareholders nice dividends.

Staff employed in residential and nursing homes have seen a change in the level of work needed to care for individuals. Initially, the need was low level, but over time has become more severe. Care and nursing staff are dealing with highly complex needs, often without the numbers of staff required, and in many cases without prior training.

Those working in the private sector are on minimum wage (or even less if they are not paid for their travel time); are often on zero-hours contracts; work long, exhausting hours, but remain dedicated to their task. Retaining staff in the care sector is difficult when supermarkets pay just as much, or more, without the huge responsibilities of caring for someone. The value and respect given to those in the caring profession is often not compatible with the skills, knowledge and understanding needed to work in elder care.

Over the last decade poor provision has been normalised, with care providers struggling with never-ending cuts to funding. District nurses (like all care staff) are too few in number and therefore also struggling to provide services to those in need. Hospital at home is similarly under pressure. There are currently around 1.4 million older people who cannot access care, meaning that their health deteriorates over time until their need becomes critical. Older people now enter their retirement years in poorer health and spend much more of their retirement in ill health than those before them. Organisations providing care at home (domiciliary care) are under-funded, under-staffed and 15 minute visits are the norm. This is no reflection on those organisations or their staff – it is the stark reality of the system in place. Care providers have suffered cumulative cuts in funding which add up to over £6bn, which makes the £60m given to local authorities recently a small drop in the ocean.

For older carers, the difficulties are multiplied several times. Currently carer's allowance is £67.60 per week, rising to £69.70 in 2022/23. However, if you happen to be claiming your state pension and it is more than the carer's allowance, then you lose it. It is then left to the individual to seek out means-tested benefits. Many older carers have health issues themselves, and also suffer from poverty. The Care Act 2014 gave carers rights to assessment of their needs separate from that of the person being cared for, followed by the appropriate support. As is normal, local authorities were not funded fully to carry this out, with the result that many family carers are desperate – certainly during and since the pandemic when support services were not there and are still not back in place. Fully funding and implementing the Care Act would go a long way to valuing those who set aside their lives to care for another.

Elder abuse has been a long-term concern with many tragic stories told in the media. However, media interest seems to have plateaued, even though elder abuse is still a feature of many older people's lives.

The effects of staff shortages

Nursing and care staff shortages and end of life care are among issues of concern. We have a shortage of social care beds and nursing staff, and more than 40,000 social care staff left the sector in the past six months. The UK is below average compared to other high-income countries, with community and mental health nurses in particularly short supply. The latest official figures show 110,000 vacant posts in the NHS, including almost 2,000 community nurses and 11,300 mental health nurses. One particular problem arising from staff shortages, which affects both health and care, is delayed discharge. This happens when the patient is ready to leave hospital but cannot go because the necessary support in the community is not available. This is associated with mortality, infections, depression, reduction in mobility, and the loss of daily activities.

Marie Curie's Better End of Life Report 2021, stated that many had endured tremendous hardships, with care being compromised by shortages of medicines and staff. One NPC member said, 'We are living and dying without adequate support'.

No wonder that, as the *Lancet* reports, in the five years before the pandemic (2014-2019) life expectancy went down in almost one in five communities for women, and one in nine communities for men. Patients, family carers and staff deserve better.

Radical policy change is needed

There is no doubt that in today's climate of increased poverty across all generations, with inflation raging on essentials like food and fuel, older people having to sell their homes to pay for care and the retention of the means-testing system, that radical changes to policy are needed.

The current system in England means that if you have assets of less than £14,250, care is funded by the state, but depending on income, an individual may have to pay 'housing' costs if in a care/nursing home. If you have assets between £14,250 and £23,250 care is means-tested, and contributions made from assets accordingly. Those with assets over £23,250 have to pay the full cost of their care. Around 300 individuals a week sell their homes to pay care fees.

The system will change in 2023 when care will be funded by the state for people with assets of less than £20,000. For those with assets between £20,000 and £100,000 care will be self-funded, with some state help after means-testing. The proposed 'lifetime 'cap' of £86,000 on care costs only covers the care element, leaving individuals to pay 'housing costs', which can reach thousands a year. The new cap is not back-dated, so care costs prior to 2023 are not eligible for inclusion. Access and the quality of care provided will still depend upon a person's ability to pay for it. The value of a house dictates how much you keep after the cap is applied.

From April 2022, an increase of 1.25% on National Insurance Contributions will come into effect. In reality, this means workers subsiding the wealthy – this is the wrong way to fund care. In 2023, the increase reverts to a 'health and social care levy' and will include those pensioners who continue to work. This is a concern, since the majority of pensioners continue working because the state pension is inadequate and not enough to pay their bills, which for many also include the cost of care for partners or relatives.

We need a National Care Service

In 2020 the NPC produced its policy booklet 'Goodbye Cinderella – A New Settlement for Care'. This policy is a radical change to the way in which social care is funded and managed. It calls for a National Care Service to be set up, separate from the NHS, funded through progressive taxation, publicly owned and publicly accountable, free at the point of need.

A National Care Service would put people at the heart of services, with choices about independence and how their healthcare is delivered, where, and by whom, with support and advocacy for family carers and those being cared for. Prevention services should be fully funded, to enable the health of the nation to improve and give a better quality of life. We call for public sector contracts, conditions of service and mandatory training for all care workers (including managers) with a pay scale linked to a point on the NHS grade. It should be independently monitored at a national level, with community services responding to local needs of the time; and it must work collaboratively with the NHS.

The NPC argues that this is affordable, but the political will for such a progressive reform is sadly missing. We need a national debate on moving to a publicly funded care service that is for everyone.

General practice: holding the frontline

David Wrigley

A GP in Lancashire and deputy chair of BMA Council

How are we going to be able to cope with this? Will my family be OK? Will my patients survive? Those were the anxieties that rushed through my mind in March 2020, when the reports from Northern Italy demonstrated the full horrors of Covid-19 and the likely wave of infections coming our way.

In Bergamo, Lombardy, hospitals were beyond full, health professionals were being forced to choose between patients, and death tolls were rising. Coffins were stacked on the back of army trucks. The horror at the indignity suffered by so many in Italy was swiftly followed by the fear of what was to come in the UK.

The truth is that we were worried not only because of what was to come, but also because of what had already been.

Prior to the Covid-19 pandemic general practitioners were already working in an incredibly difficult environment – an environment which made staff unwell and in which patient care was, through no fault of our own, often unsatisfactory and sometimes unsafe.

Our communities had been broken by a decade of austerity politics. Our workforce was burned out by the demands of those increasingly needy populations and the dwindling resource provided by a government who chose to make empty promises rather than take serious action.

For many years before the pandemic in my own surgery, in

Lancashire in the North-West of England, we collected food parcels at our reception to distribute to the most needy in our area. This was a community which had lost its Sure Start centres, its social care workers and its police community support officers, once visible on local streets – all due to political choices and austerity politics leading to savage cuts to the public sector. Our hospitals were full due to staff and bed cuts, and as GPs we often had to send patients inappropriately to A&E rather than admit them to a hospital bed for further investigations that they needed. We saw the impacts of vast health inequalities in our waiting rooms every day – patients whose life circumstances prevented them from being healthy, patients whose poverty had suffocated their opportunities and starved them of wellbeing or fulfilment.

We had been promised thousands more GPs by our political leaders, but they never arrived. The latest figures highlight that struggle. We now have the equivalent of 1,516 *fewer* qualified full-time GPs compared to 2015. That statistic is damning enough but the grim context is that our practices have had on average 2,222 more patients in the same time period and yet we have still managed to set new records for patient contacts and appointments.

Amid these terrible trends the use of private provision grew in the NHS, and even in general practice firms like the US healthcare insurer Centene were growing in influence and taking over the running of GP surgeries. Unsurprisingly, in some areas, when profits dried up or their attention was grabbed by another opportunity, large PLC companies pulled out, handed back responsibilities for NHS services, and neighbouring practices or groups of GPs had to step in to provide care for patients.

In general practice it has always felt like we are part medical professionals and part social workers. But it had never been more the case. On bad days we were trying to hold our communities together. But when the waiting lists for mental health support run to years rather than days or weeks and social care is decimated there is, frankly, only so much we could do. In some cases our role was little more than to listen and support. Ultimately though, we were listening to dozens of these stories every single day, often feeling helpless, isolated and alone ourselves.

This is the context for a pandemic which would place unprecedented strain on our profession, and wreak tragedy upon communities already struggling through life.

The weeks of warnings from Italy and elsewhere were wasted in this country. When the pandemic arrived with force we were unprepared. Arguably the greatest shame among the eventual litany of failings was that doctors did not have the basic protection we needed. We had to fight tooth and nail for proper, in-date, effective Personal Protective Equipment (PPE). Our trade union, the British Medical Association, was forced to demand on a daily basis that the government take action on this most basic and fundamental of issues. In general practice we were left to see patients in cramped buildings, totally unfit for purpose even prior to the pandemic, and my colleagues put their lives on the line to ensure our communities were cared for when they needed it most. We relied on local community knitting groups to make our PPE when the government should have been there for us and prepared many years in advance for such a situation.

In the months to come there were many failings from the government. Scandals around PPE continued but we were also let down badly over risk assessments for staff when it became clear this was a disease which left some of us more vulnerable than others. We also had to deal with the government's continued failure to communicate effectively, whether directly to the profession or to the public at large. These simple failings in communication often meant we were left little to no time to prepare for required action and the public were confused and scared.

Often, people show themselves most honestly during times of crisis. And during this great public health crisis the Conservative government did exactly this. In those early days when general practice and public health teams could have been empowered to lead the response to the pandemic, the government instead turned to its friends and colleagues in the private sector. Instead of building capacity in primary care and public health and utilising existing expertise, billions of pounds of public money were handed to companies which had so often in the past failed to deliver public services. Some of these companies had links to government politicians. Their eventual failures were no surprise to anyone working in the health service.

It is tempting to look back and consider the overarching theme – the enduring narrative – of the Covid-19 pandemic to be one of government failure. That tale of inaction, ill preparedness and complacency would not be inaccurate. But I believe there is also another story. A story of a profession which showed the very best of itself in the most challenging of times.

In the early days of the pandemic general practice rapidly changed the way we worked. Suddenly consultations were conducted remotely where possible and both doctors and patients were protected as much as we could as we reconfigured our premises and our pathways. We rebuilt relationships with health leaders in Clinical Commissioning Groups and other stakeholders and worked together to ensure the IT infrastructure was in place to rapidly meet the needs in our communities in an entirely different way.

General practice has always been rooted in the community. Since 1948 and, in fact, long before, we have been the bedrock of our neighbourhoods, the fixed point in our patients' turning worlds.

Our place at the heart of our local areas, the trust of our populations, enabled us to drive the vaccination programme which was such a great success for the country – a vital boost for morale for a long-suffering public, a source of protection for the NHS and the most important step in returning to the freedoms lost due to Covid-19.

Outsourced Test and Trace, with its eye-watering budget running into the tens of billions of pounds, bungled from one misstep to the next. In contrast the NHS-led vaccination programme, delivered in large part by general practice and supported wonderfully by other health professionals and community volunteers, succeeded, under great time pressure and amid the devastating waves of the pandemic. It was a miraculous achievement. We have our NHS, its staff and local communities to thank for the success of the vaccine campaign.

The vaccine rollout showed what can be done when doctors and our colleagues are given the flexibility to lead and the responsibility to deliver for our patients. At the time of writing 139.5 million vaccinations have been delivered in this country, with 91.4 per cent of the population over 12 years old covered by at least one jab. This is a truly incredible achievement.

I have never been more proud to be a general practitioner. My colleagues gave everything to help our patients and our communities when they needed us most. We showed, once again, that when we are challenged we respond proactively and efficiently, guided by compassion and expertise.

By the latter months of 2021 my profession was on its knees. My colleagues were anxious, beleaguered and burned out. Doctors in their early 50s, doctors who had ambitions to be serving their communities into their 60s, were leaving the profession, and the rigours of the Covid pandemic had left most of us questioning how long we could possibly continue in our vocations.

The efforts of those working in general practice, and our colleagues across the health and care system, should have been met with genuine recognition, and a determination we would never be left so vulnerable again. Instead, what we got was a government-backed campaign from the *Daily Mail* and other Conservative-leaning newspapers attacking GPs and their staff, and demanding all patients had to have access to face-to-face appointments with their GPs. It was a campaign which wilfully ignored the continued emergence of Covid variants, the need to protect vulnerable staff, and doctors pushed to breaking point. It was a campaign which chose to blame GPs for strain on capacity and limitations on access rather than successive governments who had repeatedly ignored our cries for help and our warnings of what was to come.

Inevitably, the abuse and the attacks followed. Members of the public spoke of GPs as if we hadn't been bothering to turn up at work and the government seemed happy to hang us out to dry, even though we had more than earned support and recognition. Anti-GP graffiti was painted on the walls of a surgery in Bristol and in Manchester a horrific attack left a GP with a fractured skull and practice staff suffering deep cuts.

Every day my colleagues and I wondered whether that would

be us next. We worried about the safety of our staff. We heard the aggression and abuse aimed at our receptionists and patient advisors. It was the lowest time in my professional career.

While abusive and aggressive behaviours are obviously utterly unacceptable, some patients are justifiably anxious. This pandemic has taken every problem we had in our society and exacerbated it beyond measure. I am tired, and my colleagues are tired. The burden of all this unmet need in our communities is huge, and the risk we are managing in general practice is already unmanageable for many professionals. Recently, a patient told me she was in too much pain to make herself a cup of tea; but she will likely have to wait over a year for her operation. Others are considering selling their homes or taking out loans to have treatment privately because they can't cope anymore.

This simply cannot go on. Whatever happens with the ongoing Covid-19 pandemic – and we must not forget this pandemic is ongoing – general practice and the NHS need urgent attention. The government and NHS leaders have all the evidence they need of the commitment and dedication of staff, the effectiveness of primary care and the impact of underfunding services. They also have all the evidence they need of the dangers of choosing private providers over the real experts in public service. If action is not taken urgently then the future for patients, communities and this country could be very bleak indeed.

In the short-term the government must provide consistent public statements of support for GPs and deliver on its commitment to work with our unions and healthcare organisations to stop the abuse of NHS staff. In the longer term we need to see urgent and sustained investment in general practice and the removal of the numerous barriers to providing the best patient care possible.

That means much more proportionate and compassionate regulation of GPs and ring-fenced monies for clinical and support staff. And it also means investment in buildings, facilities and equipment. It is beyond nonsensical for GPs to be delivering 21st-century care in converted Victorian houses. Alongside capital investment we need a radical programme of investment in the training, recruitment and retention of primary care teams. These steps should all be seen as investment in continuity of care, which we know to be incredibly effective, and investment in a model of primary care which is viewed as being the gold standard around the world.

Bereaved families still have no justice

Lobby Akinnola

Covid-19 Bereaved Families for Justice (CBFJ)

It's December 2019, and I am stacking chairs at the end of the office Christmas party. Despite the seasonal merriment and my boss's impromptu singing with the live band, my heart sinks into my stomach. The election results have been announced and Boris Johnson has been named as the prime minister of the UK. A well-meaning American friend tries to console me that 'Things won't be that bad. Nothing really changes'.

'It is bad, this is going to cost lives,' I replied. I had no idea how close to home this prediction would hit.

On the 26th of April, 2020, I lost my father, Olufemi Akinnola, to Covid-19. A father of five, he was 60, in good health, and looking forward to spending his 61st birthday in Paris with my mother, his wife of 30 years. I will never forget receiving the call from my mother to tell me that, despite all hope and expectation, dad had died. The sound of my sister's agonised wailing echoes in my mind still as I try to rebuild a life that fell apart that Sunday morning. My father was the cornerstone of our family. His caring and devoted nature had built a close family who needed nothing but each other's company. His wisdom and encouragement made us all feel like everything was ok as long as we were together. His smile brought us such joy.

My father's death is a loss that extends beyond my immediate family, however. Family and friends around the world wept as they watched the recording we had made of dad's funeral, unable to say goodbye to a beloved brother and uncle. Members of our church sent cards and flowers to honour the man who had been both counsel and comfort. The charity Mencap, where my dad worked, called to pay respects to a man who would spend his days off visiting his clients in hospital, just to make sure they were doing well. Just as it is impossible to encapsulate the entirety of a person in one paragraph, it is impossible to quantify the lives that have been affected by my father's death. He truly was one of a kind, and yet his death was heartbreakingly common.

At the time of writing, my father is one of 180,033 people that have died with Covid-19 on their death certificate. 180,033 families have been devastated by the sudden loss of their mothers and fathers, their brothers and sisters, their children. People from all walks of life have been lost to this terrible disease, snatched away suddenly from those they loved. These people were carers, like my father, putting their lives at risk to protect the most vulnerable in society. They were key workers, who kept the nation running during this crisis. They were grandparents, living in care homes where they were supposed to be safe and protected. They were nurses and doctors striving without rest to save as many lives as they could. They were people who, with or without underlying health conditions, were not dying but living life to the fullest. 180,033 lives, ended too soon.

After losing my dad, I became a member of the Covid-19 Bereaved Families for Justice (CBFJ) campaign. It is a campaign that was started by Matt Fowler and Jo Goodman, both of whom lost their fathers to Covid. The people we have lost during this pandemic can no longer advocate for themselves. It is on their behalf and on behalf of those that love them that CBFJ has sought a Statutory Inquiry into the Covid-19 response in the UK. For there to be justice there must be accountability, and for there to be accountability there must be a full account.

It is impossible to look at the death toll and claim that the government's handling of the pandemic has been a resounding success, yet this is all that is ever mentioned in response to questions over decisions made or rules broken. While we gratefully recognise the impact the vaccine rollout has had, we must also recognise where mistakes have been made. Our government has made decisions which put the lives of the British public at risk, and we have all dealt with the consequences. Those responsible must reckon with the consequence of their choices, rebuild the trust of the nation, maintain a just system, and ensure their mistakes are not repeated.

This was and remains the objective of the campaign: first to save lives, and then to get the justice our loved ones deserve. The campaign welcomed the government's announcement of an inquiry and the appointment of the chair, but if there is one thing that has become clear during this crisis, it is that time is of the essence. The preparatory work to begin the inquiry must begin now if we are to have any hope of starting to hear evidence this year.

We are also working hard to ensure that bereaved people have a voice in this inquiry. When appropriate, we will be requesting Core Participant status in the inquiry. Our members have seen first-hand the mistakes in the government's response to Covid and we are all too familiar with the consequences. We have questions that must be answered so that no one else has to suffer the same fate.

These questions formed the basis of our 'Learn Lessons, Save Lives' report published in November 2021. By speaking to our members and experts from major charities, trade unions, and public health institutions, we created the report as a non-exhaustive guide to the concerns the inquiry must address. Questions surrounding the UK's lack of preparedness to face a pandemic: why were there apparently no systems in place? Why were the findings of Exercise Cygnus ignored? Why were our doctors and nurses left unprotected due to a lack of PPE?

Questions surrounding those most affected by the pandemic: why were BAME communities so greatly impacted? What protections were there for the disabled and clinically vulnerable? What support was given to our frontline workers? What systemic inequality led to the disproportionate loss of life in the North of England?

Questions surrounding the government's decisions during the pandemic: why was community testing halted? Why were we so slow to lock down or monitor our borders? Why were people sent, untested, from hospitals into care homes? How were contracts for crucial resources awarded?

Questions around why, with hundreds of people dying daily from Covid and the government planning to remove the isolation period after testing positive, are these mistakes being repeated again and again?

These questions represent only some of those raised by members of the campaign in the 'Learn Lessons, Save Lives' report.

The pandemic has pervaded every household in the country and its impact will be felt for decades. Likewise, the investigation into the pandemic response and outcomes needs to be just as comprehensive and broad in scope. The factors that contributed to our experience of Covid-19 did not start in March 2020 but had been in place for many years beforehand. We cannot hope to make the necessary changes to protect future generations if we do not fully comprehend what went wrong in the first place.

Furthermore, once those mistakes have been identified, we must make sure change is implemented. Too often the results of inquiries and investigations are confined solely to the pages they are printed on. After any tragedy, there is a strong desire to move forward and not be held captive by the pain of the past. We all wish to return to some semblance of normality in our lives and to begin to enjoy the freedoms afforded us by the vaccine and the hard work of our NHS staff. However, we must be cautious in how we progress and be vigilant to make sure the learning opportunities created by the unfathomable tragedy this country has experienced do not go to waste. Covid-19 has highlighted systemic issues that need to be addressed, otherwise the UK will find itself holding another inquiry to answer the same questions, and all of this tragedy would be for nought. No, change must be borne from this loss, we have to make tomorrow better than yesterday. This is what CBFJ fights for and why I am proud to be a member.

For that is what I am, one member. One of six Akinnolas missing my dad, one of 6,000 campaign members pushing for change, one of millions grieving a loved one in this country. It is easy, with such large numbers, to become numb to the loss the British people have experienced. Yet we must not forget that behind every heart on the Memorial Wall, behind each statistic there was a person. A person who laughed and who cried, had hopes and dreams for a tomorrow that will never come, a person who loved and was loved. We are those they have left behind. Only we can honour them, only we can advocate for them. I will never get to ask my dad for help again, or tell him how proud I am to be his son. What I can do, however, is carry on his legacy of caring for others by making sure his story is heard and fighting for the changes that could have saved him. I hope, in doing so, I can say he would be proud of me.

Legal perspective: still waiting for the public inquiry

Michael Mansfield, QC

Chair of People's Covid Inquiry

The People's Covid Inquiry (PCI), organised by the campaign group Keep Our NHS Public (KONP), shone a singular searchlight during the exceedingly dark days of pandemic pain and anguish, suffered by large numbers of UK citizenry. The final findings of the Inquiry are contained in a full report, delivered on December 1st 2021.

It was a gargantuan achievement by a highly skilled team who volunteered their time and talent for the public good. From inception to the point of delivery was barely one year. It provides a model of what can be accomplished, even in the absence of statutory powers, funding, or the courtesy of acknowledgement from a consistently chaotic government. Around the world, citizens have convened such Commissions and Tribunals where state institutions have been found wanting and the rule of law flouted.

Here, throughout, the so-called lawmakers were prime lawbreakers. Way beyond kissing in corridors, drinking wine and eating cake à la 'party gate,' or spotting Barnard Castle, it was the quite appalling vista of arrogance and corruption which pervaded the handling of the pandemic. The Gray report may have finally galvanised the Metropolitan police (the Met) into a police investigation concerning a Downing Street systemic culture of disregard for essential norms accompanied by smirking avoidance, but the problem runs far deeper and wider than that.

This is evidenced in the PCI Report, entitled 'Misconduct in Public Office,' which was provided to the Commissioner of Police for the Metropolis, Cressida Dick, before Christmas 2021. There was a moment when this was thought to be a somewhat ambitious title, but that moment has long gone in the light of recent exposures. The title is entirely appropriate. There is misconduct in the colloquial sense as well as the legal.

In terms of the law it is what is known as a non-statutory common law offence. Its elements have been honed by case law over a number of years. The latest is contained in the Attorney General's Reference No 3 of 2003 [2004] EWCA Crim 868. The offence is committed by a public officer who, without reasonable excuse or justification, willfully (not accidentally) neglects to perform his/her duty to such a degree as to amount to an abuse of the public's trust in the office holder. Anyone who has read the PCI report will appreciate the potential application of this definition to those responsible for UK public health and safety for the last decade.

The Commissioner has acknowledged receipt, and it is hoped matters will progress with alacrity and due diligence, because there is a risk that the spectre of a judicial public inquiry might be used as an excuse to dismiss or defer any investigation. Equally the resignation of Cressida Dick herself might provide yet another reason. It is claimed the party gate (Hillman) investigation will not be delayed, and is continuing apace with questionnaires to 50 people including the Prime Minister.

This also gives rise to fundamental questions of compromise, since the Met are responsible for security in Downing Street by means of a physical presence and electronic surveillance. One imagines they will at least have been aware of gatherings outside in the garden in breach of regulations, but did nothing, while others who did similar things were fined thousands of pounds.

The whole point of the rapidly assembled People's Inquiry was to avoid delay and obfuscation, so that the causes, the mistakes, the misconduct, could be identified and addressed, especially in the context of one of the highest global death rates. The problem with many statutory Inquiries, however well intentioned, is the time lapse between inauguration and a final report containing a raft of recommendations. Invariably this takes years, by which time the urgency and need have passed.

Interestingly, the long overdue Public Judicial Inquiry into Covid has already amply demonstrated this shortcoming.

In the summer of 2020 the Prime Minister glibly accepted that there might have to be an Inquiry at some point. Then, all went quiet until nine months later when the bereaved, who had been singularly ignored by the Prime Minister, justifiably wanted to know what was happening. The answer was … nothing. Because it did not suit the Prime Minister who felt the time was not right. This led to a vocal protest from a number of notable bodies and individuals including the Archbishop of Canterbury. Something had to be said: so the Prime Minister opted for the Spring of 2022. Not exactly therefore a top priority or a matter of urgency or necessarily an actual start date.

Once more all went quiet on the Westminster front. Those familiar with major Judicial Inquiries know that if it were to commence as mooted, there would have to be a great deal of immediate preparation. With less than a year to go at that time, the very first step would have been to expedite the appointment of a high court judge who might have to be available for the foreseeable future. Then discussion would have to have taken place, alongside public consultation, about the terms of reference (ToRs). Put another way, how was the scope on a subject as vast as the pandemic to be determined if it were to begin to answer the pressing fundamental questions on everyone's lips - what has happened … how and why did it happen … what went wrong … who is responsible – and, most important, how can this be remedied and recurrence prevented? How could these pressing questions be managed sensibly?

Should it be one Inquiry split into phases and module? Or several parallel but interlinked Inquiries or Commissions?

Just on these issues alone during the ensuing months in 2021 nothing happened until the bereaved raised a further challenge. They were assured informally that the chair would be appointed before Christmas 2021, one and a half years after the original announcement – and two years from the start of the pandemic. On the December 15

Baroness Heather Hallett was switched from the Salisbury Novichok poisonings Inquiry (originally inquest) upon which she had been Coroner/chair for best part of a year, to head the Covid Inquiry.

At the time of writing (February 2022) there has been a public information vacuum for the third time. The government website suggests that the Prime Minister will be consulting with ministers from the devolved administrations and Baroness Hallett on the terms of reference, and will publish them in the new year. No mention in this context of any consideration being given to public consultation. And, so far, no indication of what is being formulated.

Quite how this fits with Baroness Hallett's published intention of seeking 'views from those who have lost loved ones and all other affected groups about the Inquiry's terms of reference' is far from clear. KONP approached the Cabinet Office, which has charge of this, to obtain information and clarification.

In a response dated February 7 the direction of travel by government is amplified. There will be two stages in relation to the ToRs. An initial draft will be drawn up after consultation between the Prime Minister, the devolved administrations and the Chair. This precedes any public consultation, which is contained in the second stage prior to the terms being finalised. It is to be hoped that stage 1 does not circumscribe the whole exercise by attempting to set the scope of parameters within which the public are asked for their views on terms.

Already the tenor of government pronouncements is that scope will be focused on future policy rather than the historical context of missed opportunities, deficient preparation, depletion of health and social welfare networks, and past errors or misconduct. Were this to be the case it would be totally unacceptable and a betrayal of the bereaved.

Meanwhile on 12 November 2021, altogether out of sync with all this, and before any public announcement about the chair or scope, it appears (from criticism mounted by the Labour Party via Angela Rayner) that the renowned company Deloitte has been engaged to form a 'knowledge management system' in preparation for the public inquiry 'including an evidence generation strategy'.* If this is right it is an unprecedented preemption of process, which should be determined by the chair once the terms of reference are decided and approved.

Secondly it presents a serious conflict of interest. Deloitte (one of four major financial audit firms) profited from huge sums from the Treasury in relation to test and trace schemes during the pandemic – in the region of £280m. They assisted government in preparing Parliamentary answers to defend the schemes which were heavily criticised for their ineffectiveness and waste of resources. For them to be handed another £900,000 to prepare for a public inquiry which has the potential to scrutinise their activities is entirely inappropriate.

This has become even more contentious since the recent revelations contained in the annual accounts of the Department of Health and Social Care, which disclose that nearly £9bn has been wasted on overpriced or unusable PPE. Gareth Davies the auditor general of the NAO observed that normal competitive tender processes had been suspended and multi-million pound contracts for PPE had been awarded to many companies with no previous experience.

The other aspects which need to have been sorted for an Inquiry starting this Spring, include a venue (actual and virtual), a team of lawyers to essentially advise and represent the chair, a panel, assessors, a secretariat, identification of potential witnesses both lay (especially bereaved and frontline workers) and experts, identifying and securing documentary evidence in digital and paper forms, issues of disclosure, the recognition and authorisation of Core Participants together with their legal representatives, live streaming and recording. This list is by no means exhaustive.

It is only now, in the February edition of an in-house lawyer magazine (*Counsel*) that an advertisement has appeared on behalf of the Inquiry for the purpose of recruiting the team of Counsel to deal with the matters described in the preceding paragraph: 8 silks, 15 senior juniors and 20 juniors. Such calculations cannot be made unless someone has a clear handle on scope.

* This information was allegedly derived from an article in *Private Eye*, and has not been contradicted.

If nothing else this whole narrative reinforces the case for a pre-existing fast track model like the People's Covid Inquiry, endowed with statutory powers of enforcement.

There is another dimension and function of Judicial Inquiries (and Inquests) which can be underestimated. They provide an invaluable opportunity for relatives and loved ones to describe the lives of those who have died. This is important for the professionals as well as the public at large to appreciate and recognise the human repercussions of the event being examined. It informs and begins the process of rebuilding confidence and trust, essential for a respectful community. A practice has grown over the last few years of starting inquests and inquiries** with what has become known as a 'pen portrait 'of the deceased drawn by those who were close friends and relatives. There should be no hesitation just because of the numbers. There are many inventive ways in which this evidential memorial can be erected.

The magnitude of the occasion, and its clear significance for the nation as a whole, may merit something akin to a Truth and Reconciliation Commission. The best-known example of this took place in South Africa under the guiding hand of Archbishop Tutu following the overthrow of apartheid and the release of Nelson Mandela. Over 50 other countries have used this model, especially where social division and hostility has erupted.

The People's Inquiry found that the pandemic exacerbated the economic and social divisions in UK society and was disproportionately harsh upon the poor and disadvantaged. This has dire repercussions now in the face of a massive rise in the cost of living driven by rising energy costs. For many it has become a matter of 'heat or eat'. At which point the response of the Governor of the Bank of England is to implore workers not to seek pay rises which might provoke inflation! Tell that to the oil companies who are raking in unprecedented profits and relishing negative tax liability.

A truth and reconciliation exercise, in which compassion builds back better, is long overdue!

February 2022

** notably in the Hillsborough and London bombing Inquests, and the current Grenfell Tower Inquiry.

Health unions face up to post-pandemic challenge

Sara Gorton
Head of Health, UNISON

As my contribution to this post-pandemic assessment of the NHS, I want to focus on two topics which have been the cause of regular industrial conflict in England in the last decade – privatisation, and pay and earnings.

Both are themes within the ambit of central government, and on which decisions made in Whitehall can have an immediate and direct impact on both individual workers and employment relations in the NHS. They are also themes where a progressive approach – and joint work with unions – would have a huge and positive benefit for those who work in the NHS, those who lead it and those who depend on it.

For both themes, I'll set out the current situation as I see it, flag some key considerations and describe how these might manifest as active trade union campaign issues over the next few years.

The threat of privatisation

In some ways, we should feel confident that privatisation is on the wane in the NHS. The big bang provider-takeover route was fatally discredited by Circle's failure at Hinchingbrooke;[1] the Wholly Owned Subsidiary (Subco) model has been largely halted by a combination of union action and changes to regulations and process; and traditional outsourcing is being reversed in many key providers.

The level of private provision funded by the NHS increased

by only £50m between 2018 and 2019. Even when the sort-of independent services like General Practice and dentistry are factored in, 75% of the NHS budget is spent on direct provision of services by NHS organisations.[2]

When the Health and Care Bill gets assent in 2022 the legislative requirement for NHS clinical services to be competitively procured will be removed from the statute book and decisions about who provides what in the NHS should be placed outside of competition law. These are important steps in protecting services from direct privatisation.

But we should be wary of overconfidence.

In the context of a waiting list of over six million treatments, pressure on the health service to reduce the backlog will grow. The obvious exhaustion of staff and the goodwill that followed from pandemic efforts meant that targets for reducing waiting lists set at the start of 2022, while hugely ambitious, were not as stiff as some had feared. But, as more of us experience the ongoing consequences of delays and missed targets, understanding may turn to impatience. Politicians may then seek to blame or punish the health service and its staff, and to establish routes to funnel more work towards the independent sector.

As things stand, we can anticipate a surge in the number of NHS procedures carried out in private hospitals over the next three years, weaving the independent sector into the fabric of 'normal' healthcare provision and increasing its status, profits and strategic importance to the sector. Commercial ventures are already securing contracts to provide new services for testing and imaging under the Community Diagnostic Services initiative, critical for meeting the targets for cancer treatment. And as the demand for temporary staffing continues to grow, commercial agencies and 'banks' will not be short of work, potentially increasing the proportion of staff working in the NHS outside of direct employment.

We also face the risk that an increasing number of people could opt to go outside of the NHS for their treatment.

If the current backlog does not reduce as planned (or if there is agitation for targets to be ramped up as we approach the next general election), more people may fall prey to companies offering the chance to 'jump the queues' through private health insurance and services. At this point in time, 1.7 million people in the UK have private health insurance.[*] That's more than one in 40 of us. Insurers predict 5% year on year growth in the sector,[3] so that proportion could increase during the time it takes to get through the backlog.

Last year's drop of seven percentage points in public confidence in the NHS[4] is another indicator that we cannot take continued high levels of citizen support for granted. Pro-market think tanks like the Institute of Economic Affairs continue to push for the UK to move to an insurance-based health system,[5] and their ideas will gain traction if public dissatisfaction with the NHS increases. If the number of people paying for and using the private sector grows, and the pro-market lobby is able to mobilise people who perceive they are 'paying twice' for healthcare, then political pressure to freeze, or cut funding for the NHS at the end of this current financial settlement could rise.

At best, a drop in public support would remove pressure on politicians to increase the share of funding for the NHS above what is currently in place. At worst it would result in cuts to budgets and increase pressure on the Department of Health and Social Care to meddle with structures, restrict access to services and reopen debates about how provider organisations get paid.

This worst-case scenario is, however, made less likely by three core factors. The cost-of-living crisis is being experienced across the economy, so people may not be willing or able to spend more money on expensive health insurance or treatment. Second, despite the dip in confidence the NHS is still the highest public priority for additional spending.[6] Third, private hospitals are also subject to staffing challenges and many have contracts in place to pick up NHS surgeries and treatments. This means the large private chains may well find their capacity severely stretched by returning to the levels of activity they were providing for the NHS in 2019, with the availability of staff a brake on their potential expansion.

---

[*] Including workplace insurance medical cover, subscribers comprise 11% of the population.

The workforce crisis – the problems of recruitment and retention

Staffing is a crisis in common across both the private and statutory health sectors.

The nature and scale of the workforce crisis we face as the NHS moves out of the pandemic has been covered in a wide range of statistics, reports, commissions and surveys – establishing the high levels of burnout, quantifying the staffing shortages and describing the human toll this situation takes on staff working in the health service and those waiting in pain for treatment or surgery.[7]

I don't intend to cover that ground; suffice to say that when a Conservative cabinet minister, the Chief Executive of the NHS, trade unions and think tanks all agree that there is a problem with staffing in the health service, we can be pretty sure that the workforce crisis is a phenomenon and not a rhetorical device.

So what is the problem? While anything involving the web of motivations, ambitions, feelings and family situations of over a million people is bound to be complex, the current workforce crisis can be simplified into two core aspects.

Problem number one is recruitment. As the numbers of people waiting for treatment goes up, the gap between the numbers of staff we need and the numbers in post (the vacancy rate) gets bigger.

Problem number two is retention. As demand goes up so too do the conditions that cause more people to resign, so the number of those retiring, moving to new NHS or care roles, leaving to start families, etc., is supplemented by those who feel they have no opportunities for progression; those who do not feel fairly treated or rewarded and those who are no longer able to cope with the toll of an unmanageable workload on their health.

Nuffield Trust analysis[8] showed 40% of the 140,000 staff leaving the NHS in the year to September 2021 resigned, with a steep rise in the proportion of these exits prompted by aspects of work (including hours, reward, opportunity). As the pandemic blends seamlessly into the mountainous recovery period, these numbers may climb as staff burnout persists.

UNISON's own survey work undertaken at the end of 2021 showed that 3 out of 10 staff from across the full range of nonmedical occupations were actively planning to leave the NHS in 2022. Low staffing levels are not only increasing workloads but are making staff unhappy with the quality of care they are able to give. Those on professional registers feel particularly vulnerable, worrying about compromising the standards of their registration and codes of practice.

While the range of issues that impact on retention are complex, there are some very common themes and concrete actions that can be taken to resolve these. And this is where my second core theme – pay and earnings – comes in to play.

The importance of fair pay and earnings

The NHS needs to restore services to meet public expectations. This requires not only attracting more people in, but also urgent action to stop people leaving, so that we are making gains, not just plugging gaps in the numbers. That means using pay and earnings strategically to support, not hinder, efforts to hang on to staff.

Each pay round provides the government with an opportunity to meaningfully engage the NHS workforce. Last year this was squandered. The tone, timing, approach and value of the pay award damaged morale. The constant delays, the government's insulting 1% opening position, the bungling of the announcement and the actual value and structure of the award damaged the trust and confidence of NHS staff in both the government and the process. To reverse this situation, the government must provide for a meaningful pay rise, and it must commit to additional measures to stop staff leaving.

For 2022, UNISON and other trade unions have identified five key actions that, along with a meaningful pay rise, we think could give the NHS the best chance of preventing more avoidable resignations over the next few years. These include ensuring that pay banding outcomes reflect job content; rewarding additional hours fairly; preventing burnout by limiting excess hours; supporting progression and career development; and using recruitment and retention premia to tackle the most acute shortages.

These actions will have the biggest impact if they are deployed as central policies, but employers are also in a position to deliver some of these changes locally. So issues linked to earnings may overtake privatisation as key themes for localised campaign activity for health unions.

Dissatisfaction with NHS pay has not translated into widespread industrial unrest in recent history, in part because health workers have not been convinced that taking action at employer level is an effective way of changing the minds and policy of a remote Westminster government.[9] Attitudes may differ if health workers feel their immediate employer is withholding a reasonable and achievable local claim on, say, the Living Wage or a re-banding for staff in a specific department. So perhaps a failure to put in place a much-needed post-pandemic pay and earnings settlement will be a spur to employer-level activism across the health service?

Conditions in the wider labour market – low unemployment, high vacancy rates, skills shortage – create a climate where the bargaining power of staff is high.

The current process through which NHS pay is determined makes it much easier for government to ignore non-pay earnings issues, like banding, working time and hours. If the NHS had a collective bargaining structure, where unions were able to negotiate on pay and terms on a regular basis, these issues could be considered in the round. As it is, pay is atomised and settled via the Review Body process,[10] a mechanism with which health workers are increasingly voicing dissatisfaction. The Review Body has a tightly controlled remit, can have its recommendations overridden by government and pays great attention to government pay policy in giving advice. In years where the PRB is not able to deliver a pay rise that will outstrip costs, it is not able to offer health workers any progressive action on other aspects affecting their payslip.

Achieving post-pandemic improvements

To make progress on earnings issues, unions must persuade the government into talks. This can be done (as happened in late 2017) but is not easy and requires a combination of political circumstances that are not predictable or reliable. Members of health unions will increasingly question the effectiveness of the present system, leading potentially to agitation for changes in the way pay is settled.

Unions have been cautious to date about this approach, wary of the high risk of regionalized pay and breakaways from the collective structures. However, the current labour market in the wider economy, the long path to recovery of capacity in the NHS and the time it will take to fill the 100,000+ vacancies may give unions the confidence to manage those risks. With the government in Scotland already committed to collective bargaining, frustration with the Review Body mechanism is likely to increase elsewhere. Pressure will mount if members in Scotland get better settlements than their colleagues in the rest of the UK over the next couple of pay rounds. If alternative routes for pay settlement are not immediately available, that will also contribute an increase in employer-level activity and disputes on earnings issues.

Trade unions have a crucial role to play in this space. Whether through central negotiations or local activity, unions can support health workers to achieve post-pandemic improvements to earnings. If governments refuse to listen, health unions that can provide members with the means and support to achieve positive change are likely to thrive.

At some point, perhaps the penny will drop in Westminster that negotiating a post-pandemic retention package with unions now is their best route to avoiding a whole heap of trouble down the line.

NOTES

1   https://www.unison.org.uk/news/article/2015/01/hinchingbrooke-privatisation-was-guaranteed-to-fail/
2   Centre for Public Health Interest, 'For whose benefit?', September 2021
3   Figs from the Association of British Insurers 2021 www.mordorintelligence.com/industry-reports/united-kingdom-health-and-medical-insurance-market
4   British Social Attitudes survey (last data set collected mid 2020) showed a drop of 7 percentage points in satisfaction with the NHS https://natcen.ac.uk/our-research/research/british-social-attitudes/
5   https://iea.org.uk/publications/universal-healthcare-without-the-nhs/
6   British Social Attitudes Survey 2020 https://natcen.ac.uk/our-research/research/british-social-attitudes/
7   Summarised in the following publications:
    Health and social care select committee report 'Clearing the backlog caused by the pandemic', January 2002 https://publications.parliament.uk/pa/cm5802/cmselect/cmhealth/599/report.html

NHS Digital statistics on vacancies in the NHS, March 2022 https://digital.
nhs.uk/data-and-information/publications/statistical/nhs-vacancies-survey/
april-2015---december-2021-experimental-
Kings Fund 'NHS Workforce: Our position' February 2022 https://www.
kingsfund.org.uk/projects/positions/nhs-workforce?utm_source=The%20
King%27s%20Fund%20newsletters%20%28main%20account%29&utm_
medium=email&utm_campaign=13016322_NEWSL_The%20
Weekly%20Update%202022-02-25&utm_content=Button_Position&dm_
i=21A8,7QZGI,FLXGNR,VLGC3,1

8   https://www.nuffieldtrust.org.uk/resource/the-long-goodbye-exploring-
rates-of-staff-leaving-the-nhs-and-social-care

9   In contrast, health workers in Northern Ireland were mobilised to take
industrial action in 2019 when funding to implement the 3-year deal had
been passed to Stormont but not distributed to staff due to the Assembly
not sitting.

10   England, Northern Ireland and Cymru/Wales are currently covered by PRB
remits, with the government in Scotland agreeing to settle pay for 2022-23
through negotiation with trade unions.

Key workers can't live on claps

Rehana Azam
GMB National Secretary

When times are tough we find out who we can really rely on. In Covid the country came to realise that our key workers are our most precious resource.

'Clap for carers' started as a beautiful thing, a national recognition of the scale of their sacrifice. Personally, I had seen this before, in the cities, towns, and villages I passed through back in 2014 as I walked from Jarrow to London on the 'People's March for the NHS'.*

Our key workers can be counted across the economy, in many different industries and at the most diverse pay levels, but the common thread that ran through them is very human; they did whatever they could to keep us safe and alive.

We had been conditioned to treat income levels as a measure of workers' intrinsic value. Covid should have blown that perception apart. We cannot go back to the way things were, but the government has been quick to forget the role of our key workers.

When the GMB union challenged the government on NHS pay during the pandemic, ministers such as Dominic Raab mumbled dismissive responses. Matt Hancock, then Secretary of State for Health and the man who couldn't make healthcare workers safe, said it was 'not the time' to talk about pay, despite the fact that NHS workers had already endured a real terms 15% pay cut.

Hancock also admitted that he himself could not afford to live on the UK's Statutory Sick Pay rate (the lowest in Europe), and yet the

* https://www.independent.co.uk/life-style/health-and-families/health-news/
thousands-join-new-jarrow-march-in-protest-at-nhs-cuts-9716618.html

government has chosen to continue to ignore the crisis in sick pay.

After the bankers crashed our economy and austerity was unleashed, we were told that 'restraint' had to come before pay. It took a decade of campaigning to bust the 'pay-freeze', which was in plain language a year on year devaluation of public sector pay.

Without an industrial response, key workers' pay may never recover. Not only that, with rising inflation the reality is that more NHS staff will be driven into poverty wages and the use of food banks.

Some policy-makers told us before the pandemic that we couldn't afford to pay key workers what they were worth, and the same arguments are being made today.

They don't want to talk about key workers, who are disproportionately low-paid, women and people of colour, or recognise their value. But during the pandemic our well-being depended on those workers carrying on, putting their lives on the line every day, and many died keeping us safe.

The risk is that society forgets that it can't function without nurses, porters, refuse workers, healthcare workers, food workers, and there are those facilitating this social forgetting with distracting and soporific 'whataboutery'.

The Home Office's updated immigration policy contains no reference to key workers, and no revision of the positions deemed 'skilled'. The 'low-skilled' category remains what it was before, dismissing the importance of the people we utterly rely on in the sectors from care to logistics.

We will never forget. That is why it was so important that GMB called for an independent public inquiry to do justice to the workers who died, or who are suffering from long Covid. They, and their loved ones, need answers and justice.

The government's policies on skills and social value must be challenged. Successive governments have deliberately and systematically privatised jobs across public services. As a result, yet more of those essential workers on whom we depend get classified as low-skilled and employed on poverty terms and conditions.

The GMB union exposed the true face of bosses and ministers who mistake human cost for pounds and pence. Private companies operating in the NHS exploit workers already predominately from backgrounds heavily discriminated against. As the pandemic struck, profiteering employers refused to provide protection, or social distancing, and threatened workers with the sack if they didn't attend work.

Care workers, mostly women, are exploited for their skills while they risk everything to look after the elderly and most vulnerable. Our contract workers are predominately low-paid, and are exploited, threatened and bullied in the name of profit margins.

As a general union, GMB fast emerged as a campaigning union for key workers. Our priority throughout the pandemic was to get our members protected. We launched the #GetMePPE campaign.** We called for mass testing.

Our bread-and-butter demand was to call for 'Pay Justice' and the need to reset the pay of key workers to its true value – to redress the real terms pay cuts – and a commitment to job evaluation that recognises the intrinsic values of key workers' skills.

GMB tabled the need for a 'Key Worker's Allowance' to the government but this was dismissed. Our public services have been under siege by the market and profiteers, and there is a huge danger we are emerging from this crisis with pay policy unchanged.

Throughout the pandemic, ministers and their friends in business collaborated to convert misery into profits – that's why we can never stop fighting for our NHS. The NHS is precious. It is the embodiment of what we are capable of. Its backbone is the immeasurable bravery, compassion and selflessness of its staff. It is not a commodity to be bought and sold.

As one of the most senior trade unionists in the country, the fight for the NHS is a professional issue for me, but it is also personal. After I lost my dad, all I could see were bleak days ahead. I still recall the day when I got the call to say that North West Ambulance Service paramedics were trying to resuscitate him. On the same day, I was going to lodge a formal dispute against ambulance employers

** https://www.gmb.org.uk/news/get-me-ppe-protect-protectors

for trying to impose a 25% pay cut via a reduction in Annex E payments.***

Looking back, GMB's ambulance members put a blanket around me. They saved me at my lowest point, and inspired me to fight back. That's why I went out to march for them. That's why the skills and experience I learned through People's March for the NHS means so much to me all these years on, and that's why the fight has to go on – because our NHS remains under siege.

In the midst of the most severe public service cuts in living memory, thousands upon thousands of people joined that march and took a stand to say 'Beyond this line, they shall not pass!' But then as now, when the cheering died away and the politicians saw people returning to their homes, the political dismantling began again, and the broken promises piled up like patients in corridors.

We know this from standing up for our members. We all hear it on social media. The message can be heard from nurses and doctors, porters, care workers and cleaners, from the ambulance staff who have to live and work through it. The NHS is sick to death of meaningless words and lack of resources. The NHS can't survive on applause alone.

Those politicians who sacrifice the health of this nation on the altar of market forces know that their actions are the opposite of what we hold dear. Injecting the profit motive into our public services is harming the delivery of those services.

The divorce of health and social care has been a profit-driven disaster. The complex care that is delivered to the elderly cannot be maintained by underpaid minimum wage workers whose skills are undervalued socially and financially.

Why has the struggle against this pandemic been so much harder than it needed to be? Our high death rate compared to most other countries shows that the outsourcing, devaluing and exploitation of

*** Ambulance staff Annex E is a 'prospective' system of unsocial hours payments, used mainly in the ambulance service. Under this system a percentage supplement is made to pay, reflecting the working pattern and proportion of unsocial hours. This differs from the 'retrospective' system that applies to other NHS staff where an agreed 'per hour' enhancement to plain time hourly rates is applied.

our key workers does not work.

We urgently need an integrated health and social care system where social care is no longer the poor relative. We must recommit to a truly National Health Service. No slogans, sound bites or hiding behind 'NHS' pin-badges, but a serious and genuine commitment to merge health and social care and arrange for them to be delivered as a seamless service through a valued, professionalised, well trained, well paid workforce.

Reconnecting health with care will recreate the cradle-to-grave pathway that was the guiding principle behind the NHS. It will ease capacity in the NHS and move us away from a perpetual cycle of crisis.

The marketisation of health and social care is a historic failure that must not be allowed to continue to determine the future of our essential services.

When we count the final cost of the Covid crisis, and we see all the faces of the departed that represent the underinvestment, the undervaluing, the stark inequalities that have been heaped upon the shoulders of the NHS and all workers, then know this. We will not look away.

Our fight to rescue the NHS

Colenzo Jarrett-Thorpe
National Officer, Unite the Union

Permanently under siege

NHS staff in England have not just been under siege during the pandemic, their conditions at work have been akin to a siege-like existence since 2010. They have had to endure staffing shortages, down banding[1] and downgrading, working longer hours, not being able to provide the quality of services they want to deliver to their patients, and legislation and organisational changes driven by the market. On this road to perdition they have also seen real term decreases in pay and meddling with their pensions.

The morale of staff is very low and those who can, leave, or have already left the NHS, spiralling the workforce into further disarray. And yet, among the debris of destruction, there is hope – that those who believe in the principles of the NHS can come together and forge alliances with the public and with prospective decision-makers to provide a new future for the NHS and restore the confidence of the public and the morale of NHS workers.

Improving pay and conditions is vital

Unite is a key trade union in the National Health Service and

1 The current National Health Service (NHS) grading and pay system, Agenda for Change, covers most NHS staff other than doctors, dentists, apprentices and very senior managers. It allocates posts to set pay bands. There were initially nine numbered pay bands, subdivided into points, ranging from the lowest Band 1 (now discontinued for new entrants) up to senior management level. Dropping staff down a band represents a cut in pay and in recognition of their knowledge and skills.

A

represents approximately 100,000 health sector workers.[2] Our primary objective is to protect our members by ensuring that their pay, and terms and conditions of service are protected and enhanced.

The NHS workforce numbers more than a million people in England. This is a tremendous economic lever which powers local communities and business in every village, town and city. On the whole, NHS workers spend their hard-earned pay close to home: they do not seek financial refuge in offshore bank accounts, although we are also aware that NHS staff from outside the UK do their best to help their families and relatives all over the world by sending money back home. So NHS pay is important to many people across the globe.

How our members feel about their pay is summed up best by their own comments; here are a couple from our Unite in Health members' pay survey, which was conducted in January 2022:

> When I started at the NHS over twenty years ago, the pay was good and got better after training and time served, ten years to get to the top of band two. My husband who works in a warehouse has passed my hourly rate by a third in his fifteen years in post. I save lives for ten pounds an hour, he gets £15 an hour to load chips onto a lorry?
> Health Care Assistant, Band 2

> Being short staffed frequently we are working in several areas, so less time in each area. It's been very difficult for the front line workers, doctors, nurses – all staff really – coping with the Covid-19 pandemic. I feel we deserve more, and especially with the cost of living increases most people are barely getting by.'
> Ancillary worker (porter, cleaner, caterer), Band 2

There is no doubt that NHS basic pay rates have lagged behind inflation over the last decade. According to the Retail Price Index (RPI) an NHS worker who has not been promoted and has remained

2   This includes seven professional associations and members allied health professions, healthcare science, applied psychology, counselling and psychotherapy, dental professions, audiology, optometry, building trades, estates, craft and maintenance, administration, ICT, support services and ambulance services.

at the top of their pay banding since 2010 has had their basic pay decreased by 19% in real terms. By contrast MPs have seen their pay increase by 2% in real terms over the same period. Even if the Consumer Price Index (CPI) is used, occupational groups whom Unite represents in the NHS have been some of the worst hit by real pay decreases. Nurses and health visitors have seen a 5% decrease since March 2011, and scientific, therapeutic and technical staff have seen an 8% decrease in their real terms pay in the same period.[1]

The current system of resolving NHS pay in England is broken. Because of its recent pay recommendations, support for the NHS Pay Review Body (PRB) process is at rock bottom amongst Unite members. In the same recent Unite survey of health members in England, 78% of respondents said that they did not feel fairly paid for the work that they do, while an overwhelming 88% did not think that the PRB process is delivering fair pay for themselves and their colleagues.

This last figure is damning. Members were asked to explain why they felt this way, with hundreds expressing exasperation and frustration while calling into question the independence of the PRB. A new solution is needed, since whatever the intentions of the PRB, it is not delivering a pay system fit for the challenges the NHS workforce faces. It appears to many to be constrained by government austerity policies.

For 2022/23 Unite stands with sister staff side trade unions in demanding the following:

- An inflation-busting increase so that NHS staff can cope with rising and rapidly fluctuating costs which may change significantly over the pay year;
- A pay increase which absorbs the impact of increases to pension contributions and national insurance;
- A guarantee that the minimum NHS wage does not ever fall below the government's National Living Wage.

Boosting NHS pay is not only about putting money in the pockets of NHS staff; it can be a tool in addressing low morale and the growing issues of recruitment and retention of NHS staff, establishing safer working, and delivering better outcomes for patients. This is essential for our NHS to recover after the pandemic and to address the growing waiting lists.

Unrealistic demands

NHS England set out its elective recovery plan in February 2022, pledging to deliver 30% more elective activity by 2024/25 than before the pandemic. But how is this possible when NHS staff cannot give any more, and the workforce are already stretched beyond their limit?

Of the respondents to the Unite in Health survey from January 2022, 99% reported staff shortages in their workplace over the previous year, with 75% reporting frequent staff shortages. 66% had raised concerns about safe staffing levels in their workplace and department. Unsurprisingly the impact of the Covid-19 pandemic continues to be a major driver of this crisis, with 74% of respondents reporting that their service is 'overwhelmed' or 'stretched'.

We know that the NHS is already one of the most efficient health services in the world with just 2p in the pound being spent on administration, compared to 5p in Germany and 6p in France.[2] It is clear that there are no further cuts and efficiencies to be achieved. NHS bosses are therefore relying on work being conducted differently in order to meet this challenge without further overwhelming staff. But how differently can the NHS work after almost a decade of funding increases of little over 1% per year? For the next three years funding is to increase at 3.8% per year – but this is still short of the amount needed to ensure quality of care and to meet the rising demands in the system.[3]

If there is not sufficient funding of our NHS how can a 30% increase in elective appointments over the next three years be possible? We are told that the workforce underpins the recovery plan, but where is the comprehensive and funded workforce plan? How do we tackle the growing NHS vacancy rate which at the time of writing stands at 8.3%, or 110,000, in England?[4] More than a quarter (28%) of nurses and health visitors leave the NHS within the first three years of their service,[5] suggesting that not only do we need plans to recruit NHS workers, we have to ensure they stay in the NHS.

Instead things are getting worse. Three quarters (76%) of respondents to our Unite members' survey say that morale and motivation is worse or a lot worse compared to the previous year; and 66% of respondents are 'very' or 'fairly' seriously considering leaving their current NHS job.

Though sincere and earnest, last year's NHS People Plan and the NHS People Promise have had little cut though with the NHS workforce. But initiatives during the pandemic like extending free parking to NHS staff and extending support for mental health and access to counselling for NHS staff were noticed; they all help NHS staff to feel valued and to handle the pressures of their jobs. The UK government also has to make a positive commitment, by reinstating NHS bursaries that paid tuition fees for healthcare professions, by offering existing NHS staff substantive training and educational opportunities without facing prohibitive costs, and by attracting new entrants to work in the NHS.

The Health and Care Bill

England's NHS has devoted all of its policy bandwidth to the Health and Care Bill, which is expected to come into effect in July 2022. The bill scraps section 75 of the 2012 Health and Social Care Act (which committed commissioners to competitive tendering for clinical services) and instead introduces a duty to collaborate between NHS organisations, local authorities and other non-health agencies. However, Unite believes this bill is the wrong prescription for the NHS, since it does not go far enough to roll back decades of privatisation and marketisation.

The bill seeks to introduce sweeping new powers of control and decision-making for the Secretary of State. It does *not* bring back the duty of the government to provide a universal health service, nor to sustainably fund NHS and social care services. It restructures the architecture of the English NHS, putting 42 new Integrated Care Boards (ICBs) at the heart of the new system. Unite has concerns about the democratic accountability within these new bodies, with only a limited role for local authorities, and increased central government powers to intervene and appoint board directors. Provisions for private providers to sit on the ICB boards were only dropped from the legislation after campaigning by Unite and health activists.

Though collaboration is welcome among the various agencies operating in the NHS, we fear that the lack of funding and of workforce plans will mean a reduction in the quality of the services for the public in England, with few levers for local people to hold anyone accountable for what is happening. It could mean the break-up of the NHS as some areas slide unchecked towards further privatisation. This piece of legislation does not restore the original Bevanite values to our NHS in England, which is almost unrecognisable compared with other systems in the UK. We believe ICB is best translated as 'Incapable, Crushed and Broken'.

The way forward

Access to health services is globally recognised to be a fundamental human right. Health should not be treated as a commodity or a commercial good, but as a benefit for all. That's why sustained investment in our NHS is essential for our well-being and indeed our existence. Unite will continue to demand:

- a publicly owned, comprehensive and free-to-use NHS.
- all outsourced services are brought back into the public sector.
- agenda for change terms and conditions for all NHS and health staff.
- safe staffing limits for all clinical care.
- investment in training and developing NHS staff throughout their careers.
- comprehensive training/education bursaries for nurses, midwives and allied health professionals.
- provision of mental health support for NHS staff.
- the creation of a working environment within the NHS that is safe, flexible and free from harassment, bullying or violence.

We will form alliances and partnerships with other organisations that share these principles. This is why it is important that we continue to have a strong relationship with the Labour Party to make them aware that there is another way for the NHS, and to attempt to build a consensus on its future going forward.

It will take many years of investment in the NHS to make up for the last lost decade. We should come together to develop a blueprint for what a newly elected Labour or Labour-led government should do in its first 100 days in office in order to repair the damage of the last 12 years.

That way, changes can be made that are rooted in institutions and culture, and not easily swept away if the Conservatives again return to power.

NOTES

1   https://www.health.org.uk/news-and-comment/charts-and-infographics/how-has-nhs-staff-pay-changed-over-the-past-decade

2   https://www.england.nhs.uk/2022/02/nhs-publishes-electives-recovery-plan-to-boost-capacity-and-give-power-to-patients/

3   https://www.hsj.co.uk/finance-and-efficiency/extra-65bn-next-year-falls-short-of-what-nhs-says-is-needed/7030848.article

4   https://files.digital.nhs.uk/93/495EE9/nhs-vac-stats-apr15-dec21-eng-tables.xlsx

5   https://www.theguardian.com/society/2020/sep/23/growing-numbers-of-nhs-nurses-quit-within-three-years-study-finds

To recruit and retain staff the NHS must treat them better

Roger Kline

Research Fellow at Middlesex University Business School

> 'We know – intellectually – that confronting an issue is the only way to resolve it. But any resolution will disrupt the status quo. Given the choice between conflict and change on the one hand, and inertia on the other, the ostrich position can seem very attractive.'
> Margaret Heffernan, *Willful Blindness: Why We Ignore the Obvious at Our Peril*

How healthcare staff are treated substantially influences the quality and safety of care, the health and wellbeing of staff, as well as organisational performance. We know, for example, that when staff are managed with respect and compassion, that then correlates with improved patient satisfaction, infection and mortality rates, Care Quality Commission (CQC) ratings and financial performance as well as lower turnover and absenteeism. Creating a 'culture of wellbeing' in the workplace is crucial for employee health and productivity,[1] as well as lower turnover and absenteeism'[2]

At a time when the NHS has 100,000-plus vacancies it can ill afford to lose staff, yet the factors that research tells us prompt low morale, waste of talent, unsafe practice and staff turnover exist in plain sight, both locally and nationally.

Take bullying. Bullying is a threat to patient safety because 'it inhibits collegiality and cooperation essential to teamwork, cuts off communication, undermines morale and inhibits compliance with and implementation of new practices.[3]

Despite convincing evidence of its detrimental impact, the last NHS staff survey (500,000 responses) found 24% of NHS staff in England reported that they are subject to bullying, harassment or abuse by fellow workers and managers, impacting on increased intentions to leave, job satisfaction, organisational commitment, absenteeism, presenteeism, productivity and the effectiveness of teams, costing the NHS very conservatively at least £2.28 billion annually.[4]

Take discrimination. NHS workforce and NHS staff survey data show many staff experience discrimination in many aspects of their NHS working lives, notably in recruitment, career progression, disciplinary action and through bullying, all of which are likely to adversely impact on patient care and safety.

A decade ago Robert Francis blamed the failings of Mid Staffordshire NHS Foundation Trust on a culture which put the 'business of the system ahead of patients'. Evidence to his Public Inquiry concluded there was:

a pervasive culture of fear in the NHS and certain elements of the Department for Health. The NHS has developed a widespread culture more of fear and compliance, than of learning, innovation and enthusiastic participation in improvement.[5]

Francis concluded that:

there lurks within the system an institutional instinct which, under pressure, will prefer concealment, formulaic responses and 'avoidance of public criticism' and 'an institutional culture which ascribed more weight to positive information about the service than to information capable of implying cause for concern'.

The pressure to search out 'comfort seeking' rather than 'problem sensing' information is still strong. Despite a neverending stream of reports and recommendations, staff who raise concerns about safety of patients or the treatment of staff still risk sanctions. At the heart of almost every NHS Inquiry into harm caused to patients or staff there exists a culture of avoidance and denial despite the sustained efforts of some Trusts to do better.

The causes of a culture that is often sub-optimal are no secret. The mismatch between demand and resources after a decade of austerity and two decades of 'control totals', 'savings targets' and staff shortages have left local leaderships under immense pressures, often fearful of blame, knowing senior leader turnover is astonishing. Those pressures are compounded by the steep authority gradient within individual professions and between occupations.

To cap it all, the human resources paradigm which, until recently, has dominated much NHS practice on tackling discrimination, bullying, and 'whistleblowing' on unsafe practice is a dud. Research strongly suggests that its reliance on 'policies, procedures and training' will not be a safe, effective means whereby individual staff can raise concerns about bullying, discrimination, unfair disciplinary action and unsafe practice. This approach is fundamentally flawed as a means of improving organisational culture.[6]

We rarely ask of interventions on bullying, whistleblowing, discrimination or discipline, 'why do you think this is likely to work?' For example, in response to bullying or discrimination, the default answer until very recently has been more 'training'. Yet, the largest study of diversity initiatives found that attempts to reduce managerial bias through diversity training and diversity evaluations were the least effective methods of increasing diversity in management.[7] Similarly, Unconscious Bias Training, widely used in the NHS, may be helpful but the evidence that in isolation it changes decision-making is very limited.[8]

In the decade when the NHS Employers' guidance on bullying at work (2006–2016) stated 'employers can only address cases of bullying and harassment that are brought to their attention',[9] bullying levels rose sharply. The focus on (unsuccessfully) protecting those individuals who raise concerns, rather than changing the organisational climate in which such concerns are ignored or rejected is doomed to failure.[10]

Similarly, until recently, an approach to discrimination which largely relied on individuals raising concerns was undermined by the likelihood that legitimate complaints will not be upheld and almost certainly not change institutional discrimination. An alternative model emphasising proactive use of research evidence to transform recruitment and career progression by removing bias from processes and inserting accountability at every stage is being adopted by numerous Trusts,[11] but without wholehearted endorsement by national bodies.

A further challenge is that the behaviours of national bodies do not match their exhortations to local bodies on all these issues. Their data on workforce race equality or bullying is worse than for most Trusts.[12] Indeed, NHS Improvement hasn't even published its most recent data at time of writing. When Covid began, NHS Improvement initially stopped collecting workforce race equality data ('not a priority') even when it was clear BME staff would be especially at risk.

The government's contribution to this workforce car crash? Hopeless workforce planning, outdated infrastructure, an obsession with targets, a refusal to invest sufficiently in prevention and public health, and a macho bullying culture from the very top, which inevitably leads to embedded tensions between trying to deliver targets without resources on the one hand and the staff and employer duty of care on the other.

To make matters worse, this and previous governments have sought to contract out to private companies a substantial portion of 'support services' – most notably cleaning, portering, kitchen, transport, security and administrative staff. These staff are largely female and disproportionately of Black and minority Ethnic heritage. The growing rumbles of industrial action from newly formed unions, and the absence of any benefits to patients from such contracting out, alongside evidence of their crucial role during the Covid pandemic, has led some NHS Trusts to start to reverse the trend. The Equality and Human Rights Commission have concluded a review of the treatment of low paid workers in the NHS, and it may be that this report when finally published may bring growing numbers of these crucial staff back into direct NHS employment.

So what does good look like for the workforce?

Serious national workforce planning would be a start in order to reduce the huge staffing shortfall. A national strategy, modelled by national regulators of evidenced interventions on key topics such as recruitment and career progression, bullying, whistleblowing, and discipline would help. Leaders who themselves practiced the inclusive compassionate behaviours they promulgate for others and substantially closed the gap between the treatment of white and BME staff.

Culture, or 'how we do things round here', is shaped by formal organisational values (NHS Constitution and local policies), by values, behaviours and knowledge that staff learn, and (crucially) by how an organisation's leaders behave. What leaders focus on, talk about, pay attention to, reward and seek to influence, tells staff what leadership values they should take note of.[13] Where leaders don't welcome those who speak truth to power why would others do so?

We know effective interventions and leadership are possible. On discipline, for example, applying 'human factors' science and incentivising a learning culture not blame, emphasising early informal intervention, can transform outcomes, saving 2% of staffing costs in one Trust alone.[14]

Nationally, insertion of an accountability nudge has helped cut disciplinary cases by 28% from 2017-21 and substantially closed the gap between the treatment of white and BAME staff.[15]

We know that leaders who demonstrate a commitment to high quality and compassionate care directly affect clinical effectiveness, patient safety and experience, the health, well-being and engagement of staff and the extent of innovation. Evidence of the links between psychological safety, supportiveness, positivity, empathy, leadership (in aggregate compassionate leadership) and innovation is deep and convincing.[16]

Inclusive and compassionate leadership helps create a psychologically safe workplace where staff are more likely to listen and support each other. This leads to fewer errors, fewer staff injuries, less bullying of staff, reduced absenteeism and (in hospitals) reduced patient mortality.

Improved demographic diversity at more senior levels is a precondition for improving healthcare and achieving social justice. But, unless the teams which those newly-recruited staff join are also characterised by inclusion and psychological safety, that diversity will neither be sustainable, nor add the value it can and should.

Covid risk assessments

The reliance on an over-individualised approach to risk was evidenced in the NHS approach to Covid-19 risk assessments. Instead of an emphasis on a preventative, proactive approach which could have identified which factors would place staff at greater risk of infection, the initial focus was primarily on identifying which individual staff might be most at risk if they were infected. Individual staff risk assessments were important, but insufficient effort went into preventing exposure through identifying whether some staff groups might be disproportionately at risk through organisational factors such as poorer BAME staff access to appropriate PPE, agency staff being both at greater risk and being a risk, how safe so-called 'safer' areas really were, and whether social distancing was actually possible in many communal areas. Such prevention was possible as witnessed by the absence of fatalities in the most obviously dangerous area, ICU. The staff groups particularly at risk from organisational shortcomings (BAME staff) were also those most at risk if they became infected.[17]

Staff are entitled to know their employers have taken all reasonably practicable steps to assess risks and mitigate them, as required by the Management of Health and Safety at Work Regulations and the Personal Protective Equipment at Work Regulations. Had these assessments, and Equality Impact Assessments, been carried out, they would have shown some groups of staff were probably at greater risk of infection than others. Even when risk assessments were started they emphasised individual staff health rather than a key cause of occupational exposure: the racialised patterns of staff treatment. That failure made doing timely individual health risk assessments so important.

Early data confirmed a disproportionate number of BME people died as a result of Covid-19. 20% of the NHS workforce are of BME heritage. By late April we knew that 63% of NHS staff who died from Covid-19 were from BAME background: 71% of the nurses and midwives, 94% of doctors and dentists, 56% of healthcare support staff and 29% of other staff.[18]

Quite astonishingly, NHS England/Improvement did not ask NHS Trusts to undertake risk assessments till 29 April 2020. They published updated guidance on 28 May and when it became clear progress was far too slow, finally issued a 24 June data request to all NHS organisations to ensure they were indeed risk assessing 'at risk groups'.

National bodies

The NHS has much higher trade union density than almost any other UK sector. With some honourable exceptions, trade unions nationally have been drawn into the flawed HR paradigm. Too often individual case work does not yet escalate into preventative, proactive interventions to prevent the need to raise grievances in the first place. Good lobbying on workforce culture issues does not necessarily translate into an evidence-based collective response to them.

But those shortcomings pale into insignificance alongside the huge austerity-driven staffing shortages and toxic top-down behaviours from national bodies and the Department of Health and Social Care. There are some signs of change at policy level, but many of the best practical innovations in supporting staff have come from individual organisations not from national bodies.

Speaking up can require courage, particularly in work places which do not enjoy an open, patient-centred culture. Research repeatedly demonstrates that the two main reasons why people do not report perceived wrongdoing: they don't believe it would make a difference, and they fear it might make things worse.

Overwhelmingly NHS staff enter healthcare to improve the lives of those they care for. They deserve employers who create teams that are felt to be safe for interpersonal risk taking, who recognise the deep human need to belong, and the anxiety everyone may feel when speaking up or sharing ideas in front of others for fear of saying something that may appear stupid or wrong.

The workforce challenges facing the NHS are enormous, yet research makes it clear what we should do to recruit, develop and retain staff and treat them in ways that we know will improve patient care.

NOTES

1   Dixon-Woods M, Baker R , Charles K , et al Culture and behaviour in the English National health service: overview of lessons from a large multimethod study. BMJ Qual Saf 2014;23:106–15.doi:10.1136/bmjqs-2013-001947

2   Cary Cooper (2019) How to improve workplace wellbeing https://workinmind.org/2019/10/16/how-to-improve-workplace-wellbeing/

3   Lucien Leape (2012) Perspective: a culture of respect, part 1: the nature and causes of disrespectful behavior by physicians Lucian L Leape, Miles F Shore, Jules L Dienstag, Robert J Mayer, Susan Edgman-Levitan, Gregg S Meyer, Gerald B Healy DOI: 10.1097/ACM.0b013e318258338d)

4   Kline R, Lewis D (2019) . The price of fear: estimating the financial cost of bullying and harassment to the NHS in England. Public Money Manag 2019;39:166–74.doi:10.1080/09540962.2018.1535044

5   Francis R (2013) Report of the Mid Staffordshire NHS Foundation. Executive summary. Trust Public Inquiry, 2013.https://assets.publishing.service.gov.uk/government/uploads/system/uploads/attachment_data/file/279124/0947.pdf

6   Evesson J, Oxenbridge S , Taylor D .(2015) Seeking better solutions: tackling bullying and ill-treatment in Britain's workplaces. ACAS, 2015. http://m.acas.org.uk/media/pdf/e/b/Seeking-better-solutions-tackling-bullying-and-ill-treatment-in-Britains-workplaces.pdf

7   Kalev, A., Dobbin F, Kelly E. (2006) Best practices or best Guesses? assessing the efficacy of corporate affirmative action and diversity policies. Am Sociol Rev 2006;71:589–617. doi:10.1177/000312240607100404

8   Atewologun D, Cornish T, Tresh F. Equality and human rights Commission research report 113 unconscious bias training: an assessment of the evidence for effectiveness. EHRC, 2018. https://warwick.ac.uk/services/ldc/researchers/resource_bank/unconscious_bias /ub_an_assessment_of_evidence_for_effectiveness.pdf

9   NHS Employers (2006). Guidance: bullying and harassment.

10 Tarrant C, Leslie M , Bion J , et al (2017). A qualitative study of speaking out about patient safety concerns in intensive care units. Soc Sci Med 2017;193:8–15.doi:10.1016/j.socscimed.2017.09.036

11 Kline, R. (2021) No More Tick Boxes https://mdxminds.com/2021/09/16/no-more-tick-boxes/

12 2019 WRES data analysis report for eleven arm's length bodies. https://

www.england.nhs.uk/wp-content/uploads/2020/09/WRES-Data-Report_ALBs-2020.pdf

13   http://dx.doi.org/10.1136/leader-2019-000159

14   Kaur M, De Boer RJ , Oates A , et al . (2019) Restorative just culture: a study of the practical and economic effects of implementing restorative justice in an NHS trust. MATEC Web conf 2019;**273**:01007.doi:10.1051/matecconf/201927301007

15   Workforce Race Equality Standard 2020 Data Analysis Report for NHS Trusts and Clinical Commissioning Groups February 2021 https://www.england.nhs.uk/wp-content/uploads/2021/02/Workforce-Race-Equality-Standard-2020-report.pdf

16   West M, Eckert R, Collins R. Caring to change. How compassionate leadership can stimulate innovation in health care. King's Fund, 2017 https://www.kingsfund.org.uk/sites/default/files/field/field_publication_file/Carin g_to_change_Kings_Fund_May_2017.pdf

17   Kline R. (2020)The NHS response to BME staff's covid deaths was late and lopsided https://www.hsj.co.uk/workforce/the-nhs-response-to-bme-staffs-covid-deaths-was-late-and-lopsided-/7027790.article?adredir=1

18   https://www.hsj.co.uk/exclusive-deaths-of-nhs-staff-from-covid-19-analysed/7027471.article

No peace of mind, just a lot of worry for us all

Roy Lilley
Health policy analyst

Why do you go to a restaurant?

I'd guess, as the travails of lockdown and the perils of the pandemic are on the ebb-tide, you might go, because you can. But, in the ordinary run of the things, why go?

I'd suggest, you don't go because you are hungry. That's why peanut butter and toast exist. Or, pot-noodles.

No, you go to a restaurant for fun, friendship, to seal-a-deal. For romance. For sorry. To impress. To say something that goes beyond the language of the menu. It might be, to eat your words and not the food.

Nothing is what it seems. The purpose of a restaurant goes way beyond hungry.

You don't wear a watch because you want to know the time. The purpose of a watch is a fashion statement, or a boast. People who wear a watch that will work on the moon, or thirty-thousand leagues under the sea, probably never go higher than the lift to the top floor or deeper than a ride on London's Tube.

There is another meaning, the real meaning to almost everything.

Kids join gangs for a feeling of fraternity, companionship and the support they often can't get at home. People take drugs to take them to another place. Wear clothes, drive cars, go to the game, to be part of something. To identify with a life that might never be theirs. It's all to make a statement, how they feel and what they want us to think about them.

Rich, brave, on-it, classy, in the know.

Nothing is what it seems. The real purpose, so often misunderstood. Misinterpreted.

So what is the purpose of the NHS?

The job is to find out what makes us sick, do something to fix us up, figure out if it works, what did it cost and decide if we want to do it next time.

Often, it doesn't work, often we don't get fixed up because, often, it's not possible. We are content with a return to function of sorts. 'Lucky to be as well as I am …' how often have we heard that. The best that can be managed. We are content.

Like we are content to wait, queue, take our turn.

We put up with all that because the NHS fulfils its unwritten reason for being. The NHS' real purpose?

Peace of mind.

Peace of mind, in knowing when a beginning is made there will be a midwife, and when the end has come there will be a painless passing, in tender care. In between, we tell ourselves the NHS cannot do miracles, although sometimes it seems like it, and – always – there is hope.

We tell ourselves it's worth waiting for. They will do all they can, young or old, rich or poor. There is a place for us and peace of mind.

I wonder, for how much longer will this be true?

The devastation wreaked by Covid has left the NHS damaged and vulnerable. Staff are exhausted, waiting lists reaching into millions, and the workforce depleted.

More than that, Covid has cloaked the real NHS. Covered up and obscured the truth about the NHS. Disguised its parlous state. The NHS was in a mess, long before the first person with Covid flew back from a holiday in the Tyrol, with suitcases, skis … and Covid.

Ten years of austerity government had left the NHS weakened. With fewer beds per head of population than most comparable health systems. Fewer doctors, fewer nurses and health professionals, it limped into the battle with Covid.

Somehow it muddled through. Muddled through, elegantly …

… and now, what next?

There is a mountain to climb. At least as high as the Pitztal Glacier.

There is the longest, highest, biggest waiting list for treatment the NHS has ever recorded. At the time of writing the numbers are probably north of six million. But, the real situation is much worse.

In a normal year the NHS expects to carry out ten million operations. Two million are emergencies. The other eight are what, in the trade, are known as 'electives'; people waiting for new hips, knees, cataracts, hernia repairs and the like.

We know there are seven million in the queue. Add to that the eight million routine operations carried out, year-in-year-out, that's 15 million and, don't forget, a couple of million emergencies.

But, there will be more.

Was it philosopher Slavoj Žižek, or before him a thirteenth-century Persian poet, Ibn Yamin, that inspired George W. Bush's defence secretary Donald Rumsfeld? No matter, we'll borrow from him, anyway. Pinch a phrase that is tailor made for the NHS's big worry … the 'known-unknowns'.

We know there are people who have held off consulting with the NHS, their GP, for fear of catching Covid in hospital or at the surgery. The good-hearted folk who have struggled on, because 'they don't want to trouble the NHS, because it's so busy'.

We know they are there, but we just don't know how many.

The known-unknowns. Say, two million? Three? Your guess is as good as mine.

The Institute of Fiscal Studies had a stab at a number. Their thinking is …

'… some 7.6 million fewer people joined a waiting list for NHS care in England between March 2020 and September 2021, than we would have expected, based on pre-pandemic data. This suggests that there are millions of 'missing' patients: people who, in the absence of a pandemic, would have sought and received NHS hospital care but, in the event, did not.'[1]

Some will have conditions that have resolved, some will have gone private and some just 'learned to live with it'. Who knows how many have died waiting?

This all means, we know the mountain of work facing the NHS is close-on 17 million. And, next year there will be another eight million routine operations, and the year after eight million again, and so it goes on.

And, the Rumsfeld Club? Could be five million more.

There was talk of 'clearing the waiting lists' by the next election, 2025. There are two chances; slim and none.

The NHS does not have the capacity to cope with these numbers. We know they struggle to keep up with the usual, annual 20 million cases.

For good measure, last September, the Royal College of Anaesthetists told us there was a shortage of 1,400 NHS anaesthetists, meaning more than one million surgical procedures are delayed every year[2].

Let's not forget, each operation is at the end of the line of diagnostics, tests, imaging, prescribing and, often, physiotherapy and home care. After an operation there is usually follow-up, outpatient appointments, pharmacy, occupation therapy and support at home.

Operations are the bit we all talk about. There is an army of professionals involved, and we know for certain that the NHS is short on professionals.

Even if the NHS were able to increase its operating capacity by bringing in temporary theatres and recovery suits, it simply does not have the people.

To make matters worse, there is no plan to get the people.

NHS workforce planning is a labyrinth, invented by the then Secretary of State for Health Andrew Lansley, now a Lord, whose 'reforms' of the NHS, under David Cameron, produced a disaggregated muddle of organisations and systems.

The up-shot?

Health Education England (HEE), an arms-length body, was created, responsible for workforce-planning. This year they have been allocated no budget. Without a budget they are unable to create a workforce plan. But the problems go further back than this year.

In 2014, the original Five Year Forward View, the overall NHS plan for the future, made no mention of investment in workforce.

Three years later, in 2017 HEE published a consultation on the future of the workforce and they promised a workforce strategy, to coincide with the NHS's 70th birthday.

Nothing happened.

An interim 'people-plan' emerged from the newly created 'People Directorate', created by the then Secretary of State for Health, Matt Hancock. It contained no workforce commitments.

There followed a one-year people plan. Still no workforce commitments. Last summer HEE announced it would, once again, make a start on a plan.

Since then, radio silence. Except for a statement just before Xmas. They concluded 'workforce demand will be affected by demography and disease'.

There's still no plan. HEE still have no budget, and be still, your beating heart, they indicate they might have something 'in the Spring'. They don't say which year.

I am sitting at my desk, writing all this. The London sky is slate grey and rain is sifting across the river. It's a gloomy day. A day made brighter, you might think, by the announcement from the latest Secretary of State for Health, Sajid Javid, who pledges to make England's cancer care system the best in Europe with a new 10-year plan.

He probably doesn't know that the Royal College of Radiologists tell us there are only 913 full-time clinical and consultant oncologists; there is a shortfall of around 17% in their workforce – getting on for 200 vacancies. This year's crop of newly trained consultants will only fill half the vacancies.[3]

I glance out of the window. The rain has got worse.

We are promised 50,000 more nurses by 2025. They aren't all 'new' nurses. About 20,000 are nurses who already work in the NHS, being encouraged not to leave. The rest are the ones we would be training anyway and the balance recruited from overseas.

There is a global shortage of nurses and international recruitment is getting tricky. We pay relatively low wages, our beaches aren't great and the sun doesn't shine like it does in California. Nurses can work where they chose.

Interestingly, Luxembourg, Denmark, Canada, Norway, Australia and Switzerland pay more.[4]

Peace of mind?

Not for me. Frankly, I'm worried.

Successive Conservative administrations have failed to recognise the state of the NHS and social care workforce.

A workforce the size of the NHS, dependent on highly qualified people to do the jobs, must expect ebbs and flows.

A workforce the size of the NHS, that has gone through the hammering that Covid has handed out, must expect exhausted people to leave and they have; 27,000 in the third quarter of last year.[5]

A workforce the size of the NHS, needs careful planning to dovetail demand, technology and new ways of working. It needs careful thought to work through funding, training, placements and support ... one in six nurses don't complete their training and one five nurses quit on qualifying.[6]

Peace of mind? No.

No one plans to fail, they just fail to plan. Without a workforce plan Javid's new cancer initiatives will fail. Without a workforce plan waiting list recovery plans will fail.

Without a workforce plan the NHS will fail, and that will lead us to a poor service for poor people. There is no peace of mind, just a lot of worry for us all.

NOTES

1   https://ifs.org.uk/publications/15871
2   https://www.rcoa.ac.uk/news/shortage-1400-nhs-anaesthetists-already-means-more-one-million-surgical-procedures-are-delayed
3   https://www.rcr.ac.uk/posts/new-rcr-workforce-report-shows-oncologist-shortages-continue-impact-patients
4   https://nurse.org/articles/highest-paying-countries-for-nurses/
5   https://inews.co.uk/news/health/nhs-staff-quit-record-numbers-ptsd-covid-pandemic-trauma-1387115
6   https://www.personneltoday.com/hr/one-in-five-nurses-quit-on-qualifying/

Contributors

Dr Jacky Davis is a consultant radiologist, a member of the Council of the British Medical Association, and a founder member of the national campaign Keep Our NHS Public (KONP). She has co-written two previous books, *NHS SOS* and *NHS for Sale*.

Dr John Lister has been a health journalist and campaigner for the NHS for 38 years, and obtained a PhD in health policy in 2004. He has written and co-written a number of books on the NHS as well as two books on global health policy reform, most recently *Global Health versus Private Profit* (2012) and a book on health journalism. He is a founder member of KONP.

Lobby Akinnola is a member of the Covid-19 Bereaved Families for Justice group, who lost his father Olufemi to Covid on 26 April 2020.

Rehana Azam is National Secretary of the GMB union, which represents staff working in the NHS and social care.

Kevin Courtney is joint General Secretary of the National Education Union, with 450,000 members including school teachers, further education lecturers, education support staff and teaching assistants.

Sara Gorton is Head of Health of UNISON, the public service union with the largest membership in the NHS covering all but medical staff as well as members in social care and local government.

Colenzo Jarrett-Thorpe is a national officer for the health sector of Unite which represents over 100,000 health workers in many sectors including health visiting, scientific and technical, ambulance and mental health.

Roger Kline worked for eight trade unions over 25 years, and is now a consultant on workforce culture and a research fellow at Middlesex University Business School. He authored the landmark report 'The Snowy White Peaks of the NHS' (2014).

Roy Lilley is a health policy analyst, writer, broadcaster and commentator on the NHS. His eLetter, across all social media platforms and email reaches around 300,000 in-boxes a week.

Professor Martin McKee is Professor of European Public Health at the London School of Hygiene and Tropical Medicine, former Chair of the UK Society for Social Medicine and Past President of the European Public Health Association. He has published over 1,300 scientific papers and 50 books.

Michael Mansfield, QC is a barrister. He has been involved in many notable cases including representing those wrongly convicted of the IRA's Guildford and Birmingham pub bombings and the families of the victims of Hillsborough. More recently he chaired the People's Covid Inquiry, set up by the Keep Our NHS Public campaign.

Professor Sir Michael Marmot is Professor of Epidemiology and Public Health at University College London. He has led research groups on health inequalities for nearly 50 years, and is currently the Director of the UCL Institute of Health Equity.

Professor Neena Modi is currently President of the BMA, Professor of Neonatal Medicine at Imperial College London and Consultant in Neonatal Medicine at Chelsea and Westminster NHS Foundation Trust. She has written here in a personal capacity.

Michael Rosen is a children's author and poet who has written over 140 books. He served as Children's Laureate from 2007 to 2009, and has also been a television presenter and political columnist.

Jan Shortt is General Secretary of the National Pensioners Convention, the principal organisation representing pensioners in the United Kingdom. It is made up of around 1,000 bodies representing 1.5 million members, organised into federal regional units.

Dr David Wrigley is a GP in Lancashire. He is co-author of *NHS for Sale* and was deputy chair of the BMA UK Council from 2018-2022.

Index